Consultative Jurisdiction of Supreme Court

Consultative Jurisdiction of Supreme Court

DR. AMIT SINGH
B.Sc., DCA, LL.M., LL.D. (L.U.)
Assistant Professor in P.G. Department of Law
M.J.P. Rohilkhand University
Bareilly (U.P.)

Foreword by
PROF. BALRAJ CHAUHAN
Vice-Chancellor
Dr. Ram Manohar Lohiya National Law University
Lucknow (U.P.)

DEEP & DEEP PUBLICATIONS PVT. LTD.
F-159, Rajouri Garden, New Delhi - 110 027

CONSULTATIVE JURISDICTION OF SUPREME COURT

ISBN 978-81-8450-311-1

Typeset by RAHUL COMPOSERS
358, Pocket-B, Phase-2, Sector-16B, Dwarka, New Delhi - 110 075

Printed in India at MAYUR ENTERPRISES
WZ Plot No. 3, Gujjar Market, Tihar Village, New Delhi - 110 018

Published by DEEP & DEEP PUBLICATIONS PVT. LTD.
F-159, Rajouri Garden, New Delhi - 110 027 • Phone : 25435369, 25440916
E-mail : ddpubs@gmail.com • ddpbooks@yahoo.co.in
Showroom :
2/13, Ansari Road, Daryaganj, New Delhi - 110 002 • Telefax : 23245122

INSPIRATION

"Whenever there has been a conflict between my personal interests and the interests of the country as a whole, I have always placed the interests of the country above my personal claims.

This is certain, that if the parties creed above country, our independence will be put in jeopardy a second time.

This eventuality we must all resolutely guard against, we must be determined to defend our indepèndence with the last drop of our blood."

A Great Patriot
Dr. B.R. Ambedkar

Dedicated To

All those high or low, noble or pauper,
known or unknown, who have
worked selflessly to firmly ground
The Philosophy of
The Constitution of India

Contents

Foreword

I have gone through the chapters of this book. It gives me great pleasure to write this foreword especially as *Dr. Amit Singh* is my student since 1997 when he joined Lucknow University as law graduate.

Last decade witnessed many important political and constitutional developments. These developments naturally influenced not only judicial decisions of Supreme Court but also basic thinking on the constitution of India. A new jurisprudence is being envolved by the Honorable Supreme Court in many areas. The court has made significant contribution towards the development of law through its advisory opinion under Article 143.

The primary and immediate effect of an advisory opinion is that it helps in resolving the difficulty that leads to the request for it. But there are other remoter effects that necessarily flow from its authoritative character. The opinions produce effects upon the court and like judgment, they help in developing the law. The great majority of the opinions given by the Supreme Court were effective, several of them facilitated the work of the legal system in India and some led to the settlement of disputes which has given rise to requests.

For the sake of convenience author has divided the subject matter into seven chapters. The author has examined in the introductory chapter the historical precedents of such advisory opinion and the favorable as well as adverse criticism to which it has been subject by different authors. He has then examined advisory opinion in international scenario, under which related provisions of various countries and organizations like U.N.O. and E.U. have been examined. In the concluding chapter the author has drawn some conclusions from the experience of the exercise of the advisory jurisdiction by the Supreme Court of India and has made valuable suggestions in regard to the scope and exercise of the jurisdiction.

The author being an academician has given the book a theoretical approach while at the same time he has incorporated practical aspects as well. Book has been written in a simple and lucid style and clubs the relevant topics and subjects under suitable heads. Author has used jurisdiction in a wider sense to include not only courts consultative jurisdiction as such but also all aspects of the court procedure and the nature, reception and effect of the consultative opinions.

Author has done complete justice to the subject by incorporating up to date case law and making the work comprehensive on all the important and relevant aspects. In compendium, I am sure it will not only be helpful to the bench and the bar of the Supreme Court, but also to the jurists, legislators, constitutionalists, political scientists and students as well.

So, I extend my congratulations to **Dr. Amit Singh** for making an honest endeavour in bringing out the present work, and I wish this book every success.

(PROF. BLARAJ CHAUHAN)
Vice-Chancellor
Dr. Ram Manohar Lohiya National Law University
Lucknow (U.P.)

Acknowledgements

In the consummation of this book, assistance, guidance and encouragement have been received from several persons at various levels in different forms. I wish to express my sincere gratitude to all of them.

Nothing can be as deep than the spiritual relationship between the 'Guru' and his 'disciple' it is something enternal. I feel great pleasure to evince my profound sense of veneration and gratitude to my respected teacher *Professor R.P. Singh,* Former Head of the Department and Dean, Faculty of Law, Lucknow University, Lucknow for his expert and peerless guidance, persistent encouragement, wise counseling and constant supervision during the course of present work. Prof. Singh has exercised enormous influence on my process of thinking and analysis. He has decisively moulded my career as a student, as a researcher and as a teacher. I shall remain indebted to him for his scholarly guidance.

I have paucity of words for expressing my utmost gratefulness and warmest regards to my respected teacher *Professor Balraj Chauhan,* Vice-chancellor, R.M.L. National Law University, Lucknow, who blessed, encouraged and advised whenever an opportunity occurred. Inspite of his busy academic commitments and heavy occupation, he spared his valuable time whenever I approached him. My interest in the present study could not have been sustained without the opportunity to work with him.

It is my proud privilege to acknowledge my gratitude and indebtness due to learned *Professor (Dr.) S.K. Singh,* Vice-chancellor, Raja Bhoj (Open) University, Bhopal. I would like to express high reverence to him, who always inspired me to face the hardship of life. Many of the outstanding issues of the subject were clarified and many of my ideas were crystallized as a result of long scholarly discussions with him during the years of my work.

In course of my research I have experienced that academic research is required to pass through many steps, i.e. identification of issues, analysis, interpretation of available facts, designing course of events for discovery of unknown facts, and shaping the write up of research. This all could have been possible due to my supervisor. I must impel my heartiest gratitude to my research guide *Dr. Chandra Prakash Singh,* Reader, Faculty of Law, Lucknow University whose guidance, advice and his venturesome attitude paved the way to accomplish my work. He is the person who made the project see the light of the day. I express my sincere thanks to *Dr. O.N. Mishra,* Reader, Faculty of Law, University of Lucknow who boasted my morale and provided a lot of help at each and every stage of my career.

I am deeply grateful to the Law Faculty of Dr. Ambedkar, Central University, Lucknow in particular *Prof. S.K Bhatnagar,* Dean of the Faculty, *Dr. Preety Saxena,* H.O.D. who always helped and encouraged me to achive my goal. My profound gratitude to *Prof. O.P. Tiwari, Prof. (Dr.) G.S. Tiwari* and *Prof. R.C. Srivastava* of Gorakhpur University, *Prof. J.N. Pandey* of Allahabad Central University and *Mr. Srinivas Gupta,* Reader, Department of Law, Jai Narain P.G. College Lucknow they all have been a source of constant inspiration to me.

Words are feeble to express my regards and appreciation to my senior teachers. I express my sincere thanks to all in particular *Dr. Manish Singh,* Sr. Lecturer, L.U., *Dr. Shefali,* Reader, Rohilkhand Univesity, *Mr. Aditya Pratap Singh,* Proctor and Asst. Professor, R.M.L. National Law University and *Mr. Rakesh Singh,* Civil Judge (J.D.), Uttar Pradesh.

During the course of my work I met some influencing personalities like *Shri Dharm Raj Mishra,* Additional District Judge (A.D.J.), Allahabad, *Ms. Rekha Agnihotri,* Deputy

Director, Judicial Training and Research Institute (JTRI), *Shri R.L. Kaul,* Asst. General Manager (Law), State Bank of India (SBI), *Shri Sheetla Pal Singh* Deputy Commissioner, Lucknow Development Authority (L.D.A), *Dr. V. Tayal,* former Vice-Chanceller, University of Bikaner, Rajasthan, *Shri Ram Gopal Singh,* Asst. General Manager, L.I.C., *Dr. A.K. Singh,* Assistant Director, Regional Centre for Urban Studies, Lucknow, and *Dr. K.N. Dhawan,* former H.O.D. and Dean, Deptt. of Medicine, K.G.M.U., who encouraged, motivated and accelerated the pace of my work. Although they are in no way related to my work but all have been a source of constant inspiration to me.

While making the aforesaid acknowledgement I must not fail to express my gratitude to my family members. It was the desire of my father *Late Ramakant Singh* for me to do Doctoral Research in Law. He would say that, "my son I will feel privileged the day you will put the title of Doctor before your name." He was the first person who has seen a teacher inside me. By this book I pay my sincere homage to my loving father. I am highly indebted to express my profound regards to my mother *Kalawati Singh* for their untiring dedication, affection, silent wishes and blessings which is just beyond my capacity to express in words. In the process of preparing this task I have been sustained by the good will and moral support which I have received from my sister *Kavita Singh,* and my wife *Poonam Singh* who were always so indulgent and cooperative, will I feel, but a formality, and I would not like to be formal with them.

My friends are my assets. My heartfelt thanks to all my friends, seniors and juniors for their kind consideration, support and affectionate help received from them. It will be not fair if I do not list them all it is not lack of gratitude but for lack of space that I keep my pen down to them all. I convey my deep love and affection.

I must place on record my sincere thanks to the librarians and the staff of Indian Law Institute, The Institute of Constitutional and Parliamentary Studies, Supreme Court Judges Library, Indian Society of International Law Library, New Delhi, Dr. R.U. Singh Law Library, Tagore Library, Govt. Advocate Library, High Court Judges Library, Judicial Training and Research Institute Library, R.M.L. National Law University Library, Dr. Ambedkar Central University Library, Lucknow for providing me access to the latest editions of books, research journals and study materials for writing the book.

My Publisher Deep & Deep Publications Pvt. Ltd., New Delhi deserves special compliments on accent of injecting 'adrenalin' into me by rendering encouragements. They have induced me to write this book and the painstaking cooperation and efforts in bringing it out of this excellent form.

Last but not the least, I am thankful to *Shri Asim Manohar* for taking keen interest in typing this manuscript speedily and timely.

DR. AMIT SINGH

Abbreviations

A.I.R.	:	All India Reporter
A.C.	:	Appeal Cases, House of Lords since 1890 (Law Report)
All E.R	:	All England Reporter
A.L.R.	:	Allahabad Law Reporter
Art (art)	:	Article (of the Constitution)
Bom.	:	Bombay
Cal.	:	Calcutta
C.J.	:	Chief Justice (of H.C/S.C.)
Constitution	:	The Constitution of India
Ch or Ch.D.	:	Chancery Revision since 1890 (England) (Law reports)
C.W.N.	:	Calcutta Weekly Notes
C.L.J.	:	Cambridge Law Journal
Cr. L.J.	:	Criminal Law Journal
C.P.C.	:	Civil Procedure Code, 1908
Cr. P.C.	:	Criminal Procedure Code, 1973
C.J.	:	Consultative Jurisdiction
D.B.	:	Division Bench (of H.C./S.C.)
DPSP	:	Directive Principles of State Policy
E.U.	:	European Union
ECHR	:	European Convention for the Protection of Human Rights and Fundamental Freedom
E.C.	:	Executive Council
e.g.	:	For example (exempts gratia)

F.B.	:	Full Bench (of High Court)
GDP	:	Gross Domestic Product
GATS	:	General Agreement on Trade ir Services
H.L.	:	House of Lords
Harv.L.R.	:	Harvard Law Review
H.C.	:	High Court
H.R.	:	Human Rights
Ibid	:	Ibidem (at the same place)
i.e.	:	that is
IJIL	:	Indian Journal on International Law
ILI	:	Indian Law Institute
Infra	:	Below
ILO	:	International Labour Organization
IPR	:	Intellectual Property Rights
ICSSR	:	Indian Council of Social Science Research
J./JJ.	:	Justice/Justices (Judge/Judges of H.C./ S.C.)
K.B. or K.B.D.	:	Kings Bench Division (England Law Reports)
Mad.	:	Madras
NGO	:	Non-Governmental Organization
N.H.R.C.	:	National Human Rights Commission
L.Ed.	:	Lawyers Edition, United States Supreme Court Reports
L.Q.R.	:	Law Quarterly Review
P.C.	:	Privy Council
P.I.L	:	Public Interest Litigation
Q.B./Q.B.D.	:	Queens Bench Division (England)
R.	:	Rex
S/Sec	:	Section (of the Act)
S.C.	:	Supreme Court of India
S.C.C.	:	Supreme Court Cases (Law Reports)
S.L.R.	:	Supreme Court Law Report
S.C.J.	:	Supreme Court Journal
Supra	:	Above
U.N.O.	:	United Nations Organization
U.G.C.	:	University Grants Commission
U.O.I.	:	Union of India

V.	:	Versus (Meaning Against)
Viz.	:	(Vidilicat) Namely
w.e.f.	:	with effect from
W.L.R.	:	Weekly Law Reports (English Law Reports)
W.T.O.	:	World Trade Organization
u/s	:	Under Section
Yale L.J.	:	Yale Law Journal

Author's Caveat

"Research is to see what everybody else has seen, and to think what nobody else has thought".

—*Albert Szent Gyoergi*

The present work deals with the propriety of the Consultative/Advisory jurisdiction conferred by Article 143 of the Constitution of India on the Honorable Supreme Court. The word jurisdiction in the title has been used in a wider sense to include not only the courts consultative jurisdiction as such but also all aspects of the courts procedure and the nature, reception and effect of the consultative opinions.

The primary function of a Court is to give a judicial verdict in a dispute which may arise between individuals *inter se* or between an individual and the State. To tender advice on controversial issue is not its normal function. There are countries like the U.S.A. and Australia where the highest tribunal of the land is not invested with advisory jurisdiction. Issues which may be referred to the Supreme Court for its advice are often matters of lively political controversy. It is debatable whether the highest tribunal in the country should be involved in such matters. The consultative jurisdiction, however, is often very beneficial if it is exercised with complete detachment. Several references have been made to the Supreme Court of India, since the promulgation of the constitution in 1950 and all those references were dealt with by the court in a dignified and non-partisan manner.

The present book aims at evaluating the working of the system of consultative jurisdiction in India and to record the impact it has on the process of constitutional development and also to study whether the institution has been successful in removing doubts relating to important Constitutional provisions. This work is exhaustively arranged in different topics carrying explained case laws and juristic views and approaches. Book has been divided into seven chapters under which the subject is tried clearly to elaborate.

Chapter one is introductory, it introduces the concept of Article 143 which incorporates the consultative jurisdiction in Indian Constitution. The scope and nature of advisory jurisdiction has been discussed in detail. The phraseology of the constitutional provision is quite broad to cover all types of references. The court has stated that it is well within its jurisdiction to answer the President in a reference under article 143, if the questions referred are likely to arise in future or such questions are of public importance or there is no decision of this court which has already decided the question referred.

Chapter two deals with the historical development of consultative jurisdiction. In order to evaluate the working of the institution of consultative or advisory jurisdiction an indepth study of the constitutional intent behind the provision is necessary. It was the Adhoc committee on Supreme Court which recommended the Constituent Assembly for the conferment of advisory jurisdiction upon the Supreme Court. Next heading deals with the related provisions of Government of India Act, 1935. Article 143 is a close replica of section 213 of Government of India Act, 1935. Before the advent of the Supreme Court, the Federal Court exercised advisory jurisdiction under this section. The Federal Court pronounced only four opinions all of which are discussed in the heading. The significance of the four pronouncements can be measured by the fact that they are cited in cases and various articles not only in India but also in other leading judicial systems of the world as well.

Next part of chapter is criticism and advantages of consultative jurisdiction. Firstly, the criticism of the system have been dealt with. A provision for executive consultation of the judiciary has always been subject to severe criticism mainly on account of the fear that an indiscriminate use of consultation may undermine the prestige of the court and the faith of the people in the judiciary. The opinion has also been voiced that there is the likelihood of the executive using the court as a sponge to absorb political shocks or as a shield to protect itself from any loss of prestige that may otherwise be directed against it. In heading "Assay of criticism" each point of criticism has been closely examined, it is however, submitted that there is no sufficient weightage. The advisory jurisdiction has a very useful purpose. There are quite few advantages of advisory jurisdiction. Which has been examined in the next heading.

Chapter three focuses upon consultative provisions of various countries. The system of various countries has been closely examined. Most of the democracies of the commonwealth have made provisions in their constitution for the highest courts to have an advisory jurisdiction. The discussion in this chapter is divided into two parts, first, the advisory jurisdiction of courts in the older or classical democracies of the commonwealth, secondly, the advisory jurisdiction of courts in the newer democracies of the commonwealth. In older democracies of commonwealth, the provisions of four countries—Canada, U.S.A., Australia and Britain have been discussed. Sec. 4 of the judicial committee Act, 1833 was the inspiration for article 143. This was enacted for obligating the judicial committee of the Privy Council to tender advice to the crown on any matter other than the judicial appeals presented to the committee.

Article 143 is analogous to the powers possessed by Sec. 55 of the Canadian Supreme Court Act, 1952. This jurisdiction in Canada is infact a statutory obligation on the part of the Supreme Court to answer the questions under reference. Sincc its establishment in 1875, the Canadian Supreme Court has so far pronounced advisory opinions in many cases. Whereas, in U.S.A. and Australia there is no provision in the federal constitution for seeking advice from the Supreme Court. The Courts has refused to give advisory opinion on the ground that the essential function of the judiciary is decision of disputes and not the consideration of abstract legal questions.

In the newer democracies of the commonwealth the provisions of four countries—Bangladesh, Pakistan, Sri Lanka and Malaysia have been discussed.

The second part of chapter is related to consultative jurisdiction in International Law. The International Court of justice (I.C.J.) plays an important part in the development of International Law through its advisory opinions. Article 65 of the statute of I.C.J. incorporates provisions for advisory jurisdiction. The court may give an advisory jurisdiction on any legal question to any body which has been authorized in accordance with the Charter of the United Nations or in accordance with the state. Whereas the charter under Article 96 Para 1 lays down that the Security Council and the General Assembly may request to the Court to give an advisory opinion on any legal question.

In addition to them other organs of the United Nations and specialized agencies can also request for advisory opinion on legal questions arising within the scope of their activities if so authorized by the General Assembly. The scope of the advisory opinion of I.C.J. is not to settle at least directly disputes between states but to offer the legal advice to the organs and institutions requesting the opinion and therefore, the opinion given by the court is referred to as legal advice, it does not have any binding force. The I.C.J. has delivered 22 opinions upto 2006. The opinions of the court are reparations, reservations and expenses cases and in particular opinion on WHO request are very important. All the important opinions in brief have been discussed in the later part of the Chapter.

Chapter four can be said to be the soul of the book. It contains references under article 143. So far, the President of India has made only fourteen references out of which one reference to Satluj-Yamuna Link Canal (SYL) is still pending before the court. The court answered eleven references and gave its opinion on merits. Two references have come back without any opinion. First one is Ram Janambhoomi and second is Jammu and Kashmir Resettlement Act reference, which came back without any remark. The order in which each reference has been studied is related cases, main facts, question referred and opinion delivered by the court and at the end main points of the reference in brief have been discussed.

In each reference at the top the name of the reference and citation has been quoted. If there is any related case, then it is mentioned in the side heading below it. Then comes the main facts of the reference. In this heading all the developments judicial and non-judicial of each reference have been given. In each reference President of India has put questions to the court. All the questions were referred to the court for its opinion thereon. The reference is to be heard by a bench of not less than five judges, according to Article 145(3). Order XXXVII of Part V of the Supreme Court Rule, 1966 contains the rules of procedure to be followed in the case of a reference by the court. The Registrar of the Supreme Court gives notice to the Attorney General to appear before the court and to take appropriate directions as to the parties who will be served with notices of such references. The court permits such persons or groups of persons as may be interested in the reference to intervene.

The questions so far referred to the court for its opinion under article 143 do not disclose any pattern. They cover a wide range of questions in different fields. The *first reference* was made to the court in 1951 about the validity and constitutionality of the material provision of the Delhi Laws Act, 1912, the Arjmer Marwara (Extension of Laws) Act, 1947 and Part C, States Laws Act, 1951. The *second reference* was made in 1958. This was related to the reference of the validity of certain provisions of the Kerala Education Bill, 1957, which had been reserved by the Governor for the consideration to the President. The *third reference* was made in 1959 in regard to the validity of the material provisions of an agreement between the Prime Ministers of India and Pakistan which was described as the Indo-Pakistan Agreement. The *fourth reference* was made in 1962 regarding the validity of the relevant provisions of a draft Bill which was intended to be moved in Parliament with a view to amend certain provisions of the Sea Customs Act, 1878 and the Central Excise and Salt Act, 1944.

The *fifth reference* was made in 1964 regarding the privileges and immunities of the Legislative Assembly of Uttar Pradesh. The *sixth reference* was made in 1974 seeking the courts opinion on some questions connected with the holding of election to the office of the President at a time when the

Legislative Assembly of a State was dissolved. The *seventh reference* was made in 1978, regarding the validity of the provisions of the Special Courts Bill, 1978. The *eighth reference* was made in 1982, regarding the validity and constitutionality of Jammu and Kashmir Resettlement Act which provides for the resettlement of all those persons who have migrated to Pakistan after March 1947, if they returned to Kashmir on a permanent basis. The *ninth reference* was made in 1992 about the validity and constitutionality of the tribunals order which was established to settle the dispute regarding distribution of Cauvery river water between the two states of Karnataka and Tamil Nadu. The *tenth reference* was made in 1993, which was related to a longstanding dispute of Ramjanmabhumi-Babri Masjid structure in Ayodhya. The *eleventh reference* was made in 1998, regarding appointment of judges of Supreme Court and High Court and transfer of High Court judges from one High Court to another. The *twelfth reference* was made in 2001 about the validity of the Gujarat Gas (Regulation of Transmission Supply and Distribution) Act, 2001 empowering the state to regulate transmission, supply and distribution of gas in the state. The *thirteenth reference* was made in 2002, regarding the interpretation of Article 174, in context with articles 324 and 356. The reference was with respect to assembly elections in Gujarat. The *fourteenth reference* was made in 2004 regarding dispute between Punjab and Haryana over Satluj-Yamuna Link Canal. Next heading after referred questions is opinion. In each reference the majority and minority opinions have been discussed in detail. In the end of each reference main point of opinion is given in brief.

Chapter five deliberates with new dimensions of consultative jurisdiction. 14 references in 58 years have been made to the Supreme Court. After every opinion the Honourable Court has added some new dimensions in the field of law. Some gray areas are still awaited where an authoritative answer from the Supreme Court have not come. For example, whether the opinion "Law declared" is within the meaning of Article 141? or whether the opinion is binding on the Courts? or whether the Supreme Court can modify its earlier judgment in an advisory opinion? These all have been discussed in this chapter in detail.

Chapter six throws light upon consultative jurisdictions impact on Indian Legal System. With the delivery and communication of advisory opinion, the task of the court is over. Thereafter it rests with the President to accept it and to implement it in action. The extent of this reception and the effect given to the opinion depends upon their nature, apart from political considerations. There upon depends also their effect on the court. It is important therefore to discuss the impact of the advisory opinions. The primary and immediate impact of an advisory opinion lies in the resolution of the difficulty that leads to the request for it. But there are other long range effects that necessarily flow from its authoritative character. The opinions produce effects upon the court, like judgments are a means of developing the law.

Chapter seven contains the epilogue. Conclusion of the work has been given in the first heading. The whole picture of the work in brief is incorporated. General trends of the opinion have been given. Next heading deals with the question whether the system be continued or not. Answer is affirmative. It is submitted that there is no sufficient weightage in this criticism. The advisory jurisdiction has served very useful purpose. Before enacting a law some doubts may be cleared on points of law and thereby not only unnecessary litigation may be avoided but also soundness of that law may be ensured. Last heading is related to *suggestions.* Certain modifications in the provisions have been suggested to make advisory jurisdiction more useful and less harmful.

This book is a reformative document to suggest reform in existing Laws. *Firstly,* it will strike a balance in conflicting interests between the judiciary and executive. *Secondly,* it will guide the planners and policy-makers in the effective implementation of Laws. *Thirdly,* it will foster constitutional friendly legal regime and *lastly,* it will focus gray areas for effective implementation of consultative jurisdiction. For the proposed object doctrinal methodology of research is the most suitable. The work is based on documents, commentaries, law reporters, debates in Lok Sabha and Rajya Sabha and enactments adopted in past or in present and further judicial trends of national courts will be analyzed and finally inference will be drawn.

Besides this some other methods like comparative, descriptive, applied and analytical will also be used according to the need of the study. Where things are of introductory and observatory in nature the method to be applied would be descriptive. Regarding analysis of the constitutional and legal provisions the method to be applied will be analytical. Where the research is directed to bring about improvement in the procedural aspects of consultative jurisdiction of Supreme Court the methodology will be applied. Regarding comparison of our Supreme Courts consultative jurisdiction with other countries and organizations (U.N.O. and EU, etc.) and considering their suitability with or without modification for our system, the methodology will be comparative.

The present book is dedicated to my learned teachers from whom I have derived the knowledge and the authors whose work I have consulted. *One may not always agree with all that I have written and at times there may be disagreements with my conclusion, yet this is the essence of academic freedom to formulate a reasonable judgment on the basis of known and accepted facts and authority of law.*

All efforts have been made to keep this edition free from errors. The responsibility for mistakes if any is exclusively mine. The author earnestly believes that this edition will prove to be very fruitful to the students, law teachers and legal fraternity. I will feel amply rewarded if the book is warmly received by all those for whom it is meant. I would welcome every suggestion for improvement in the book and shall incorporate the same in the next edition.

DR. AMIT SINGH

1

Concept of Consultative Jurisdiction

"The true secret of giving advice or consultation is, after you have honestly given it, to be perfectly indifferent whether it is taken or not, and never persist in trying to set people right."
—Hannan Whitall Smith

Advice! a wonderful word, is part of every one's life. It is a truthful and helpful idea, either generic or specific, flowing from someone having authority and possess the tendency of transmitting confidence and security in one at a time when he needs to take important decision. It is not just a passive passing of experiences from one to another, instead an active participation to help avoid mistakes. Good advice could be expressed in the form of suggestion or in some cases as a warning too.

Generally, there is involvement of two agencies in an advice; the advisor and the advisee. These two act independently of one-another but yet for a common object. At time, it is the advisee who goes-out, and looks for the advice, while at others the advisor chooses the time to tender advice.

An advice usually works best when the advisee experiences its inevitability. This is because the need increases the chances of its acceptability. Even if the advisee is convinced about the utility of advice, he has every right to decide whether to follow it or not.

What is true about an individual advice is equally relevant as regard to expert consultations. The idea of judicial consultation traces its origin in the Anglo Saxon World.

1. BACKGROUND

In British History upto the Middle Ages the Court was not a distinct institution as we see it today as distinct from the executive and the legislature, and there was no defined office of Judge.[1] The King reigned and governed with the aid of a big counseling body out of which the Courts of today have evolved. In course of time the functions of the King separated and became vested in distinct functional bodies viz., the legislature, executive and the judiciary. Still the Judges continued to function as "concilium regis", the King's Council in matters of law, and were bound by their then statutory oath to lawfully counsel the King in his business. Such consultation was in vogue in Britain till the middle of the 18th century.[2]

1. Constitutional History, Maitland 4th ed: "The further back we trace our History", says Maitland, "the more impossible is it for us to draw strict lines of demarcation between the various functions of the State: the same institution is a legislative assembly, a governmental council and a Court of law; . . . " (p. 05) "Besides the general Council, the King had a permanent council in constant session . . . the King can take advice in whatever quarter he pleases . . . Both in his Parliament and his Council, the King legislates, taxes and judges . . . " (p. 91) when in course of time the functions of the King separated themselves as executive, legislative and judicial and became vested in different bodies, ". . . the word curha comes to bemore and more definitely appropriated to a judicial body in which the King looks for advice and aid in the daily task of Government". (p. 91).
2. Broom's Constitutional Law 2nd ed. G.L. Denman, 1885, p. 143. The last constitution was in 1760 on the trial of George Sackville (p. 146).

Judicial consultation was the necessity of that time in Britain when law was in its fluid, formative and uncodified state. Owing to the power hunger of Kings and the subservience of the Judges this practice fell into great abuse for out of fear the Judges also gave such advice as were favourable for the extension of the King's prerogatives but adverse to the power of Parliament and welfare of the people.

Hence by an Act to which Charles I gave his assent on 7th August, 1641, the Long Parliament prohibited the practice. The Act of Settlement 1700 which made the Judges tenure during good behaviour instead of King's pleasure finally freed them from the Crown's yoke and created the environment for them to hold office without fear of the King's displeasure.

But the idea of obtaining judicially given opinions itself was not given up. Section 4 of the Judicial Committee Act, 1833, was enacted obligating the Judicial Committee of the Privy Council to tender advice to the Crown on any matter other than the judicial appeals presented to the Committee. Section 4 was the inspiration for section 213 of the Government of India Act, 1935, the precursor of Art. 143. Section 4 of Judicial Committee Act was also the genesis for similar provisions enacted by their respective parliaments in certain other territories held by great Britain viz., Canada[3] and Australia.[4]

The role of the Court which is nothing more than an institution of community life is fashioned as an answer to social need and it is not a matter of jurisprudential neatness. Even delivery of declaratory judgments was considered not the proper function of the court[5] though such power is part of the Anglo-Indian and American legal systems now. It is also interesting to note that Article 58 of the *Finnish Constitution,*

3. Canadian provision now contained in section 55 of the Supreme Court of Canada Act R.S., C. 35 was originally contained in S. 60 of Supreme Court of Canada Act R.S.C. 1906, C. 139.
4. Australian provision was contained in S. 88 Part XII, Judiciary, Act, 1903-20. It was declared *ultra vires* the Parliament of the Commonwealth of Australia in Judiciary Act, 1903-20, and *in re The Navigation Act*, 1912-20. 29 C.W.L.R. (1920-21).
5. S.A de Smit, Judicial Review of Administrative Action (1959) p. 368.

1919, provides that the Supreme Court and the Supreme Administrative Court of Finland have the right when they think that a modification or interpretation of law or ordinance is necessary, to address the President of the Republic a note requesting that such legislation be enacted, a practice not accepted as the proper activity of the courts in Britain, the U.S.A. or India.

An assessment of the validity of acts has been provided for in the Constitutions of Ireland[6] and France[7] but the reference in France is made not to any civil court but to a special court called the Constitutional Council. Such references seem to be the logical necessity of her State polity where the Civil Courts have no power of judicial review of legislations. While in Ireland and France references can relate only to the constitutionality of legislative acts the Indian references embrace a greater variety of problems, viz., questions of fact or law,[8] another difference is that the Indian opinion is in effect pruely a *responsa prudentium* on the legal status of a res while in France and Ireland, the opinions bind their executive i.e., the President and he is bound to act according to the opinion.

Chief Justice Jay and his associate judges declined to give advisory opinion to President Washington on the 27 questions on International Treaty Law the latter had referred to them on the ground that the "power given by the Constitution to the President, of calling in heads of departments for opinion seems to have been purposely as well as expressly united to the executive department."[9]

A provision for executive consultation of the judiciary had always been subject to serve criticism by the declaratory theory of judicial precedent. The theory believes that consultative function of Supreme Court is a constitutional function not in the nature of a judicial function or the exercise of any

6. Constitution of Ireland, 1927 Art. 26.
7. Constitution of the Vth Republic of France, Arts. 61, 62.
8. Section 213, Government of India Act, 1935, did not authorise the Governor.
9. *Muskrat v. United States*, 219 US 346 31 S. Ct. 250, 55 L.Ed. 246 (1911).

jurisdiction[10] though always judicially exercised on evidence between a proposal and an opposition. It is an enquiry made as to the legality of things and problems and does not result in declaratory or executable pronouncements.

According to the Classical theory :

> *"Theoretically a Court of Law should not have consultative jurisdiction because Court while giving an advice, exercises no judicial function. Lord Coke in the seventeenth century refused to give an opinion to King James I, and the American Supreme Court gave a similar answer to the President Washington in 1795, when the latter asked it to advise on certain questions arising under certain treaties. A court of law should decide issues arising out in cases and controversies duly litigated before it. A friendly litigation collusive suit, a question relating to future legislation, or a friendly and hypothetical question set for opinion must be normally outside the pale of judicial function of the court".*[11]

In spite of the theoretical objections, the advisory jurisdiction is often found necessary. The expediency of this has been recognized by Article 143 under which the President can ask the Supreme Court to give its opinion in respect of a question of public importance.

As the judges are traditionally known for adjudicating on disputes, there being counsel of the President is of great constitutional significance. Executive seeking advice from judiciary makes unique relationship between the two organs of Government in a Parliamentary System. It assumes greater significance in a federal structure where state units have nothing to do with the provisions under Article 143.[12]

Article 124 of the Constitution of India established the Supreme Court of India as the pinnacle of the Indian Judiciary.

10. Consolatory function does not involve the exercise of any jurisdiction which is "the authority which a court has to decide matters that are litigated before it or to take cognizance of matters presented in a formal way for its decision." Halsbury's Laws of England, Vol. 2, p. 340.
11. Kagzi, Constition of India, p. 312.
12. Jain, M.P., Indian Constitutional Law, p. 94.

The Constitution has conferred various jurisdiction on the Supreme Court. They are enumerated as follows:

(i) Writ jurisdiction under *article 32* for the enforcement of the fundamental rights.
(ii) Original jurisdiction under *article 131*.
(iii) Appellate jurisdiction under *articles 132, 133 & 134*.
(iv) Jurisdiction to grant special leave to appeal under *article 136*.
(v) Jurisdiction under *article 137* to review any judgment pronounced by it or order made by it.
(vi) Advisory jurisdiction under *article 143*.
(vii) Jurisdiction under *article 317 (1)* to hold enquiry and to report to the President for the removal of the chairman or the members of public service commissions.
(viii) Jurisdiction under *article 71* for matters relating to, or connected with the election of a President or vice President.

2. POWER OF PRESIDENT TO CONSULT SUPREME COURT

1. If at any time it appears to the President that a question of law or fact has arisen, or is likely to arise, which is of such a nature and of such public importance that it is expedient to obtain the opinion of the Supreme Court upon it, he may refer the question to that court for consideration and the court may, after such hearing as it thinks fit, report to the President its opinion thereon. [Article 141(2)].
2. The President may, notwithstanding anything in the proviso to Article 131, refer a dispute of the kind mentioned in the said proviso to the Supreme Court for opinion and the Supreme Court shall, after such hearing as it think fit, report to the President its opinion thereon [Article 141(2)].

The above extract of Article 143 shows that clause (1) is general in nature subject to the fulfillment of the conditions

Precedent prescribed therein. Clause (2) on, the other hand, deals with a specific matter by referring to the proviso of Article 131.

The President has been authorised by Article 143 to refer to the Supreme Court a question of law or fact which in his opinion is of such a nature and of such public importance that it is expedient to obtain its opinion upon it. The words of Article 143 are quite wide and there is no condition that it is only in respect of matters falling within the powers, functions, and duties of the President that it would be competent to him to frame questions for the advisory opinion of the Supreme Court. The only conditions are:

(i) that he should be satisfied that a question of law or fact has arisen or is likely to arise;
(ii) that he should also be satisfied that such a question is of such a nature and of such public importance that it is expedient to obtain the opinion of the Court on it.

Thus to ascertain the scope of clause (1) of Article 143, the following points must be noted:

(i) *Question of Law or fact:* It is not necessary that the question referred for opinion must be of law. It may be question of law or of fact.
(ii) *In respect of any matter:* The opinion sought by the President may be in respect of any matter. It was contended that only in respect of matters falling within the powers, functions and duties of the President he was entitled to make a reference under Article 143. The Court rejected this contention and held that the words of Article 143 are wide enough to empower the President to refer to the Supreme Court for its opinion any question of law or fact in respect of any matter.[13]
(iii) *Questions arisen or likely to arise:* The power of the President under Article 143 is wide enough to get

13. In the U.P. Legislature case, 1965 S.C.

opinion on prospective issues. It is not necessary that the dispute must have arisen. Even where a dispute is likely to arise, the President may obtain the opinion of the Supreme Court in advance.

(iv) *Public importance:* The question must be of such public importance that it is necessary to obtain the opinion of the Supreme Court. Whether the question is of such importance or not is a matter to be judged by the President. His satisfaction is sufficient.

3. PROCEDURE FOLLOWED IN A REFERENCE

Article 145 of the Constitution says about the rules of the court for their proceeding. It authorizes that the Supreme Court may from time to time, with the approval of the President, makes rules for regulating generally. Its practice and procedure, by using this power the court has made *"The Supreme Court Rules, 1966"*. Order 37 of Part V of this code contains the rules of procedure to be followed in case of reference under Article 143 of the Constitution.

On receipt of the reference the Registrar gives notice to the Attorney-General to appear before the Court to take directions of the court as to the parties why will be served with notice of such reference.[14] The Court also permits such persons and group of persons as may be interested to appear as interveners.[15]

The Court is to report after such hearing as it thinks fit. Every report shall be made in accordance with an opinion delivered in open Court with the concurrence of the majority of the judges present, with liberty to any judge who does not concur, to deliver a dissenting opinion.[16] The procedure has to be similar to that followed by the Court in the exercise of its original jurisdiction.

14. Or. 35 R. (I) of Supreme Court Rules, 1966, In re Presidential Poll. (1974) 2 SCC 33, 36 AIR 1974 SC 168 (summary of arguments).
15. Presidential Poll. Re. (1974) 2 SCC 33 AIR 1974 SC 1682.
16. 37 R.(3), Supreme Court Rules, 1966, Article 145(3), (4) and (5).

In order to effectively perform as duty under Art. 143, the Supreme Court may invoke Art. 142(2) in aid of its consultative function. Article 142(2) provides that :

> *"subject to the provisions of any law made in this behalf by Parliament, the Supreme Court shall, as respect the whole of the territory of India, have all and every power to make any order for the purpose of securing the attendance of any person, the discovery or production of any documents, or the investigation or punishment of any contempt of itself."*

Considering the unqualified usage of expression here, unlike sub-article (1) of Art. 142 which applies to situations where the Court make orders "as is necessary for doing complete justice in any cause or matter pending before it," it seems that this provision can be made use of by the Court when it sits as an enquiry tribunal under Art. 143.[17]

Further, Article 145(3) provides that a reference shall be heard by a Bench of five Judges. No report shall be made to the President save in the form of an opinion delivered in open court in terms of its cl. (4). When the parent provision for this requirement in S. 213 of the Government of India Act, 1935, was discussed in the House of Lords. *Earl Peel*[18] was of opinion that the delivery of an opinion in open Court would have a limiting effect on the freedom of reference of the Governor-General as his move that would turn on the reference could be anticipated and predicted once it was known that he had sought the opinion of the Federal Court.

He feared that a provision for public delivery of opinion in open Court would handicap and discourage the Governor-General from making use of the consultation for reasons of tact. But Archbishop of Canterbury clinched the issue by advocating for delivery of opinion in open Court substantiating the need from British History itself. It should be

17. It sits as an enquiry tribunal also under Art. 71 to decide disputes and doubts in the election of President or Vice-President and Article 317 to inquire into the removal of a member of the Union Public Service Commission.
18. Parliament Debates Lords (1934-35), Vol. 97, C, 1245-56.

remembered that the expressed reason of a judgment is so important an ingredient in it that any attempt at altering reasons publicly avowed as the reason of a judgment and handing privately to anyone other reasons in support of it, not specified in open Court is reprehensible. It is also possible that in a reference majority opinion would not be available since Judges are entitled to abstain from giving an opinion as *Sir Zafrullah Khan* did *in re Levy of Estate Duty*.[19] But cl. (5) provide " . . . no such opinion shall be delivered by the Supreme Court save with the concurrence of a majority of the Judges present at the hearing of the case . . . ." It means that where a majority opinion is not available no opinion shall be sent to the President and those opinions, which are available shall not be delivered in the open court even though a full hearing has been gone through.

4. NATURE AND SCOPE

The nature of Art. 143(1) is quite broad. There is no condition that the President can refer only such questions as pertain to his powers, functions and duties or those of the Central Government. The President can seek the opinion of the Supreme Court on any question of law or fact which appears to him to be of such a nature and of such public importance that it is expedient to obtain the Court's opinion. Of course, in this matter, the President acts on the advice of the Cabinet. Thus, questions relating to constitutional validity of the proposed legislation,[20] or 'powers, privileges and immunities' of State Legislatures have been referred to the Supreme Court for opinion.

It is not necessary that only a question which has actually arisen may be referred to the Court for its opinion. The President may make a reference even at an anterior stage, namely, when the question is likely to arise in future. It is a matter essentially for the President to decide whether the question is of such a nature and of such public importance that it is expedient to seek the Court's opinion thereon.

19. AIR 1944 F.C. 73.
20. *In re*, the Special Courts Bill, 1978.

The President is entitled to refer to the Supreme Court for its opinion any question of law or fact whether or not it has any relation to the entries in Lists I and III , or whether it falls in the Central sphere or in the State sphere. What Art. 143(1) requires is the President's satisfaction—(i) a question of law or fact has arisen or it likely to arise, and (ii) the question is of such a nature and of such public importance that it is expedient to obtain the Court's opinion on it. The satisfaction of the President on both these counts would justify reference to the Supreme Court. Questions regarding the validity of a statute in force or a proposed Bill may be referred to the Court as Art. 143(1) contemplates reference of a question of law which is 'likely to arise'.

The phraseology of the constitutional provision is quite broad to cover all types of references. The Court has stated that it is well within its jurisdiction to answer/advise the President in a reference made under Art. 143(1) of the Constitution of India if the questions referred are likely to arise in future or such questions are of public importance or there is no decision of this Court which has already decided the question referred.[21]

The Court has now clarified that it cannot be asked, under Art. 143(1) to reconsider any of its earlier decisions. The President can refer only such legal question as has not been decided by the Court earlier. The Court has reasoned that when in its ad judicatory jurisdiction, it has pronounced an authoritative opinion on a question of law, there neither remains any doubt about the question of law nor does it remain *res Integra* so as to require the President to know what the true position of law on the question is. The Court can review its earlier decision only under Art. 137.

The Supreme Court has rejected the contention that under Art. 143, the President can ask the Court to reconsider any of its previous decisions. The Court has observed that under the Constitution, the Court enjoys no appellate jurisdiction over itself. The Court cannot convert its advisory jurisdiction into an appellate one. "Nor is it competent for the President to

21. Gujarat Assembly election matter (2002) 8 SCC-237.

invest us with an appellate jurisdiction over the said decision through a reference under Article 143 of the Constitution". To interpret Art. 143(1) as conferring on the executive power to ask the Supreme Court to revise its own decision, would cause a serious inroad into the independence of the judiciary.[22]

In Art. 143(1), the use of the word 'may' indicates that the Supreme Court is not obligated to express its opinion on the reference made to it. It has a discretion in the matter and may, in a proper case, for good reasons, decline to express any opinion on the question submitted to it. Such a situation may perhaps arise if purely socio-economic or political questions having no constitutional significance are referred to the Court, or a reference raises hypothetical issues which it may not be possible to answer without a full setting of facts in which the issues are to operate. It is to ensure against such a contingency that the Article uses the word 'may' and enables the Supreme Court to refuse to answer questions if it is satisfied that it should not express its opinion having regard to the questions and other relevant facts and circumstances.

The Court has emphasized that 'abstract' or speculative or hypothetical or too general questions should not be referred to it for advisory opinion. The Court has asserted that if a reference made to it is "vague and general", or if for any appropriate reason, the Court considers it "not proper or possible" to answer the reference, the Court may return it by pointing out the impediments in answering it. The Court has said that the plain duty and function of the Court is to consider the question on which the President has made the reference and report to the President its opinion. If for any reason, the Court considers it not proper or possible to answer the question, it would be entitled to return the reference by pointing out the impediments.[23]

However, in Art. 143(2), the use of the word 'shall' indicates that the Supreme Court has to give its opinion on a reference made thereunder.[24] There is a reason for his

22. In the matter of Cauvery Water Disputes Tribunal, AIR 1992 SC 522, 553, 554 : 1993 Supp.(1) SCC 96(2).
23. *Re,* the Special Courts Bill.
24. *In re,* the Kerala Education Bill, 1957, AIR 1958 SC 956 also Keshav Singh's case, AIR 1965 SC 745.

dichotomy between Arts. 143(1) and 143(2). Whereas it may be possible to agitate before the Courts the matters falling under Art. 143(1) by adopting suitable procedures and techniques, the matters referred to in Art. 143(2) are banned from judicial scrutiny of the Supreme Court, High Court or any other Court because of the operations of Arts. 131 and 363 and there is no other way to get a judicial verdict on these matters, if it ever becomes necessary, except through the machinery of Art. 143(2). Hence the Supreme Court is constitutionally obligated to give its opinion if ever it is sought on the type of questions referred to in Art. 143(2).

2

Development of Consultative Jurisdiction in India

In order to evaluate the working of the institution of advisory jurisdiction an in-depth study of the constitutional intent behind the provision is necessary. The provision was, surprisingly, put in the Constitution without much debate. Article 119 of the Draft Constitution, which became Article 143 in the new Constitution came up for discussion in the Assembly on 6th June, 1949, which then decided to debate clause (2) of Article 119 of the Constitution.[1]

On 14th October, 1949 that Article was reconsidered by the Assembly and clause (2) was inserted in the Constitution[2] without any discussion. Hence, it becomes difficult to say anything about the reasons or intentions of the Constitution framers for adopting that Article or about the scope of Article 143.

It was the *'ad-hoc'* Committee on Supreme Court which recommended to the Constituent Assembly the conferment of

1. C.A. Debates, 6th June, 1949, pp. 642-43.
2. C.A. Debates, 14th Oct., 1949, p. 274.

advisory jurisdiction upon the Supreme Court. The Report of the ad hoc Committee[3] was added as an appendix to the Union Constitution Committee Report. A mention has been made in the report that some members of the Committee were opposed to the provision of placing on the Supreme Court an obligation to advise the Head of the State, although it is not clear in the report which of the members opposed and on what grounds. Having given their best considerations to the arguments for and against, the Committee felt that it would be on the whole better to continue the old provision[4] even under the new Constitution. Section 213 of the Government of India Act empowered the Governor General to refer a question of law to the Federal Court for advice. Clause (1) of Article 143 practically reproduces sub-section (1) of Section 213 of the Government of India Act, 1935. The adhoc Committee hoped that this jurisdiction was scarcely likely to be invoked. It was also required that the references to the Supreme Court for advice shall be dealt with by a full Court. Thus, the main reason for the incorporation of Article 143 in the new Constitution was that it had been in the old Statute which forms the basis of the new Constitution. It would be useful, therefore, to look to the Federal Court of India for a proper understanding of the constitutional intent of Article 143.

The Government of India Act, 1935 was based on the Report of the Joint Committee on Indian Constitutional Reforms, 1933-34. To trace the objects of Section 213 a study has to be made of the Committee's recommendations. The White Paper of 1933 proposed[5] that the Governor-General should be empowered in his discretion to refer to the Federal Court for hearing and consideration any 'justiable matter'. The

3. "Framing of India's Constitution," by B. Shiva Rao, Report of the *adhoc* Committee on Supreme Court, May 21, 1947, Appendix to the Union Constitution Committee Report p. 589, Sec. Appendix-I.
4. Section 2; 3 of the Government of India Act, 1935.
5. Proposals for Indian Constitutional Reforms (Published originally as Camb. 4268) p. 336, para 161, "161 : The Governor-General will be empowered in his description, to refer to the Federal Court, for hearing and consideration any justiciable matter he considers of such a nature and such public importance that it is expedient to obtain the opinion of the Court upon it."

Joint Committee accepted the proposals contained in the White Paper. The Chairman's Draft Report,[6] which was submitted to the Joint Select Committee of Indian Constitutional reforms on June 18, 1934 proposed the institution of advisory jurisdiction. Exception was made to the words any 'justiciable matter' used in the White Paper, and the words 'any matter of law' were preferred. The Chairman's Draft Report also referred to the similar jurisdiction possessed by the Privy Council under Section 4 of the Judicial Committee Act, 1833, which provided that his Majesty might refer to the Committee for hearing or consideration any matters whatsoever as His Majesty might think fit, and the Committee would thereupon hear and consider the same, and advice His Majesty thereupon.

On the point of the intentions behind proposing such jurisdiction, the Chairman's Draft Report expressed that this advisory jurisdiction may often prove of great utility. It was also mentioned that some of the British Indian delegates appeared to think of a private and confidential opinion being communicated by the Court to the Governor-General. The Chairman's Draft Report was accepted and adopted by the Joint Committee. It said, "We concour generally in the proposal and we are of the opinion that this advisory jurisdiction may often prove of great utility."

1. RELATED PROVISION OF THE GOVERNMENT OF INDIA ACT, 1935

A provision for judicial consultation in India was first devised in *Section 213* of the Government of India Act, 1935. The provision was enacted to meet certain political needs of the time when India was to become a federation of British Indian province and native states under the 1935 Act. The Governor General was entrusted in his own individual responsibility with the security of India and various other matters and in the discharge of his functions he was empowered to exercise his own individual judgment and discretion even as to override the advice of the Council of

6. The Chairman's Draft Report, p. 147, para 314. The Marquess of Linlithgo in the Chair.

Ministers. Besides, he was expected to maintain that delicate balance as it were between those who wanted more central and those who wanted more provincial powers.[7]

In face of such circumstances the British Parliament made the Federal Court to assist the Governor-General when he could not rely on the opinion of the Attorney General.[8] Hence section 213 of the Government of India Act, 1935 gave the Federal Court an additional role as legal consultant to the Governor-General.

The Federal Court pronounced only four advisory opinions. Almost in all cases it was called upon to interpret important constitutional provisions. They are as follows:

(A) In C.P. Barar Motor Spirit Reference[9]

In this first reference case, the Federal Court, firstly set principles of interpretation of the constitution. The opinion established the principle that in interpreting any particular provision of the Constitution due consideration, weight and importance should be given to the conditions, circumstances, particular environment of the time and needs of the changing society. The prevailing conditions could neither be enlarged nor be lessened when the question of interpretation was involved.

Secondly, the Court, through this advisory opinion helped in evolving the norms of Federalism. It established a definite norm regarding the principle of provincial autonomy and gave a lead to make the provinces the maters of their own houses. The Court opined that provincial autonomy without financial autonomy was a contradiction in terms. The judicial practice tells that the principle of constitutional interpretation propounded in this first reference case continues to figure prominently in even subsequent references of the Supreme Court.

7. Parliamentary Debates, Official Reports, 5th series, Lords, 1934-35, ed. 97c 1245-56 per Earl Peal C 1248.
8. Per Lord Rankeillor C. 1247.
9. AIR 1939 F.C. 1.

(B) In Hindu Women's Right to Property Act Reference

The Second reference under Section 213 of the 1935 Act to the Federal Court was that of the Hindu Right to Property Act case.[10] The Court pronounced its opinion in 1941. The Hindu Rights to property act had given rise to several doubts and difficulties and the Court was called upon to define its ambit, importance and limitations. The reference aimed at asserting whether the Act was validly enacted and could constitutionally be implemented. The Court through the opinion, upheld validity of the Act. Though the opinion could not end litigation on the subject and four years later, in a concrete case i.e., *Umayal Achi case*[11]—the same court declined to accept the stare decision effect of the advisory opinion, in subsequent cases the opinion was followed by the Federal Court,[12] High Courts[13] and the Supreme Court.[14]

(C) In Allocation of Lands and Buildings Reference[15]

This was the third reference made to the Federal Court for opinion. It was necessitated due to differences of opinion between the Union Government and the Punjab Government over the ownership of certain land. The Federal Court under this reference considered the scope of Section 213 of the 1935 Act and held that through under this Section it was not obligatory on the part of the court to entertain every reference, the court should always be unwilling decline to entertain a reference except for good reasons. The Court also observed that its sole concern had to be merely legalistic and juristic interpretation of the referred statute and the problems related thereto. The theory propounded by this opinion in respect of acceptance of reference has been followed by its successor, the Supreme Court in various reference cases.[16]

---

10. AIR 1941 F.C. 72.
11. AIR 1943 F.C. 8 at p. 11.
12. Narain *vs.* Province of Bihar, A.I.R. 1942 F.C. 8 at p. 11.
13. Nagappa Narain *vs.* Nukamba, 53 Bom. L.R. 177 Rodha Ammal.
14. Angarahala *vs.* Debarata, A.I.R. 1951 S.C. 293.
15. AIR 1944 F.C. 73.
16. *In re* Kerala Education Bill 1957 (1959) SCR 995 at p. 1015.

(D) In Re Levy of State Duty Reference

The scope of Section 213 of the Act came in for consideration also in the Fourth reference case i.e. *Re Levy of Estate Duty.*[17] The Federal Court laid down two principles contemplated and proposed legislation cannot be a good and reasonable ground for declining a reference. The advisory opinion, being advisory only, had no binding effect on the referring or giving authority. The principles laid down by this opinion have been continuously followed by the Supreme Court in various other reference cases. Though under the Government of India Act, 1935, the center was within its powers to levy Estate duty in respect of succession of property, the court in its advisory opinion held that the entry did not authorize the center to levy Estate Duty. The opinion necessitated an amendment into the 1935 Act. Consequently, the Indian Estate Duty Act, 1945 was passed which provided for the imposition of Estate Duty.

The Federal Court by announcing the four opinions under Section 213 of the 1935 Act contributed much to the process of constitutional development. Solution of complicated problems which need immediate relief has been the major object behind the exercise of the provision under Section 213. The procedure adopted by the Federal Court in rendering advisory opinions has certainly proved its worth.[18] The significance of the four pronouncements can be measured by the fact that they are cited in cases, legal materials, articles, law books and in legal documents now and then not only in India but in other leading judicial systems of the world as well.

2. CRITICISM AND ADVANTAGES OF CONSULTATIVE JURISDICTION

The utility and propriety of the Institution of advisory jurisdiction is debatable. Though the Institution is not without its advantages, it has also attracted severe criticism. The whole notion of consultation of the judiciary is, by hypothesis a contradiction. The judges do not sit in the seat of justice in

17. 1944 F.C. 73.
18. AIR 1943 F.C. 8 at P 11.

order to be consulted but in order to decide an issue. Arguments against the provision of advisory jurisdiction can briefly be put as under.

3. CRITICISM

First, criticism relates to the nature of advisory opinions. The opinions, technically, are merely advisory in nature. They bind neither the President nor the judges. An opinion given under the exercise of Article 143 is not 'law' within the meaning of Article 141 hence is not binding on lower courts.[19] Accepted theory of precedent tells that judges do not make law, only by formulation and declaration, they make law by applying it. Judicial declaration unaccompanied by judicial application is of no authority. In case of an advisory opinion, the court declares law but has no occasion to apply the same to a dispute between parties. The very fact that the subject of advisory opinions finds place in an article later than 141 is in itself an indication that an advisory opinion would be no more than opinion.

Secondly, the advisory opinions are criticized on the grounds that they are speculative and based on hypothetical, abstract and academic considerations. Justice Frankfurter took an opinion, given on the validity of prepared bills as void of any intrinsic value because of the psychologically unreal atmosphere in which the opinion moves on account of the questions being sterilized and mitilated for want of the impact of actuality and intensities of immediacy.[20]

A constitutional commentator[21] has pointed out that the expression of such opinion on any issue or issues that may be referred to it means a kind of pre-commitment on the part of the court to a certain point of view and this may create a difficult and embarrassing situation later on when a concrete case involving more or less similar issue comes before it for adjudication. Hence, the litigant concerned may not quite feel

19. *In re* Allocation of Lands and Buildings A.I.R. 1943 F.C. 13.
20. 37 Harvard Law Review (1924), pp. 1005-08.
21. Banerjee, D.N., some Aspects of the Indian Constitution, pp. 151-52.

confidence in the impartiality of the Court in such circumstances.

Thirdly, the critics are afraid of the provision under Article 143 being abused by the executive for political purposes. The executive may refer to the court questions involving political issues. Consequently, judiciary would be drawn into political controversies with the danger of loss of popular respect, impartial image and abandonment of truly judicial standards. There are instances where Presidential references arose much political controversies.—*The Kerala education bill reference* raised questions on which the public opinion in Kerala was greatly agitated. Berubari reference involved political issues. Similar situation arises *in Ayodhya reference*. The Court was asked to give opinion on whether a temple originally existed at the site, where the Babri Masjid subsequently stood. In the Presidential *reference on Gujarat issue*, segment of political parties said that ruling party is misusing the power of advisory jurisdiction. Thus, through such references by seeking advice from the Supreme Court the executive is able to drag judiciary into political controversies.

Fourthly, it is pointed out that the Court in tendering advisory opinions does not hear arguments from contesting parties but only dwells upon suggestions from the Union, the States and interveners which are allowed to by the Court. That is why, it is seen that there are less dissents in opinions that in normal judicial decisions.[22] Arguments in advisory proceedings move in unreal atmosphere and possible situations which would arise, are imagined.

Lastly, advising executive by judiciary, it is argued, violates the principles of separation of powers. Advisory function is not a judicial one. To advise executive or legislature is an executive function. The U.S. Supreme Court has consistently declined to exercise any powers other than those which are strictly judicial in their nature. It is also argued that the Order of reference to the highest judiciary amounts to a gesture of command or a threat which undermine the dignity and independence of judiciary.

22. 'Wanger, W.J., Advisory opinions in the Federal Judiciary, A Comparative Study (1958-59).

4. ASSAY OF CRITICISM

To understand the provision fully and correctly, every point of criticism has to be assessed categorically. *First,* about the non-binding nature of the opinions, it is true that technically the opinions are merely advisory, for they are not the results of judicial adjudication properly so called. But in practice, they are treated as having the same efficacy, authority and value as the judgments of the Supreme Court. *Chief Justice, Gawyer* of the Federal Court ruled that advisory opinions are not to be treated any the less binding on account of being advisory. Lower courts treat an advisory opinion to be as authoritative as a judgment in a case coming before the court in the normal manner. The referring authority, the President or practically the Union Government on the other hand, has always honored and obeyed the opinions given even in case when an opinion of the Supreme Court went against the wishes of the Union Government, i.e. the *Berubari case,* it was obeyed up to the fullest extent. The opinion in the *Keshav Singh case*[23] largely favored the High Court in Allahabad as against the Uttar Pradesh Legislative Assembly and in spite of the express dissatisfaction of the Assembly, all parties respected the opinion. The opinions practically do possess judicial character.

Secondly, the phrase 'likely to arise'[24] used in Clause of Article 143 provides room for reference to the court issues of doubtful maturity and hence attracts the criticism that advisory opinions are based on speculative, hypothetical, abstract and academic considerations. This is a real danger. But the experience with the institution so far does not present a serious threat at present. The problem of abstractness in the

23. A.I.R. 1965 S.C. 745.
24. *In re* Levy of Estate Duty certain questions regarding future Legislation on Levy Estate duty were referred to the Federal Court for opinion, but no draft Bill was submitted. Justice Zafrullah Khan, one of the judges hearing the reference, refused to give opinion because the reference was enveloped in thick fog of hypothesis and uncertainties and the opinion delivered on it could only rest 'upon a forest of assumptions' which must rob it of all value.

extreme form of the *levy case*[25] has not recurred. Besides, the Court in such cases, has the option to decline the reference. In the *Presidential Poll reference case* the court came across a hypothesis; what would be the situation if there was a malafide dissolution of a State Assembly or Assemblies or a malafide refusal to hold elections? The Court rightly refused to lend any consideration to the question at that stage.

Thirdly, by the institution of advisory jurisdiction, it is feared the President acting on instructions of the political head of the Government, can use the impartial judiciary for political ends or it may result in judicial intrusion in political affairs. This fear can be diluted in both the referring and answering authorities restrain themselves to act within the limits. The institution is not faulty, the need is that the persons who run the institution behave properly. The executive should hesitate in referring political questions for judicial advice and then the court should be careful not to entertain such references. Of course, the requirement of clause (1) of Article 143 that a question be of 'public importance' suggests that some political heat may be tolerable in the interest of judicial settlement of an otherwise unmanageable dispute.

Fourthly, it is pointed out that there are no contesting parties in a reference case and hence proceedings in reference cases lack legal representation. It is, however, a theoretical structure. Practically, the Court follows almost the same procedure in advisory proceedings as is followed in contested cases. The parties likely to be affected, generally are given notice and are allowed to be represented in Court through their advocates. In some cases *amicus curia* also are called to present the view point of unrepresented parties. A constitution commentator[26] believes that absence of briefs and oral arguments encourages the court to frame the constitutional matters more precisely, reduces the time taken to reach a decision and results in short opinions.

Finally, the argument that judicial consultation by the

25. In fact there is no instance of a reference of a question not yet in the stages of a draft bill again.
26. Field, D.P. Advisory Opinions—An Analysis, pp. 220-21, 24 ILJ 203 at pp. 220-21 (1948-49).

executive violates the principle of separation of powers. Once it is settled that advisory function of judiciary does have a judicial character, no ground is left for such argument. Even if, for arguments sake it be accepted that the principle of separation of powers is affected by the advisory opinions, we should keep in mind that the principle is designed to serve governmental efficiency not the *vice-versa*.[27] Besides, existence of a large number of Tribunals has already violated this theory and, therefore, the argument looses any weight. It is argued, further that requiring judiciary to advise executive results in loss of prestige and independence of the former. In answer to it, the singular instance of the judicial committee of the Privy Council which is an advisory body to the crown acting on judicial lines can be called to mind. On the other hand, it assists in the governance of the country by giving advice to the executive and legislature to act in accordance with the constitution.

5. ADVANTAGES OF CONSULTATIVE JURISDICTION

(i) Advisory function of judiciary has a number of advantages to its credit.

(ii) It accelerates the process of judicial review and hence saves time and energy both.

(iii) Taking advice beforehand leads to a prompt removal of doubts in the mind of the public or the Government.

(iv) It creates possibilities of judicial review where the Constitution has barred any judicial interference, i.e. proviso to Article 131.

(v) The constitution presents some situations where legal rights exist but no legal remedies are available. In atleast six situations the Constitution has created legal rights for which there is no legal remedy, i.e., *Article 31(2), 359(1), 329, 109(3), 199(3) and 363*. The institution of advisory jurisdiction can help in such situations.

27. Glovis, P.C. and Updegraff, C.M., Advisory Opinions, p. 188.

(vi) To depends solely on a real controversy for deciding a constitutional issue means that the court's jurisdiction depends on the whims of private litigants, and vital questions of constitutional law may remain clouded and unanswered by the highest Court for long till a suitable case arises and reaches the Court.

(vii) The ordinary court procedure is time-consuming and expensive as the case must pass through several courts before reaching the highest court and for this period a cloud of uncertainty would hang around the law, and the ultimate decision may very much depend on how and when a question is raised.

3

Consultative Jurisdiction in International Scenario

Most of the democracies of the commonwealth have made provision in their constitution for the highest courts to have an advisory or consultative jurisdiction. The rationale was to enable the court to render advice on crucial matters when other constitutional mechanisms are either inefficacious to resolve specific issues or when the constitution appear not to have provided any other mechanism. In order to have a clear insight into the working of the Institution of advisory jurisdiction, an assessment of the various countries on the point will not be out of place. The discussion in this chapter is divided into two parts, first, the advisory jurisdiction of courts in the classical democracies of the commonwealth, secondly, the advisory jurisdiction of courts in the newer democracies of the commonwealth.

1. ADVISORY JURISDICTION IN CLASSICAL DEMOCRACIES OF COMMONWEALTH

(A) Related Provisions of Canada

Canadian Supreme Court Act, 1952, contains the provision giving birth to the Institution of advisory jurisdiction. Section 55 of the act empowers the Governor-General-in-Council to refer to the Supreme Court for hearing and consideration important questions of law or fact touching ... any matter. Governor-General is the final authority on the question whether a matter so referred is an important question.

The Court is, under the statute,[1] bound to answer each question so referered :

> "When any such reference is made to court, it shall be the duty of the court to hear and consider it, and to answer each question so referred with the reason for each such answer."

Section 60 of the Supreme Court Act of Canada, 1906 was more explicit in this regard. It provided that it was the duty of the Court to hear and consider the references made on matters enumerated in Sec. 60 and that the court shall certify to the Governor in council for his information, its opinion each such question with the reasons for each such answer. The provision under Section 60 of the Canadian Supreme Court 1906 is significant for at least two reasons.

First, the provision requires that such opinion shall be pronounced as in the case of a judgment upon an appeal to the court and that it shall be binding on all inferior courts in the like manner as an appellate judgment of the Supreme Court. The 1952 Act has thus removed any doubt[2] as to whether such opinion on a reference shall count as an 'opinion' because there is no 'lis' and no parties, or as judgment.

Secondly, this jurisdiction in Canada is a statutory

1. Present Sec. 55 of the Supreme Court of Canada Act, 1952.
2. A.G. Ontario *v.* A.G. Canada (1912) A.C. 571.

obligation of the Supreme Court to answer the questions under reference. The jurisdiction is, thus, an exception to the general rule adhered to by the court that it will not decide abstract questions. The Canadian Supreme Court itself has upheld the constitutionality of legislation providing for such reference on abstract questions.[3]

Although it has been made obligatory on the part of the Canadian Supreme Court to pronounce advisory opinion, the judicial committee has at times, on appeal from such opinions from Canada, expressed fears of the dangers of such advisory opinions. In *cf. A.G. of Antario* v. *Hamilton Street Ry*[4] the committee observed that they would be worthless as being speculative opinions on hypothetical questions. It would be contrary to principle, inconvenient and inexpedient that opinions should be given on such questions at all. When they arise, they must arise in concrete cases, involving private rights, and it would be extremely unwise for any judicial tribunal to attempt beforehand to exhaust all possible cases and facts which might occur to qualify, cut down and override the operation of the particular words when the concrete case is not before it.

In *A.G. of British Columbia* v. *A.G. of Canada*[5] it was pointed out that under this procedure questions may be put which it is impossible to answer satisfactorily. Not only may the question of future litigants be prejudiced by the Court laying down principles in an abstract form within reference but it may turn out to be practically impossible to define a principle adequately and safely without previous ascertainment of the exact facts to which it is to be applied.

In Re-Regulation and control of Aeronautics.[6] The Committee held it undesirable that the Court should be called upon to express opinions which may affect the rights of persons not represented before it or touching matters of such a nature that its answers must be wholly ineffectual, with regard to parties who are not and who cannot be brought before it, i.e. foreign Government.

3. Dawson, R.M., Democratic Government in Canada, pp. (95-101).
4. 1903 A.C. 574.
5. (1914) A.C. 155, p. (162).
6. (1932) A.C. 54, p. 66.

Nevertheless, since its establishment in 1875, the Canadian Supreme Court has so far pronounced advisory opinions in many cases.

1. In most of these cases, the Government, seeking to introduce a bill has sought the judicial opinion on its constitutional powers e.g. as to marriage, liquor, fisheries[7] on when similar questions have arisen in relation to a Provincial Bill reserved for the assent of the Governor-General.[8]
2. The Governor-General may also refer the question of constitutionality of a Dominion or Provincial[9] statute after it has been enacted.
3. Even the validity of subordinate legislation has been the subject of reference.[10]
4. The respective powers of the Dominion and Provincial Legislatures with respect to particular matters also have been referred in the abstract, irrespective of any proposed or actual legislation.[11]
5. A reference has been made upon the very competence of Canadian Parliament to abolish appeals to the Privy Council altogether.[12]
6. Some of the references related to the interpretation of statutes, e.g. which court had jurisdiction to perform certain statutory functions.[13]

Section 55 of the Supreme Court Act, 1952 also empowers either House of the Dominion Parliament to refer any question to the Supreme Court for the advisory opinion. Provincial

7. In Cf. A.G. for Canada *v.* A.G. for Provinces (1898) A.C. 700.
8. *In re* Alberta Statutes (1938) S.C.R. 100 (Can.).
9. Cf. Ref. *Re* Alberta Debt Adjustment Act S.C.R. 31 (Can.).
10. Ref. *Re* Validity of Wartime Le asehold Regulations (1950) S.C.R. 124 (Can.).
11. Cf. Ref. Re Waters and Water Powers (1929) S.C.R. 200 (Can.).
12. Cf. A.G. of Antario *v.* A.G. of Canada (1947) 51 C.W.N. 886 (P.C.) A. 1947 P.C. 1999.
13. Ref. *Re* Adoption Act (1938) S.C.R. (Can.).

Governor also can refer similar questions to the Provincial Appellate Court for opinion.[14]

(B) Related Provisions of U.K.

We find some attempts in British History to call upon the judiciary to give advisory opinions but the Lords have refused to exercise such function. Up to the middle ages, in Great Britain, the judicial organ was not a distinct institution as we see it today, from the executive and legislature and there was no defined office of Judge. The King reigned and governed with the aid of a big advisory body out of which the courts of today have evolved. In course of time and functions of the King separated and became vested in distinct functional bodies viz., the legislature, executive and the judiciary. Still the judges continued to function as 'concilium Regis,' the King's Council, in matters of law and were bound by their then statutory oath to lawfully counsel the king in his business. Such consultation was in vogue in Britain till the middle of 18th Century.[15]

On a proper understanding, one can safely conclude that judicial consultation was the necessity of times in Great Britain when law was in its fluid, formative and un-codified condition. But, owing to the power hunger of kings and the subservience of the judges this practice fell into great abuse. The judges, out of fear, were compelled to give such advice as were favorable for the extension of the King's prerogatives but adverse to the power of Parliament and welfare of the people.

The Long Parliament, by an Act to which Charles-I gave his approval in August 1641, prohibited the practice.[16] The Act of Settlement, 1700 which made the judges' tenure during good behavior instead of king's pleasure finally freed judges from the Crown's yoke and created environment for them to hold office without fear of the king's displeasure. But the idea of obtaining judicial opinions itself was not abandoned. Section 4 of the Judicial Committee Act, 1883 was enacted providing that His Majesty may refer to the Privy Council 'any such other matter whatsoever as his Majesty thinks fit'.

---

14. *Ref. re* validity of the orderly Payment of Debts Act (1959), (1960), 23 DLR 2nd Ed., 449 (Can.).
15. Constitutional History, Maitland, 4th Ed.
16. Broom's Constitutional Law, 2nd Ed. 1885, p. 143.

The provision empowered the Crown to refer to the Judicial Committee any legal issue on which it desired advice and the Judicial Committee 'shall thereupon hear and consider the same and shall advise Her Majesty thereupon'. Use of this provision was made mostly on issues outside the United Kingdom.

In 1928, an attempt to create the advisory jurisdiction was made by the English Parliament. Members of the House of Lords seriously opposed the provisions of the proposed clause 4(1) of the Rating and Valuation Bill of that year which sought to enable a minister to submit a question to the High Court for its opinion. It was branded as a 'piece of mischievous legislation'.[17] It was argued that the proposed clause would 'make the Judiciary act in an ancillary and advisory capacity to the Executive' and confuse the working of the judicial system with the Executive administration.

(i) That it was no part of the business of the judges and never had been 'part of their business', at any rate since the Act of Settlement, to have advisory concern in the acts of the administration.

(ii) That the natural effect of associating 'the judges with the administration and attaching to them the responsibility for conclusions which are put forward by the administration' would be to 'weaken the authority of the judiciary'.

(iii) That there was no reason why the judges should be brought in 'by this side wind to help the Executive to carry on their business, to replace the Law Officers and to relieve the Executive of responsibility as to decisions they ought to arrive at upon the law'. In face of the strong opposition in the House of Lords, that clause had to be dropped.

(C) Related Provisions of United States

The U.S. Constitution has no specific provision like Art. 143(1) authorising the President to make a reference to the U.S.

17. The parliamentary debates, official report, Vol. 70, H.L. 19th April, 1928, Col. 760.

Supreme Court seeking its opinion on any question. The U.S. Constitution is based on the doctrine of Separation of Powers. Art. III, s. 2(1) of the U.S. Constitution provides that the judicial power vested in the Supreme Court shall extend to "cases" and "controversies".

The U.S. Supreme Court has consistently refused to render advisory opinion on abstract legal questions as it does not wish to exercise any non-judicial function. Giving of such an advice, it has been feared, might involve the Court in too direct participation in legislative and administrative processes. The reluctance of the Court is formally based on the doctrine of separation of powers which forms one of the bases of the U.S. Constitution.

In 1793, when Secretary of State Jefferson enquired of the Supreme Court whether it would give advice to the President on questions of law arising out of certain treaties, the Court refused saying that there was no such provision in the Constitution, and that it was not proper for the highest Court to decide questions extra-judicially.[18] Again, in *Muskrat* v. *U.S.*[19] The Court refused to give an advisory opinion arguing that under the Constitution its jurisdiction extends to a 'case or controversy' and so it cannot give an opinion without there being an actual controversy between adverse litigants. The Court has consistently refused to decide abstract, hypothetical or contingent questions. Justice William R. Day, writing for the Court, predicted that if the justice rendered a judgment in the case.

> *"the result will be that this court, instead of keeping within the limits of judicial power and deciding cases or controversies arising between opposing parties, as the Constitution intended it should, will be required to give opinions in the nature of advice concerning legislative action, a function never conferred upon it by the Constitution."*

18. Douglas, "Marshall to Mukharjee" at pp. 25-26, Thayer Legal essays, (1923) at p. 53.
19. Frank Furter, "A Note on Advisory Opinion", 37 H.L.R., 1002, 1005 (1924).

Echoing the convictions expressed in Muskrat, Supreme Court Justice Felix Frankfurter, writing on advisory opinion, stated,

> *"Every tendency to deal with constitutional questions abstractly, to formulate them in term of barren legal questions, leads to . . . sterile conclusions unrelated to actualities."*

While courts are typically limited in issuing advisory opinion, the attorney general of the United States and state attorneys general frequently issue opinions that are advisory in nature. By statue, the president or head of an executive department may require from the US attorney general an opinion on questions of law arising from the administration of that office or department.[20] Most states charge attorney general with similar responsibilities. Although advisory opinions issued by attorneys general are not typically binding in nature, in some circumstances the opinions may bind the authorities that request them.

However, some of the State Constitutions (e.g. Massachusetts) empower the Legislature and the Executive to seek opinion of the State Supreme Court 'upon important questions of law'. The opinions so given are not taken as precedents in subsequent litigations relating to the same question.

It has only been supposed that a federal court set-up under Article III of the U.S. Constitution should not take up an advisory role, there being no bar to a Court set-up by statute to give an advisory opinion at the request of either the Legislature or the Executive. Thus the judicial Code of 1942 provides that the Court of Claims shall have the jurisdiction to reports (i) to either House of the Congress on any Bill referred to the Court by such House except a Bill for pension, (ii) or to any executive department as to any claim or matter involving controversial questions of law or fact.

20. 28 U.S.C.A., 511-512 [1993].

(D) Related Provisions of Australia

The Australian High Court has refused to give advisory opin:ion on the ground that the essential function of the Judiciary is the decision of disputes and not the consideration of abstract legal questions.[21] Even the legislature cannot require the Court to exercise any such function.[22]

For under Section 76 of the Constitution, the Court can only decide 'matters', i.e. judicial proceedings and not abstract questions and a statute which requires the Court to determine such questions must be held to be invalid. But declaratory action lies at the instance of the Attorney General of the Commonwealth or of a State to test the validity of the statute even though no private individual has yet been affected.

(E) Related Provisions of Japan

There is no provision in the constitution of Japan to give advisory opinions and Chief Justice 'Tanka' had announced that the Supreme Court of Japan will follow the American Supreme Court on this point.[23]

2. ADVISORY JURISDICTION IN NEWER DEMOCRACIES OF COMMONWEALTH

The newer constitutional system of the commonwealth, the precedent of Canada, rather than of Australia appears to have been followed. However, unlike Canada where the Supreme Court's advisory jurisdiction has been conferred by legislation, and Australia where the attempt was also legislative, most of the constitutional systems of the 'New Commonwealth' entrench this jurisdiction in their respective Constitutions. In countries of South and South-East Asia, provisions for advisory or consultative jurisdiction are found in every Constitution. The common features are that the president, in most of the newer constitutional systems of the Commonwealth, or the Yand di-Pertuan Agong (King) in

21. *In re* Judiciary and Navigation Acts, 29 C.L.R. 25 (1921).
22. *Attorney Gen. for Victoria* v. *Commonwealth*, 71 C.L.R. 237 (1945).
23. Cf. Douglas, from Marshall to Mukherjee, (1923) at p. 26.

Malaysia is constitutionally empowered to ask the Supreme Court for an advisory opinion.

The grounds entitling the seeking of an advisory opinion vary from one jurisdiction to another. In Pakistan, India, Bangladesh and Sri Lanka acquisition of law or fact' of 'public important' which has 'arisen' or 'likely to arise' can be the basis for seeking an advisory opinion. It is also specified that the ground of 'expediency' be also attendant. The respective provisions are as follows:

(A) Related Provisions of Pakistan

If, at any time, the President considers that it is desirable to obtain the opinion of the Supreme Court on any question of Law which he considers of public importance, he may refer the question to the Supreme Court for consideration. The Supreme Court shall consider a question so referred and report its opinion on the question to the President.[24]

Reference of 1954:

> The Governor-General of Pakistan after dissolving to constituent assembly (Provisional Parliament) and suspend the constitution on 24 October 1954, made a reference to the Federal Court of Pakistan under S. 213 of the Government of India Act, 1935. One of the questions so referred was "whether the Constituent Assembly was rightly dissolved."[25]

In this reference, the Governor-General had made, the following three averments which, despite their being unproven according to judicial procedure by letting in evidence, the Pakistan Court made its assumptions.

1. That though the Constituent Assembly functioned for more than 7 years, it was unable to carry out the duty of providing a Constitution and for all practical

24. Article 186, Constitution of Pakistan, 1973, now it is Article 209 of new Constitution.
25. All-Pakistan Legal Decision 1955 (I) 455.

purposes assumed the form of a perpetual legislature;

2. That the Constituent Assembly was dissolved by the Governor-General because by reason of repeated representations form the resolutions passed by representative public bodies throughout the country, he formed the opinion that the Assembly had become wholly unrepresentative of the people; and
3. that the Constituent Assembly from the very beginning asserted the claim that the laws passed by it under sub-sec. (1) of S. 8 of the Indian Independence Act, 1947, did not require the assent of the Governor General.[26]

The learned Chief Justice Muhammed Munir observed on the objection taken by the opposition as to the manner in which the reference was made: "...Whether, if the Governor-General had the authority to dissolve the Constituent Assembly, it was properly dissolved, is not a legal but a political issue which cannot be referred to Court for opinion." *Mr. Pritt,* however contends that the question must be answered in the form in which it has been framed and that the Court should go into the facts on which the propriety or impropriety of the dissolution may depend. He has, therefore, referred to the affidavits which were filed on behalf of the Government and the counter-affidavit put in by Mr. Tamizuddin Khan[27] in an endeavour to show that the dissolution was not justified on the facts and that it was ordered with more ulterior motives.

We cannot, on this reference, undertake this enquiry or record any findings on the disputed question of facts because any such course would convert us into a fact finding tribunal which is not the function of this Court when its advice is asked on certain questions of law. The answer to a legal question always depends on facts found or assumed and since we cannot try issues of fact the reference has to be answered on the assumption of fact on which it has been made. . . . The

26. *Ibid.*, p. 461.
27. Cf. A.K. Brohi, Fundamental Law of Pakistan, p. 641.

Governor-General has taken the responsibility of asserting certain facts and has merely asked us to report to him what the legal position is if those facts are true."

Relying on the three averments and without considering them on merits, the Court concluded that the dissolution was valid and legal.

Presidential Reference against the CJI of Pakistan

On March 9, 2007, President Parvez Musharraf filed a reference against the Chief Justice of Pakistan, Mr. Justice Iftikhar Muhammad Chaudhary, under Article 209 of the Constitution, on charge of misconduct. On the same day, the Chief Justice was rendered "non-functional" by presidential decree, which declared without citing any specific law, that the Chief Justice could not carryout the functions of his office while the reference was pending against him. On the same day, the President also appointed the next senior most available judge on the Supreme Court. Mr. Justice Javed Iqbal as the Acting Chief Justice.[28]

On July 20, 2007, the thirteen-member bench of the Supreme Court has set aside the Presidential reference against the Chief Justice. The Supreme Court has restored the Chief Justice of his post by declared invalid the presidential action of sending him on force leave.[29]

(B) Related Provisions of Bangladesh

If any time it appears to the President that a question of law or fact has arisen, or is likely to arise, which is of such a nature of such public importance that it is expedient to obtain the opinion of the Supreme Court upon it, he may refer the question to the Appellate Division for consideration and the Division may, after such hearing as it thinks fit, report to President its opinion thereon to the President.[30]

---

28. Gazette of Pakistan Extra-ordinary, Part III, Islamabad, p. 675.
29. Nasir Iqbal : "CJI Challenges reference in Supreme Court : New twist to raging Controversy" available at www.dawn.com accessed on 25.04.2007.
30. Article 106, Constitution of Bangladesh.

(C) Related Provisions of Sri Lanka

If at any time it appears to the President that a question of law or fact has arisen or is likely to arise which is of such nature and of such public importance that it is expedient to obtain the opinion of the Supreme Court upon it, he may refer the question to that Court for consideration and the Court may, after such hearing as it thinks fit, within the period specified in such reference or within such time as may be extended by the President, report to the President its opinion thereon. Every proceeding under paragraph (1) of this Article shall be held in private unless the Court for special reasons otherwise directs.[31]

(D) Related Provisions of Malaysia

In Malaysia, only a 'constitutional question' is fit for invoking the advisory jurisdiction of the Supreme Court. Also, 'expediency' is not named as a factor in the Malaysian Constitution.

Yang di-Pertuan Agong may refer to the Federal Court for its opinion any question as to the effect of any provision of this Constitution which has arisen or appears to him likely to arise, and the Federal Court shall pronounce in open court its opinion on any question so referred to it.[32]

Despite the difference in phraseology, the important issues to note in regard to these constitutions is that first, only the head of state, the President or the king like the "Governor of Council" in Canada is empowered to seek an opinion from the Court. Secondly, the practical use of the advisory jurisdiction in the other constitution system. In Malaysia, the provision has not been utilised since Independence in 1957. A similar situation exists in Sri Lanka. In Bangladesh, the advisory jurisdiction was invoked only once and the Pakistan Supreme Court was called upon advice only an rare occasions.

3. CONSULTATIVE JURISDICTION IN INTERNATIONAL ORGANIZATION

The advisory jurisdiction of the International Court has

31. Article 129, Constitution of Sri Lanka, 1978.
32. Article 131, Constitution of Malaysia.

acquired a significance which was not contemplated originally. In the beginning it was criticized as likely to undermine the judicial character of the Court. However, the Permanent Court exercised this power with such judicial care that its advisory opinions have been considered by the States as well as the International organizations to be as authoritative statements of law as the Court's judgments. What was considered in its inception to be of doubtful quality, in practice developed into a perfected judicial procedure.[33]

It provided international organizations with a means of access to the Court and enabled them to bring before it legal questions which, in their particular circumstances, were unlikely to have come up for judicial consideration. So useful, in fact, this jurisdiction proved in the course of the working of the Court that, when the Charter of the United Nations and the Statue of the International Court of Justice were being drafted, its retention was favoured in these constitutional instruments indeed the Charter has further provided for authorizing many more organizations to request the Court's advisory opinions. The International Court of Justice has already given a number of opinions. Some of these have provided to be controversial, as were some of the opinions of the Permanent Court. But the soundness and value of the Court's advisory jurisdiction has never been doubted.[34]

4. ADVISORY JURISDICTION OF I.C.J.

According to *Article 65* of the Statue, the Court may give an advisory opinion on any 'legal question' to any body which has been authorized in accordance with the Charter of the United Nations or in accordance with the Statue. The Charter under *Article 96, Para 1* lays down that the Security Council and the General Assembly may request to the Court to give an advisory opinion on any legal question. In addition to them, other organs of the United Nations and specialized agencies

33. Hambro : "The auhority of the advisory opinions of the I.C.J.", p. 5: and Rosenne, I.C.J., p. 441.
34. Hudson : *The Effect of Advisory Opinions.* (Oxford University Press, London) at p. 631.

may also request for an advisory opinion on 'legal questions' arising within the scope of their activities if so authorized by the General Assembly. It may be noted that the above bodies may seek the advisory opinion only on legal questions. But there is a difference in the seeking of advisory opinion of the Court by the General Assembly and the Security Council, and by the other organs of the United Nations. While the former may seek advisory opinion on any 'legal question', latter can do so only on such 'legal questions' which arise within the scope of their activities.

It is to be noted that the Court will give advisory opinion even if a question bears legal as well as political character. *In the legal consequences of the Construction of a Wall in the Occupied Palestinian Territory,*[35] it was contended that the question posed before the Court for the advisory opinion is of political character, and therefore it has no jurisdiction. The Court did not accept the view by stating that the fact that a legal question also has political aspects, does not suffice to deprive it of its character as a 'legal question' and to deprive the Court of a competence expressly conferred on it by its Statue, and the court cannot refuse to admit the legal character of a question which invites it to discharge an essentially judicial task.[36]

5. DISCRETIONARY POWER TO GIVE ADVISORY OPINION

The power to give the advisory opinion conferred upon to the Court is discretionary. Article 65(1) of the Statue of the Court clearly states that "the Court may give an advisory opinion".[37] The use of the expression "may" denotes that the Court is not obliged to give an opinion, and can decline to do so, even where it would unquestionably have the right to

35. The Judgment was delivered by the Court on July 9, 2004.
36. Legality of the Threat or Use of Nuclear Weapons, ICJ Reports 1996 (1) p. 234 para 13.
37. Article 65, Para 1 of the Statue of the Court says that the Court may give an advisory opinion on any legal question at the request of whatever body may be authorized by or in accordance with the Character of the United Nation to make such a request.

comply with the request for an opinion. However, in principle the Court does not refuse such a request provided the opinion is sought appropriately from the organ or organization on any legal question. *In the case of Reservations to the Genocide Convention* the Court stated that "A reply to a request for an opinion should not, in principle, be refused".[38] However, the Court may decline to give an opinion, in the following cases:

1. Where the opinion given by the Court is likely to amount as a decision of the Court in a contentious case. In *Eastern Carelia case*[39] the Permanent Court of International Justice declined to give an opinion on the ground that answering the question would be "substantially equivalent to deciding the dispute between the parties."[40]
2. When the Court considers that even on legal questions the opinion is likely to raise serious political issues. *In the Certain Expenses case*[41] the Court stated that "even if the question is a legal one, which the Court is undoubtedly competent to answer, it may nonetheless decline to do so" on compelling reason. One of such reasons is that the opinion given by the Court may have far reaching political implications.
3. Where the Court does not have adequate information on the issue on which the opinion has been sought.
4. If the Court considers that it lacks jurisdiction to give advisory opinion on a particular question. *In the case concerning the Legality of the Use by a State of Nuclear Weapons in Armed conflict*, the Court refused to give the advisory opinion to the World Health Organisation, on the ground that the request for an advisory opinion submitted by the WHO does not relate to a question which arises "within the scope of (the) activities" of that Organisation. The Court

38. ICJ Reports (1951), p. 19.
39. PCIJ Series B, No. 5.
40. PCIJ, Series B, No. 5 at p. 29.
41. ICJ Reports (1962) at p. 155.

> observed that 'an essential condition of founding its jurisdiction in the present case is absent and that it cannot, accordingly, give the opinion requested'.

Although the Court may decline to give an advisory opinion on the basis of 'proprietary' it has to be cautious is doing so. The Court in principle does not decline to give an advisory opinion. It refuses only on 'compelling reasons'. If the Court adopts the practice of not to give the opinion without any convincing reasons even on legal questions, its image is likely to be lowered down. It is to be noted that in the history of the International Court of Justice there has been no refusal to act upon a request for advisory opinion. The Court for the first time refused to give advisory opinion to the WHO in the case concerning the Legality of the Use by a State of Nuclear Weapons in Armed Conflict

6. ADVISORY OPINIONS OF THE COURT

The advisory opinions of the International Court of Justice have greatly encouraged the progressive development of International Law and have helped the functions and development of the International Organisation.[42] Between 1946 and 2006, the court dealt with 23 requests for advisory opinions, delivering 22 opinions and making 24 orders in the cases concerned. Following advisory opinions of the court deserve special mention in this connection:

1. *Conditions of admission of the State to the United Nations (1948).*[43]—In its advisory opinions on the Conditions of Admission of a State to the Untied Nations, the World Court ruled that a member State of the United Nations while casting its vote either in

---

42. "By several of its Advisory opinions the Court has made an important contribution to the development of the legal status of International organisations and international civil servants". Nagendra Singh, note 12, at 14. "Codification and progressive development of International Law". I.J.I.L., Vol. 18 (1978) at p. 8.
43. I.C.J. Rep. (1948), p. 4.

the General Assembly or in Security Council, cannot make its consent or vote depending upon the conditions which are not mentioned in the Charter. Thus in view of the Court, in regard to the admission of the State, essential conditions mentioned in the Charter are exhaustive and no other conditions can, therefore, be validity imposed.

2. *Competence of General Assembly regarding Admission of a State to United Nations (1950)*[44]—After the repeated failure of the Security Council to make its affirmative recommendation in respect of the applications of certain States for the membership of the United Nations, some States expressed the opinion that in such a situation the General Assembly can by its decision admit a State to the United Nations. But in its advisory opinion given in 1950, the World court ruled that for a State to be admitted to the United Nations both the affirmative recommendations of the Security Council as well as the decision of the General Assembly are necessary. The Court also made it clear that it is competent to interpret the provision of the Charter.
3. *Reparation of the injuries suffered in the service of the United Nations (1949)*[45]—In this advisory opinion the International Court of Justice ruled that the United Nations is a legal person and has capacity to claim compensation for injuries suffered by the persons who are in the service of the United Nations.[46]
4. *International Status of South West Africa (1950)*[47]—In this case the Court helped the development of International law relating to succession of

44. I.C.J. Rep. (1950), p. 4.
45. I.C.J. Rep.(1949), p. 174.
46. The court also observed, "Under International Law the Organisation must be deemed to have those powers, which, though not expressly provided in the Charter, are conferred upon it by necessary implication as essential to the performance, of its duties". *Ibid.*, at p. 182.
47. I.C.J. Rep. (1950), p. 128.

International Organisation. The Court ruled that the succession of International Organisation takes places if the objects and nature of the predecessor and successor International Organisations are same. In this case the Court ruled that the trusteeship system of the United Nations succeeded to the rights and duties of the mandatory system of the League of Nations.

5. *Reservations to the convention on the Prevention and Punishment of the Crime of Genocide.*—In this opinion the court propounded compatibility test relating to reservations to a multilateral treaties which was later on adopted in the Vienna Convention on the Law of Treaties, 1969.
6. *Effects of Awards of Compensation made by the U.N. Administrative Tribunal.*[48]—In this case, the court held that though established by the General Assembly, the U.N. Administrative Tribunal was an independent and truly judicial body pronouncing final judgments without appeal within the limited field of its functions and not merely an advisory or subordinate organ. Its judgments were therefore binding on the U.N. Organization and thus also on the General Assembly. Later in Application for Review of Judgment No. 158 of U.N. Administrative Tribunal[49] and Application for Review of Judgment No. 273 of the U.N. Administration Tribunal[50] also, the court upheld the decision of the Tribunal.
7. *Certain expenses of the United Nations (1962)*[51]—In this case the Court had to decide whether the expenses incurred by the United Nations Suez Crisis 1956 and Congo Operations (1960-61) apportioned by the General Assembly among the members were to be regarded the expenses of the Organisation, in accordance with the provisions of Article 17(2). The

48. L.C.J. Rep. (1954), p. 47.
49. Advisory opinion of 12th July, 1973.
50. Advisory opinion of 20th July, 1982.
51. I.C.J. Rep. (1962), p. 151.

Court answered in affirmative. The Court also made it clear that the United Nations is capable of doing anything which is not prohibited under the Charter and if done to achieve the purpose contained in Article I of the Charter. Thus the Court indirectly sustained the validity of Uniting for Peace Resolution, 1950.

8. *Advisory opinion concerning the legal consequences of the continued presence of South Africa in Namibia (i.e. South-West Africa), notwithstanding Security Council Resolution 276 (1970).*[52]—In this case, the World Court held the following:

   (a) That the continued presence of South Africa in Namibia being illegal, South Africa is under obligation to withdraw its administration from Namibia immediately and thus put an end to its occupation of the territory.
   (b) That State Members of the United Nations are under obligation to recognise the illegality of South Africa's presence in Namibia and the invalidity of its acts on behalf of or concerning Namibia and refrain from any acts and in particular any dealings with the government of South Africa implying recognition of the legality of lending support or assistance, to such presence and administration.
   (c) That it is incumbent upon States which are the Members of the United Nations to give assistance in the action which has been taken by the United Nations with regard to Namibia.[53]

9. *Advisory opinion of the International Court of Justice in the Western Sahara Case.*[54]—In this case the Court, dealt with, *inter alia*, the question of decolonization and the principle of self-determination. During the course of judgment, the Court made it clear that in

52. I.C.J. Rep. (1971), p. 16.
53. *Ibid.*, at pp. 315-16.
54. I.C.J. Rep. (1975) reprinted in L.J.I.L., Vol. 15 (1975), pp. 390-441.

consequence of General Assembly Resolution 1514 (xv) of 14th December, 1960 and other resolutions, the principle of self-determination has become a binding principle in the context of colonialism. The court concluded that the materials and information presented to it do not establish any tie of territorial sovereignty between the territory of Western Sahara and the Kingdom of Morocco or the Mauritanian entity. Thus the court has not found legal ties of such a nature as might affect the application of Resolution 1514 (xv) in the decolonization of Western Sahara and, in particular of the principle of self-determination through the free and genuine expression of the will of the peoples of the Territory.[55] The court also clarified its own competence to give advisory opinion.[56]

The court observed :

"its competence to give an opinion did not depend on the consent of the interested States, even when the case concerned a legal question actually pending between them. However, the Court proceeded not merely to stress its judicial character and the permissive nature of Article 65, paragraph 1 of the statue, but to examine, specifically in relation to the opposition of some of the interested States, the question of the judicial propriety of giving the opinion. In short, the consent of an interested State continues to be relevant, not for the court's competence, but for the appreciation of the propriety of giving an opinion".[57]

55. I.C.J. Rep. (1975) reprinted in I.J.L.L., Vol. 15 (1975), para 162 at p. 441.
56. *Ibid.*, paras 18, 23, 28, 32, 33 and 39; Interpretation of Peace Treaties with Bulgaria, Hungary and Romania, First Phase, I.C.J. Reports 1950, p. 72; Legal Consequences for States of the Continued Presence of South Africa in Namibia (South Africa in Namibia (South West Africa) notwithstanding Security Council Resolution 276 (1970), I.C.J. Repots, 1971, p. 27; Application for Reviews of Judgments No. 158 of the United Nations Administrative Tribunal, I.C.J. Reports (1973), p. 172.
57. *Ibid.*, para 32.

Further, In certain circumstances, therefore, the lack of consent of an interested State may render the giving of an advisory opinion incompatible with the court's judicial character. An instance of this would be when the circumstances disclose that to give a reply would have the effect of circumventing the principle that a State is not obliged to allow its disputes to be submitted to judicial settlement without its consent.[58] But according to the court, in the present case the object of the request was to obtain from the Court an opinion which the General Assembly deems of assistance to for the proper exercise of its functions concerning the decolonization of the territory.[59]

Further the court observed:[60]

"What the Court said in a similar context, in its advisory opinion on Reservation to the Convention on the Prevention and Punishment of the crime of Genocide, applies also to the present case. The object of this request for an opinion is to guide the United Nations in respect of its own action."[61]

10. *Interpretation of the Agreement of 25th March, 1951 between the WHO and Egypt*[62]—In this case the court clarified the legal position relating to determination by the court of the meaning and implications of question submitted for advisory opinion and the need to ascertain and formulate legal questions really in issue.
11. *Application for Reviews of Judgment No. 273 of the U.N. Administrative Tribunal*[63]—In this case the Court dwelt

58. *Ibid.*, para 33.
59. *Ibid.*, para 39.
60. *Ibid.*, para 41.
61. I.C.J. Reports 1951, p. 19.
62. Judgment of 20th December, 1980.
63. Advisory opinion of 20th July, 1982.

upon the competence and propriety of Court's giving advisory opinion, nature and scope of opinion, requested and the need for Court to ascertain and state legal questions really in issue.

12. *Advisory opinion on Applicability of the obligation to Arbitrate Under Section 21 of the United Nations Headquarters Agreement of 23rd June, 1947*[64]—In this advisory opinion the World Court interpreted Section 21 of the Headquarters Agreement in the context of U.S. decision to close down PLO Observer Mission at New York and unanimously held that the U.S. is under an obligation, in accordance with Section 21 of the Headquarters Agreement of 26th June, 1947, to enter into arbitration for the settlement of the dispute between itself and the U.N. This case has also been discussed in Chapter on "Definition, Nature, Functions and Evolution of International Organisation".
13. *Advisory Opinion requested by the World Health Organisation (WHO) (1996)*[65]—World Health Organisation (WHO) on August 27, 1993 asked to the Court for the advisory opinion on the question "In view of the health and environmental effects, would the use of nuclear weapons by a State in war or other armed conflict be a breach of its obligations under International Law including the WHO Constitution?"

The court gave the advisory opinion on July 6, 1996. First of all, it considered that there are three conditions which must be satisfied in order to found the jurisdiction of the Court when a request for an advisory opinion is submitted to it by a specialized agency. Firstly, the agency requesting the opinion must be duly authorized under the Charter; secondly, the opinion requested must be on a legal question; and thirdly, the question must be one arising within the scope of the activities of the requesting agency.

64. Advisory Opinion of 26th April, 1988.
65. Advisory Opinion Delivered on July 06, 1996.

The Court was of the opinion that the first two conditions had been met. With regard to the third, the Court found that according to the Constitution of the WHO, it is authorized to deal with the effects on health of the use of nuclear weapons, or of any other hazardous activity, and to take preventive measures aimed at protecting the health of population in the event of such weapons being used or such activities engaged in. The question put to the Court in the present case relates not to the effects of the use of nuclear weapons on health, but to the legality of the use of such weapons in view of their health and environmental effects. The Court pointed out that the Constitution of the WHO does not expressly refer to the legality of any activity hazardous to health and none of the functions of its dependant upon the legality of the situations upon which it must act. The Court observed that the question put to it in the present case relates not to the effects of the use of nuclear weapons on health, but to the legality of the use of such weapons in view of their health and environmental effects. The Court pointed out that whatever those effects might be, the competence of the WHO to deal with them is not dependent on the legality of the acts that caused them. In view of the Court, therefore, the question is not being capable of being considered as arising "within the scope of the activities of the WHO".

The Court pointed out that international organisations are subjects of the International Law which do not, unlike States, possess a general competence. International Organisations are governed by the principle of 'specialty', that is to say, they are invested by the States which create them with powers, the limits of which are a function of the common interests whose promotion those States entrust to them. The Court is of the opinion, however, that to ascribe to the WHO the competence to address the legality of the use of nuclear weapons even in view of their health and environment effects would be tantamount to disregarding the principle of specialty.

The Court therefore concluded that the responsibilities of the World Health Organisation are necessarily, restricted to the sphere of public 'health', and that there is no doubt that question concerning the use of force, the regulations of armaments and disarmaments do not come within the scope of the WHO, and therefore the request for an advisory opinion by the WHO does not relate to a question which arises within the scope of activities of that Organisation. The request for an advisory opinion was therefore dismissed.

7. NATURE OF THE ADVISORY OPINION

The purpose of the advisory opinion is not to settle at least directly disputes between States, but to offer the legal advice to the organs and institutions requesting the opinion, and therefore, the opinion given by the Court is referred to as 'legal advice', it does not have any binding force, primarily because the objective of procedure contained in Articles 65-68 of the Statue of the Court is purely advisory. *In the Peace Treaties case,*[66] it was stated by the Court that the opinion is only of an advisory character and 'as such it has no binding force'.

However, the opinion of the Court as an authoritative statement of International Law as it comes from the highest judicial authority. The opinion of the court is cited by the court itself in the subsequent cases and also by the publicists and writers of International law.

Further, provisions of many instruments, other than the charter and the statute, characterize the opinion requested the court as a 'decision' in relation to the dispute at issue; that is they confer binding force on the opinion for the parties to the dispute. Examples of such provisions may be found in some of the Headquarters agreements between these organizations and the States on whose territory they carry out their activities,[67]

66. Interpretation of Peace Treaties, ICI Reports (1950) p. 71; Reservation to the Convention on Genocide, *op. cit.*, p. 20; Certain expenses of the United Nations, *op. cit.*, p. 168.
67. Agreement between United Nations and Chile Regulating Conditions for the Operation of the Headquarters of the United Nations Economic Commission for Latin America of 1953 (Article XI, Sec. 21); Agreement between United Nations and Thailand Relating to the Headquarter of the Economic Commission for Asia and the Far East of 1954 (Article XIII, Sec. 26); Agreement establishing a radio-isotope center in Cairo of 1967 (Article XVI, Sec. 39) between Egypt and International Atomic Energy Centre.

general conventions on the privileges and immunities of the United Nations, the specialized agencies and the International Atomic Energy Agency.[68] The above implies that the Court's advisory opinions are to be regarded as inherently capable of pertaining, of the nature of a judicial decision.[69]

The advisory jurisdiction of the International Court has proved to be of considerable importance. The judicial character of the advisory opinions has given them a far greater significance than was originally contemplated. Mr. Rosenne also considers that the advisory procedure has proved its worth and that its value has been strengthened by the fact that since the establishment of the present Court it has not been asked to settle disputes between States but has been used to give answers to legal questions. According to him this conforms to the true conception of advertise jurisdiction.[70]

The League Council requested a large number of opinions, the majority of which were helpful in solving the differences which had led to the requests being made.[71] The number of requests from the present Court has, however, been small. With increase in the number or organs and agencies

68. Article VIII Sec. 30 of the Convention on the Privileges and Immunities of the United Nations of 1946; Article XI, Section 33 of the Convention on the Privileges and Immunities of the Specialized Agencies of 1947 and Article X, Sec. 34 of the Agreement on the Privileges and Immunities of the International Atomic Energy Agency of 1959.

69. Roberts Ago, 'Binding Advisory Opinions of the International Court of Justice', AJIL, 85 (1991), p. 439.

70. The Law and Practice, p. 755, Cf. the statement of Judge Read to the effect that 'the procedure of the World Court, in its advisory jurisdiction, is unsuitable for dealing with contentious issues; there is no provision for reply, no machinery for the orderly dialogue between parties in conflicting interest which is essential to justice', *The Canadian Yearbook of International Law*, 1964, p. 168.

71. The reasons for the success of the opinions were the authoritative judicial character of the opinions, the disputes being marginal to the major sources of international tension prevailing during the period between the two world wars (Rosenne, *The Law and Practice*, p. 15), and the dominant position in the League System of Powers who favoured pacific settlement of disputes through resource to the Permanent Court; *Ibid.*, p. 108.

how authorized to request the opinions, it was reasonable to expect an increased number of requests being made. But, in fact, there have been fewer requests for opinions of the present Court than were requested from the Permanent Court in the comparable period.[72] There have been many cases and groups of cases in which proposals for requesting advisory opinions made in the principal organs of the Untied Nations have not been adopted.[73]

There are several reasons for this situation. Perhaps the main difficulty lies in the attitude of the States.[74] Most of them are concerned with pursuing their own policies than with securing the settlement of disputes on merits.[75] There is either 'ill-concealed mistrust' or an attitude of indifference towards the Court on their part. This attitude is the result of the tensions produced by the Cold War and violent changes taking place in the political structure of the international society.[76] There is also a general feeling on the part of the Members of the United Nations that law has little relevance to the problems involved in the maintenance of peace and security under existing conditions.[77]

There is also the view of the Permanent Members of the Security Council that they carry the real burden of maintaining international peace, and for that purpose are obliged to use whatever means suits them at the give moment.[78] All this results in the situation that in the General Assembly and the Security Council the Members are reluctant in supporting proposals for reference of a question to the Court; and these

72. *Ibid.*, p. 755.
73. Jenles, *The Prospects*, pp. 32-34, Rosenne, 'On the non-Use of the Advisory Competence of the International Court of Justice', 39, *B.Y.I.L.*, p. 1.
74. Wilcox and Marcy, *Proposals for Change in the United Nations*, 1955, p. 130.
75. Vallat, 'The Peaceful Settlement of Disputes', *Cambridge Essays in International Law in Honour of Lord McNair*, 1965, p. 165.
76. Waldock, 'General Court on Public International Law'.
77. Anand, 'Survey of Recent Research; International Law, Attitude of the "New" Asian-African Countries toward the International Law Court of Justice', 4, *International Studies*, 1962-3, p. 132.
78. Rosenne, *The Law and Practice*, pp. 93-4.

organs have been prevented from referring ever their own legal problems to the Court. *In the case of specialized agencies,* the very small number of requests can be explained by the fact that they have their own machinery to solve most of their special problems which they feel cannot be resolved through recourse to the advisory procedure of the Court.[79]

There are some procedural drawbacks as well to the effective use of the advisory procedure. Mr. Rosenne has pointed out the fact that questions are not drawn with sufficient care; the voting system whereby only a majority is required for a resolution requesting an opinion; and the absence of formal legal rules determining the legal consequences in terms of permissible conduct for States arising out of an advisory opinion.[80]

Some writers have put forth suggestions with a view to increasing the advisory work of the Court. Dr. Jenks makes a number of proposals, both for granting liberal access to the Court and for improving the procedure.[81] He discusses the two objections to the granting of liberal access to the Court,

---

79. Three reasons have been given for this attitude: (i) fear that support for a reference to the Court would be a sign of weakness, (ii) fear that reference would in some way prejudice a State's position, and (iii) fear that reference would involve delay or accusations of delay. Vallat, *op. cit.*, p. 165. Goodrich, Hambro and Simons in *The Charter of the United Nations,· Commentary and Documents* enumerate six reasons; political nature of the question, Court should not be asked to interpret the Charter, subject-matter within domestic jurisdiction, issue is clear or should be decided by the Assembly or Council, other procedures for setting disputes have been agreed upon, and the request would delay the work of the Assembly or the Council or cast doubt upon their previous actions, pp. 565-5.
80. Rosenne, *The Law and Practice,* p. 756.
81. Proposals for the possible development of the advisory procedure without involving and amendment of thc Statue:
    (a) A readier course by the bodies already authorized to request opinions of the Court;
    (b) Advisory proceedings to be held before a Chamber of the Court, and through recourse to summary procedure—as under Art. 82(2) of the Rules;
    (c) Extension of the range of bodies so far authorized to any nuclear tests or disarmament supervision agency or space agency established as an autonomous U.N. body;

namely, the danger of overburdening the Court with a large volume of unimportant work and the undesirability of encouraging the specialized agencies to litigate upon problems involving mutual relations.

He comes to the conclusion that they are unfounded.[82] Another suggestion would like the Art. 96 to be amended so as to empower the General Assembly to authorize other public international organizations, whether general or regional, to request the Court's opinion.[83] It has also been said that if the organizations of States were to be permitted to appear as parties before the Court in contentious cases this would clearly induce complementary changes in the advisory procedure.[84] A third suggestion would require the Court to give 'plurilinear' advisory opinions which would be likely to increase the number of requests.[85]

All these suggestions for increasing the advisory work of the Court do not appear to be practical propositions, and are not likely to yield any appreciable result in the present atmosphere obtaining in international relations. In the final analysis the ability of the Court to perform its functions depends on the readiness of the States to make use of the Court,[86] but they are in no mood to resort to the judicial decisions as a means towards pacific settlement of their

---

(d) tribunals which may be established for a special purpose as an or gan of the U.N. could be authorized, and be instructed to treat the opinion as a declaratory judgment;

(e) on the precedent of the Administrative Tribunal Judgment Review Committee, the General Assembly could also create an organ of the U.N., specially for the purpose of requesting advisory opinions in defined circumstances, instruct such an organ to request an opinion, and make such an opinion binding on the parties substantively interested in the matter. *The Prospects*, pp. 160-1.

82. *Ibid.*, pp., 200-3.
83. Eagleton, 'Report of the Committee on the Uses of the Waters of International Rivers, International Law Association, Meeting at Dubrovnik', August-September, 1956, 51 A.J.I.L., 1957, pp. 89-91.
84. Rosenne, *The Law and Practice*, p. 757.
85. Cheng, 'The First Twenty Years of the International Court of Justice', *The Year Book of World Affairs*, 1966, pp. 255-6.
86. Rosenne, *The Law and Practice*, p. 100.

differences. Apart form this the size of the Court's docket is no indication of the role it has played in the peaceful settlement of disputes.[87]

Besides, the desirability of very frequent requests for opinions on all kinds of problems is questionable.[88] It has been rightly pointed out that there is need for caution and room to ask whether the Court's pronouncement is or is not likely, regardless of its content; to form the basis for the ultimate settlement of the problem and relaxation of the tension.[89] There are many political problems with legal aspects which cannot be resolved by settlement of legal issues involved therein.[90]

Moreover, not much harm seems to have been done merely by the fact that a number of legal questions pending before the political organs have not been referred to the Court for its opinion. Either a political solution has been found for them or else they have been left unsolved because the parties were not willing to resolve the difference. Such questions do not appear to have adversely affected international peace to any appreciable extent.

It appears to be much more desirable that the International Court of Justice with limitations and with limited volume of advisory work should be left untouched. There is in existence a perfected advisory procedure. If, and when, there is need of the assistance of the Court, and there is willingness to submit the legal issues involved in a difference to the Court's wisdom, the procedure will be readily available.

8. ADVISORY JURISDICTION OF THE EUROPEAN COURT OF HUMAN RIGHTS

The European Court of Human Rights was established by the *"Convention for the Protection of Human Rights and Fundamental Freedoms"*. In the year 1950 the court was set-up in January, 1959. *'Protocol–XI'* which comes into force on 1st

87. Hackworth, 'Address to the American Association of International Law', 50 A.J.I.L., 1956, p. 115.
88. Bowett, *The Law of International Institutions,* p. 128.
89. Rosenne, *The Law of Practice,* p. 94.
90. Wileos and Marcy, *Proposals for Change in the United Nations,* p. 129.

November, 1998 has changed the existing test of Sections II to IV of the convention (Articles 19 to 56) which is related to European Court. The related provisions of Advisory opinions are here under:

> Article 20 of the European convention says that the court consists of a number of judges equal to that of the contracting parties. To consider case before it the court shall sit in committees of three judges, in chamber of seven judges and in Grand chamber of seventeen judges.

The Grand chamber consists of seventeen judges. The Grand chamber shall also include the President of the court, the Vice-Presidents, President of the chamber and other judges chosen in accordance with the laws of the court. As regards the powers of the Grand chamber, Article 31 of European convention provides that it shall consider requests for advisory opinions submitted under Article 47. The General chamber renders advisory opinions at the request of the Committee. Article 32 provides that the European Court may have following three types of jurisdiction:

(i) Inter State cases (Article 33)
(ii) Individual application (Article 34)
(iii) Advisory opinions (Article 47)

Article 47 which deals with advisory opinions provides that the court may at the request of the committee of Ministers, give advisory opinions on legal questions concerning the interpretation of the convention and the protocols thereto.[91]

Such opinions shall not deal with any question relating to the content or scope of the rights or freedom defined in Sec. 1 of the convention and the Protocols thereto, or with any other question which the court or the committee of ministers might have to consider in consequence of any such proceedings as could be instituted in accordance with the consequence.[92]

91. Article 47, para 1.
92. Article 47, para 2.

Further, decisions of the committee of ministers to request an advisory opinion shall require a majority vote of the representations entitled on the committee.[93] Article 48 provides that the Court shall decide whether a request for an advisory opinion submitted by the committee of Ministers is within its competence as defined in Article 47.

Article 49 of the European Convention provides that the court shall give reasons for its advisory opinion. If the advisory opinions do not represent in whole or in part, the unanimous opinion of the judges, any judge shall be entitled to deliver a separate opinion. Further advisory opinion of the court shall be communicated to the committee of ministers.

European Convention for Protection of Human Rights and fundamental freedom (1950) in the first important regional convention on human rights which goes beyond the Universal Declaration of Human Rights and gives effect to civil and political rights contained therein by binding commitments. It provides machinery for the implementation of rights, namely (a) commission, (b) the court and (c) The Committee of ministers. Later on (i.e. on 31st October, 1998) the commission was abolished by 'Protocol-XI'. Amendment of the convention by Protocol XI has enlarged the powers and jurisdiction of the Court. The final judgment of the court shall be transmitted to the committee of Ministers which shall supervise its execution.

93. Article 47, para 3.

4

References for Consultation to the Supreme Court

During the last fifty nine years, since the constitution came in force, 14 references have been made to the Supreme Court under Article 143(1).

1. *In re* the Delhi Laws Act, in 1951,[1]
2. *In re* the Kerala Education Bill, in 1958,[2]
3. *In re* the Berubari, in 1960,[3]
4. *In re* the Sea Customs Act, in 1962,[4]
5. *In re* the Keshav Singh's case in 1965,[5]
6. *In re* Presidential Poll, in 1974,[6]
7. *In re* the Special Courts Bill, in 1978,[7]

---

1. A.I.R. 1951 SC 332.
2. A.I.R. 1958 SC 956.
3. A.I.R. 1960 SC 845.
4. A.I.R. 1963 SC 1760.
5. A.I.R. 1965 SC 745.
6. A.I.R. 1974 SC 1682.
7. A.I.R. 1979 SC 478.

8. *In re* the Jammu & Kashmir Resettlement act, in 1982,[8]
9. *In re* the matter of Cauvery Water Disputes in 1992,[9]
10. *In re* the matter of Ram Janamabhoomi in 1993,[10]
11. *In re* on the Principles and Procedure regarding appointment of Supreme Court and High Court Judges in 1998,[11]
12. *In re* the Gujarat Gas Regulation Act, in 2001,[12]
13. *In re* Gujarat Assembly Election Matter in 2002,[13]
14. *In re* the Satluj-Yamuna Link Canal, in 2004.[14]

(FIRST REFERENCE) IN THE DELHI LAWS ACT REFERENCE (Special Reference No. 1 of 1951)[15]

1. Main Facts

On January 7, 1951 the President of India exercised for the first time his powers under Article 143 of the Constitution. The first reference case, popularly known as the Delhi Laws Act case was unique in many ways. Firstly, the highest Court of the land was asked to speak on an issue of great constitutional significance, the ruling on which was to have immense influence upon the shape of future legislation in independent India. Secondly, all the seven judges who constituted the Bench hearing the Reference pronounced their separate opinions discussing elaborately the various issues on different grounds. Thirdly, the Reference was the result of a ruling in a Federal Court case i.e., *Jatindra Nath Case*.[16] More interestingly, all the five judges, (Justices Kania, Fazal Ali, Patanjali Shastri, Mahajan and Mukharjee) who gave the judgment in *Jatindra*

8. Sp. ref. no. (1) of 1982.
9. A.I.R. 1992 SC 522.
10. (1993) 1 SCC 642.
11. A.I.R. 1999 SC 1.
12. SCC (2004) 4 at p. 489.
13. (2002) 8 SCC 237 : (2002) 8 JT 389.
14. Sp. ref. no. (1) of 2004.
15. A.I.R. 1951, S.C. 332.
16. Jatindra Nath Gupta *v.* The Province of Bihar (1949-50), F.C.Q. 595.

Nath's case were occupying the Supreme Court Bench which heard this reference.

The President put forward three question regarding the validity of certain provisions of the Delhi Laws Act, 1912, Ajmer Marwar (Extension of Laws) Act, 1947 and Part C States (Laws) Act, 1950. The three questions were all in respect of delegation of legislative power and the three particular Acts were selected to raise the question in respect of the three main stages in the constitutional development of India.

The reason for making the reference were set out in the letter of reference. It was stated in the letter that the reference was necessitated because the Federal Court in *Jitendra Nath case* held by a majority that the proviso to sub section (3) of Section I of the Bihar Maintenance of Public Order Act, 1947 was 'ultra vires' the Bihar Legislature *'inter alia'* on the ground that the said proviso conferred power on the Provincial Government to modify an Act of the Provincial Legislature and thus amounted to a delegation of legislative power. As a result of this decision of the Federal Court, doubts were raised regarding the validity of Section 7 of the Delhi Law Act, 1912, Section 2 of the Ajmer-Merwara (Extension of Laws) Act, 1947 and Section 2 of the Part C States (Laws) Act, 1950 and other orders and instruments issued under the Acts so extended. Under such circumstances, the President referred the following three questions to the Supreme Court for its opinion:

2. Questions Referred

1. Was Section 7 of the Delhi Laws Act, 1912,[17] or any of the provisions thereof and in what particular or particulars or to what extent 'ultra vires' the legislature which passed the said Act?

17. Section 7 of the Delhi Act ran as follows:
"The provincial Government may, by notification in the official gazette, extend with such restrictions and modifications as it thinks fit to the province of Delhi or any part thereof, any enactment which is in force in any part of India at the date of such notification".

2. Was the Ajmer-Merwara (Extension of Laws) Act,[18] 1947 or any of the provisions thereof and in what particulars or to what extent 'ultra vires' the legislature which passed the said Act?
3. In section 2 of the part C States (Laws) Act, 1950[19] or any of the provisions thereof and in what particular or particulars or to what extent 'ultra vires' the Parliament?

3. Opinion

A full bench of the Supreme Court consisting of seven judges heard the arguments. Each judge pronounced a separate opinion of his own discussing elaborately the various issues involved and numerous English American, Australian, Canadian and Indian case law.

The Supreme Court had two precedents before it on the issue of delegation of powers. The two approaches differ from each other rather fundamentally.

One is the British approach.[20] The Parliament in Great Britain is a sovereign body with no limits over its power. It, therefore, is in a position to delegate as much authority as it pleases and the courts have no power to question any parliamentary enactment, whatsoever the quantum of

18. Section 2 of the Ajmer-Merwara (Extension of Laws) Act, 1947 ran as follows:
"Extension of Enactments of Ajmer-Merwara: The Central Government may, by notification in the official gazette, extend to the province of Ajmer-Merwara with such restrictions and modifications as it thinks fit any enactment which is in force in any other province at the date of such notification".
19. Section 2 of the part C States (Laws) Act, 1950 ran as follows:
"Power to extend enactments to certain part C States: The Central Government may by notification in the official gazette, extend to any part C State (Other than Pondicherry and Andaman Islands) or to any part of such State, with such restrictions and modification as it thinks fit, any enactment which is in force in a part A State at the date of the notification and provision may be made in any enactment so extended for the repeal or amendment of any corresponding law (Other than a Central Act) which is for the time being applicable to that part 'C' State.
20. *Supra* n. 15 at p. 340.

delegation may be. The other is the American approach where the theory of separation of powers places restrictions on the power of the legislature to delegate an unlimited amount of power. However, the courts having realised that in modern times the doctrine of separation of powers can not be enforced rigorously and, therefore, it can not be insisted that only the Congress and no one else should exercise legislative powers, developed the view that the Congress should state the policy within the delegating legislation and the task of filling in detail within the framework of the policy statement may be left to the executive or administrative.

Out of the two approaches, the Court had to select one as applicable to the Indian Parliament. Following the British Model,[21] it could be held that the Indian Parliament was free to delegate as much power as it liked. There were no limits to it. If the American scheme of Constitution was to be followed, the Court could hold that the Parliament could not give to the delegate unlimited powers and that it should prescribe the policy within which the delegate was to legislate.

On a comparative study of the British and the Indian Constitutions we find that there is one similarity and one dissimilarity between the two. The similarity is about the form of Government, i.e., the parliamentary type, where the executive is an integral part of the legislature. The dissimilarity between the two is that whereas in Great Britain the Parliament functions under no-charter and it derives its power from the common law, customs and conventions. As a result, the Parliament has unlimited powers, making it all powerful. In India, Parliament functions within the framework of a Constitution which defines its powers, functions and obligations and it cannot go beyond the limits prescribed by the Constitutions. The Courts have been given the power to review the acts of the Parliament.[22]

The same is the case with India and America. There is one similarity and one dissimilarity between the two. The similarity is that both the Indian Parliament and the U.S. Congress function under a written code. Their acts may be

21. *Ibid.*, at p. 368.
22. *Supra* n. 15 at p. 348.

judicially reviewed and if anything against or beyond the written Constitutions is found in their enactments, the Courts have the power to declare them 'ultra vires'. The dissimilarity between the two systems is that whereas in the U.S. scheme of administration, the theory of separation of powers is in force leading to a presidential from the government, in India no such doctrine is recognised atleast between the executive and the legislature. The parliamentary form of government is a negation of the doctrine of separation of powers.

Justice Patanjali Shastri[23] pointed out that the American political scene in the 18th century was dominated by the ideas of Montesque and Locke; that the concentration of legislative, executive and judicial powers in a single organ leads to tyranny. It was, therefore, provided that each of the departments of the State would not exercise the powers of others hence, the doctrine of separation of powers placed restrictions on the Congress to delegate its powers to the executive or any other administrative agency. The historical background and the political environment which influenced the making of the American Constitution were entirely absent in India and beyond the creation of the three organs of the government there is not the least indication that the framers of the Indian Constitution made the American doctrine of separation of powers an integral and basic feature of the Indian Constitution. On the contrary India has a system in which the legislative and executive organs work in cooperation and unison so much so that the executive is an important part of the legislature. The doctrine of separation of powers was thus ruled out of the way as a restriction on Parliament's power to delegate its legislative functions.

Justices Mukharjee and Kania[24] also made similar observations. The doctrine of separation of powers was thus refused recognition as a feature of the Indian Constitution and consequently as a restriction on Parliament's power to delegate its legislative functions.

The doctrine of '*delegatus non potest delegare*' is a necessary corollary of the doctrine of separation of powers. This doctrine

23. *Supra* n. 15 at p. 361.
24. *Ibid.*, at p. 368.

signifies that a delegate cannot further delegate its powers. Resource has been taken to this doctrine to restrict the delegation of powers by the Congress in the U.S.A. Shree N.C. Chatterjee, advocate for the Maiden's Hotel, urged that having regard to the Preamble to the Constitution, whereby the People of India resolved, in exercise of their sovereign right, "to adopt, enact and to give to themselves the Constitution," Parliament must be deemed to be a delegate of the people and this fundamental conception attracts the application of the maxim 'delegatus non potest delegare' and operates as an implied prohibition to the delegation of legislative power by the Parliament. But Justice Patanjali Shastri held that the Indian Parliament could not be regarded as a delegate of the people so as to attract application of the doctrine against delegation. This maxim, according to him, could have no constitutional status but could only have the force of a political percept.[25]

Justice Mukharjee[26] considered the doctrine at great length and then rejected it. He explained the theory as one which prevents a person upon whom a power has been conferred or to whom a mandate has been given, from delegating his powers to other people. He elaborated thus;

> *"To attract the application of the this maxim; it is essential that the authority attempting to delegate its powers must itself be a delegate of some other authority. The legislature as it exists in India at the present day, undoubtedly is the creature of the Indian Constitution, which defines its powers and lays down its duties; and the Constitution itself is a gift of the people of India to themselves. But it is not a sound political theory that the legislature acts merely as a delegate of the people. This theory ones popularised by Locke and eulogized by early American writers is not much in favour in modern times."*[27]

One more point is worth-mentioning here. There is no express provision in the Indian Constitution Prohibiting

25. A.I.R., 1951, S.C. 332 at p. 370.
26. *Ibid.*, at p. 372.
27. 1951 S.C. 527 at p. 644.

Parliament to delegate its legislative functions to any other authority. The Courts, therefore, had to dwell upon general constitutional principles and theories to arrive at the conclusion in the matter.

4. Main Points of Opinion

(1) Doctrine of separation of powers is not a part of the Indian Constitution.
(2) Indian Parliament was never considered an agent of anybody, and therefore, doctrine of delegates 'non potest delegare' has no application.
(3) Parliament cannot abdicate or efface itself by creating a parallel legislative body.
(4) Power of delegation is ancillary to the power of legislation.
(5) The Limitation upon delegation of power is that the legislature cannot part with its essential legislative power that has been expressly vested in it by the Constitution. Essential legislative power means laying down the policy of the law and enacting that policy into a binding rule of conduct.

On the basis of this reasoning, the Supreme Court came to the conclusion that :

(1) Section 7 of the Delhi Laws Act, 1912 is valid.
(2) Section 2 of the Ajmer-Merwara (Extension of Laws) Act, 1947 is valid.
(3) Section 2 of the Part 'C' States (Laws) Act, 1950 is valid except that part of the section which delegated power of repeal and modification of legislative policy as it amounted to excessive delegation of legislative powers.

Even though seven judges gave seven separate judgments but it will not be correct to hold that no principle was clearly laid down by the majority of judges. Anyone who survey the whole case comes to an inescapable conclusion that there is a similarity in the views of the judges at least on three points.

(i) Legislature cannot give that quantity and quality of law which is required for the functioning of a modern state, hence delegation is necessity.

(ii) In view of a written constitution, the power of delegation cannot be unlimited.

(iii) The power to repeal a law or to modify legislative policy cannot be delegated because these are essential legislative functions which cannot be delegated.

The Supreme Court has now made it abundantly clear that the power of delegation is a constituent element of the legislative power as a whole under Article 245 of the Constitution and other relative Articles.

(SECOND REFERENCE) IN THE KERALA EDUCATOIN BILL REFERNECE (Special Reference No. 1 of 1958)

5. Main Facts

The second Presidential Reference unlike the first one, was made in a politically heated atmosphere. A bill passed by a State Legislature was first reserved by the Governor for consideration of the President and then it was referred to the Supreme Court for opinion. The things can be understood in the light of the fact that the State being governed by a different political party than the one which was at the Centre.

The Congress Party was in minority in the State Assembly, and having lost in the House, it attempted to reverse the decision of the majority with the help of the provision under Article 143 of the Constitution. The reference raised the question whether the President should be empowered to refer issues falling in a State's jurisdiction to the Supreme Court. Such a power can be abused by the President or Practically by the Union Government when there was an opposition party Government at a State.

The Kerala Education Bill, 1957 was passed by the Kerala Legislative Assembly on 2nd Sept. 1957. Doubts were raised about the constitutional validity of certain provisions of the Bill on the pleas that these provisions were violative of some of the fundamental rights[28] and some other provisions of the Constitution. The State Assembly, in exercise of its powers under Articles 245 and 246 read with Entry 11 of List II in the Seventh Schedule to the Constitution, passed the Bill for the better organisation and development of educational institutions of the State of Kerala. The Governor, in exercise of his powers under Article 200 of the Constitution, reserved the Bill for the consideration of the President.

It would be fruitful, at the very outset, to give a brief account of the Kerala Education Bill.[29] On the basis of order of the questions referred to the Supreme Court for its opinion, the Bill can be studied categorically, Firstly, 'a provision related to the subject of recognition of schools'.

The provision, among other things empowered the Kerala Government to recognise any school established and maintained by any persons or body of persons for the purpose of providing the facilities for general education, special education and for training of teachers.[30]

It also provided that any new school established or any higher class opened in any private school, after the Bill became an Act and it came into force otherwise than in accordance with the provisions of the Act and the rules made under them were not entitled to get recognition by that Government of Kerala.[31] It was feared the Clause 3 (5) of the Bill gave the government an unguided power of recognition of new schools and opened possibilities of the power being used in a arbitrary and discriminatory manner violative of Article 14 of the Constitution and that the provisions of clause 3 to establish and administer educational institutions violated Article 50(1) of the Constitution.

28. Articles 14, 28, 29 and 30 of the Constitution of India.
29. A.I.R. 1958 SC at p. 956.
30. The Kerala Education Bill, 1957, clause 3(2).
31. Sub clause 5 of clause 3 of the Bills ran as follows:

    "3(5) After the commencement of this Act, the establishment of a new school or the opening of a higher class in any private school shall be subject to the provision of this Act and the rules made thereunder. Any school or higher class established or opened otherwise than in accordance with such provision shall not be recognised by the government".

Secondly, the Bill made provision for the collection of fees. Clause 8(3)[32] of the Bill required all fees and other dues, other than special fess, to be made over to the Government of Kerala even if there was any agreement or arrangement to a contrary effect.

Thirdly, Clauses 9 to 15 of the Bill conferred on the government certain powers of administration in aided schools. These provisions were feared to be violative of Article 30.[33]

Fourthly, Clause 15 of the Bill empowered the State Government to take over, by notification in the Gazette, any category of aided schools in any specified area, if it was satisfied that for standardizing general education in Kerala or for improving the level of literacy in any area or for more effectively managing the aided educational institutions or bringing education of any category under its direct control, it was necessary to do so in public interest. The government could do so only on payment of compensation on the basis of market value of the schools so taken over after deducting the amounts of aids or grants given by that government for requisition, construction or improvement of the property of the school. The doubt, here was whether this provision gave such power to the Government which could be exercised in an arbitrary and discriminatory manner to the violation of Article 14 of the Constitution.

Lastly, Clause 33(I) of the Bill made a very sweeping provision.[34] It barred the courts from granting temporary

32. Clause 8(3) of the Bill Ran as follows:
'8(3) All fees and other dues, other than special fees, collected from the students in an aided school after the commencement of this section shall not withstanding anything contained in any agreement, scheme or arrangement, be made over to the Government in such manner as may be prescribed".

33. Clause 2(1) of the Bill defines 'aided school' as 'a private school recognised by and is receiving aid from the Government.'

34. Clause 33 of the Kerala Education Bill ran as follows:-
"Courts not to grant injunction notwithstanding anything contained in the Code of Civil Procedure, 1908, or in any other law for the time being in force, no court shall grant any temporary injunction or make any interim order restraining any proceedings which is being or about to be taken under this Act".

injunction restraining any proceedings taken or proposed to be taken under the Act notwithstanding anything contained in the Code of Civil Procedure, 1908. Doubts were expressed that this provision violated Article 226 of the Constitution so far as it related to the jurisdiction of the High Court.

A brief account of the, various provisions of the Kerala Educational Bill clearly establishes that the Bill contained many provisions which imposed considerable state control over the management of educational institutions in the state. As a result, it was greatly expected that the affected schools will take the matter to the courts for final adjudication involving considerable litigation. Besides, the width of the power of control thus sought to be assumed by the State, in the opinion of the President, raised doubts as to the constitutional validity of the provisions on the ground of apprehended infringement of some of the fundamental rights guaranteed to the minority communities by the constitution. The President, therefore, referred following questions, to the court.

6. Questions Referred

1. "Does sub-clause (5) of clause 3 of the Kerala Education Bill read with clause 36 thereof or any of the provisions of the said sub-clause offend Article 14 of the constitution in any particulars or if any extent?
2. Do sub-clause (5) of clause 3, sub-clause (3) of clause 8 and clauses 9 to 13 of the Kerala Education Bill, or any provisions thereof offend clause (I) of Article 30 of the constitution in any particulars or to any extent?
3. Does clause 15 of the Kerala Education Bill, or any provisions thereof, offend Article 14 of the constitution in any particulars or to any extent?
4. Does clause 33 of the Kerala Education Bill or any provisions thereof offend Article 226 of the constitution in any particulars or to any extent?"

7. Opinion

The Supreme Court was not unanimous in its opinion on

the reference. The majority opinion was delivered by Chief Justice Das on behalf of himself and five other judges. Justice Venkataraman Aiyar, while agreeing with the opinion of Chief Justice Das in respect of questions 1, 3 and 4, delivered a separate opinion as he did not agree with the opinion 'of the Chief Justice' on question No. 2. The majority opinion delivered by Chief Justice Das should be studied first.

As regards the point raised by Mr. Frank Anthony (Advocate of Anglo Indians and Roman Catholics Associations) the Chief Justice opined that it was for the President in the first instance to determine what questions should be referred to and if he did not entertain any serious doubt on other Provisions, it was not for anybody else to say that doubts also arose out of them. The Court could not go beyond the Reference. The point that the president did not think fit to refer other questions as to the constitutional validity of some of the clauses of the Bill could not be a good or cogent reason for dealing to entertain the reference.[35]

A. Answer of Question No. 1 and 3

A point about the scope and ambit of question No. 1 and 2 had been raised during the course of arguments. These questions challenge the constitutional validity, inter alia, of clause 3(5) of the Bill. The Attorney general, on the one 'hand, argued that provision of clause 3(5) of the Bill, namely, that the establishment of a new school shall be subject to the provisions of this Act and the rules made thereunder, attracted all other clauses of the said Bill. Therefore, the two questions called in question the validity of even other clauses of Bill. On the other hand, the counsel for the State of Kerala opposed the stand of the Attorney General. He maintained that clause 3(5) attracted only clauses 3(3) and the rules made under clause 36(2)(a) and no other clause of the Bill and, therefore, no other clause could be included within the scope of the question unless of course, they were specially mentioned therein. After weighing the two rival contentions, Chief Justice, on behalf of the majority of judges, opined that to accept the restrictive argument that clause 3(5) attracted only clause (3) would be putting a too

35. A.I.R. 1958 S.C. 956 at p. 965.

narrow construction on sub-clause (5). Therefore, a discussion of the validity of other clauses came within the purview of questions 1 and 2.

The Chief Justice took two questions, first and third, together for consideration. The two questions challenged the validity of clause 3(5) read with clauses 36 and 15 of the Bill in respect to Article 14 of the constitution. A number of cases[36] on the point were referred. He specially quoted on paragraph from *Mohd. Hanif Qureshi* v. *State of Bihar*[37] which ran as follows:

> "It is now well established that while Article 14 forbids class legislation it does not forbid reasonable classification for the purposes of legislation".

Two conditions, however, were set to test the permissible classification. One, the classification must be founded on an intelligible differentia which distinguished persons or things that are grouped together from others left out of the group and, second, such differentia must have a rational relation to the object sought to be achieved by the statute in question. The issue was to be decided in the light of the principles laid thus.

A possibility of discrimination, it was argued, arose as a result of the application of the same provisions of the Bill to all schools which were not similarly placed. As for example, only Anglo Indian schools were entitled to get grant under Article 337 of the Constitutional and no other schools. So also, minority institutions were protected under Articles 29 and 30 of the Constitution. As a result, such institutions were different from all other educational institutions established by majority communities and the Bill sought to treat all institutions in the same manner and placed equal burdens on unequals and thus violated Article 14. In support of this contention reliance was placed on a decision[38] of the American Supreme Court. It was,

36. For example, Chiranjit Lal *v.* Union of India, 1950 S.C.R. 869; Budhan Chaudhary *v.* the State of Bihar, 1955 S.C.R. 1045; Ram Krishna Dalmia *v.* Justice S.R. Tendolkar, C.A. Nos. 455 to 457 of 1957, 23-3-1968; A.J.R. 1958 S.C. 538.
37. S.C.R. 1959, p. 629.
38. Cumberland Cole Co. *v.* Board of Revision, (1931) 284 U.S. 23.

however, held by the majority opinion that decision did not apply in the present context because in that case discrimination was an integral part of the mode of taking and that was not the position here in as much there was no discrimination in the provisions of the Bill.

As regards the argument that the, Bill did not lay down any policy or principle for the guidance of the Government, the Chief Justice opined[39] that the policy and purpose of the Bill could be deducted from the long title and the title thereof. In the present Bill general policy was to provide for better organisation and development of educational institutions, providing varied and comprehensive educational service throughout the State of Kerala. Every clause of the Bill was to be interpreted and read in the light of the policy. Therefore, any discretion of the Government under any clause of the Bill has to be exercised in accordance with this policy. It was, therefore, incorrect to argue that there were no guidelines for the executive to exercise any power under the Bill.

The Chief Justice further pointed[40] out that the general policy was reinforced by more definite statements of policy in different Clauses. For instance, the power under clause 3(2) could be exercised only for the purpose of providing facilities for general education, special education and for the training of teachers. The various provisions in the Bill established that in matters of granting permission or recognition, the Government was to be guided by the consideration as to whether the giving of such permission or recognition would ensure for the better organisation and development of educational institutions; whether it would facilitate the imparting general or special education or the training of teachers, and if it did, permission or recognition must be given; if it impeded that purpose, permission must be refused.

It was the Court's concern to see whether purposes of the Bill were good or bad that as was a matter of State policy, observed the Chief Justice while considering clause 15 of the Bill. This clause provided for taking over schools. He opined that the provision certainly did not violate Article 14 of the

39. A.I.R. 1958 SC 956 at p. 976.
40. A.I.R. 1958 SC 955 at p. 978.

Constitution. Many safeguards were provided against arbitrary exercise of power under clause 15 of the Bill. An educational institution could be taken over only if it appeared to the Government that the manager of any school had neglected to perform the duties imposed on him and that the exercise of that power was necessary in public interest. Likewise, power under clause 15 (I) could be exercised only if the Government was satisfied that it was necessary for standardizing general education in the State or for improving the level of literacy in any area or for more effectively managing the aided institutions in any area or for bringing the education of any category under the direct control of the Government. Further, the power could not be exercised unless the proposal for taking over was supported by a resolution of the Legislative Assembly. It was also opined that discretionary power was not necessarily a discriminatory power and the abuse of power by the Government was not to be rightly assumed.[41]

The Chief Justice on the basis of the above reasoning ruled that the charge of unconstitutionality of several clauses of the Bill coming under questions 1 and 3 founded on Article 14 could not be sustained.

(B) Answer of Question 2

The President, by way of question No. 2 of the Reference called upon the Supreme Court to interpret the word 'minority'. The Court, however did not express a full and a full and final opinion as to the meaning of a minority community. It declined to opine whether 'minority' should be taken in the context of the population over which the law in question applied, i.e., State population for a law extending all over the State or local population if the law applied to a particular locality.[42]

The reason given by the Chief Justice was that in the present reference, the Bill applied to the whole of the State and the minority was to be determined in the context of the entire population of the State. By this test, Christians, Muslims and Anglo-Indians were held minorities in Kerala by the Chief

41. A.I.R. 1958 SC 955 at p. 978.
42. *Supra* n. 29 at p. 968.

Justice. He also reminded that the second question in the Reference was, framed on the basis that certain minority communities in Kerala who were entitled to the protection of Articles 29 and 30 and, therefore, it was held that for answering question no. 2 the Court need not enquire what was meant by a minority or how was it to be determined. The issue to be decided was what was the scope and ambit of Article 30(1)?

The Chief Justice rejected the argument that Article 30(1) extended only to the educational institutions established after the commencement of the Constitution. The Article, of course, protected all the minority institutions whether established before or after the commencement of the Constitution.

It was also not true, in the opinion of the Chief Justice that the protection of Article 30(1) was available to only those minority institutions which were established exclusively for their own community. He rejected the contention that Article 30(1) did not protect a minority institution if single member of any other community was admitted to it. It was not possible, in fact, to read that condition into Article 30(1) of the Constitution.[43]

While considering the content of Article 30(1), the Court noted first that the Article gave certain rights not only to religious but also to linguistic minorities. In the next place, the right conferred thus on minorities was to establish educational institutions of their choice. However, that Article does not provide that such institutions shall be established for teaching religion only or that linguistic minority should have the right to establish educational institutions for teaching their language only.

There was no limitation placed on the subjects to be taught in such institutions. The institutions under Article 30(1) may be classified into three categories : (i) those which did not seek aid or recognition from State, (ii) those which sought aid, and (iii) those which wanted recognition only.

As to the first category of institutions the Chief Justice ruled[44] that such institutions were outside the purview of the

43. A.I.R. 1958 SC 955 at p. 978.
44. *Supra* n. 29 at p. 978.

Bill by virtue of clause. 38 of the Bill and there was nothing for or against them and, therefore the question of violation of Article 30(1) in their case was out of place.

The institutions of the second category could further be divided into two categories (i) those which were entitled to grant by virtue of the Constitution itself, for instance Anglo-Indian educational institutions, and (ii) those which were not entitled to any grant by any express provision of the Constitution but still sought aid from the State.

The educational institutions established by Anglo-Indians are entitled to grant by virtue of the provisions under Article 337,[45] subject to the limitations imposed under the Constitution itself. The State of Kerala making a distinction between the grant under Article 337 and 'aid' as used 'in the Bill, pleaded to have the power to impose' additional restrictions on the educational institutions, than those already prescribed by the Constitution. The Chief Justice rejected this theory and held that imposition of stringent terms as fresh or additional limitations on educational institutions of this category violated their rights not only under Article 337 but also under Article 30(1) and thus the provision of the Bill referred in question No. 2 were void against them.

There were other educational institutions, falling under the third category, which were not entitled to any grant by any constitutional provisions but even then sought it from the State. Article 337 coveted only those educational institutions which were established by the Anglo-Indians prior to the year 1948. No such constitutional provisions existed for the ones established after that time by any other minority community. If these institutions wanted aid from the State, they were naturally made to fulfil the stringent conditions laid down in the Bill.

45. Article 337 runs thus; "Special provision with respect to educational grants for the benefit of Anglo-Indian Community—During the first three financial years after the commencement of this Constitution, the same grants, if any, shall be made by the Union and by each State for the benefit of the Anglo-Indian community in respect of education as were made in the financial year ending on the thirty-first day of March, 1948".

These institutions pleaded that if they were to fulfil these conditions for receiving aid under the Bill, the provisions thereof virtually deprived them of their rights under Article 30(1). These conditions were laid down in clauses 2, 5 to 12, 14, 15 and 20 of the Bill. They included the provisions requiring the managers to submit annual statements to the Government, fixed assets of schools were to be frozen and could not be used without permission of the Government, restriction on appointment of managers, fees, etc. to be paid to the Government, payment to the teachers by the. Government, appointment of teachers only through the public service commission, etc. Here, on the one hand there was the fundamental right of the minority under Article 30(1) and, on the other hand, there was an obligation on the part of the State under Article 45 of the constitution to provide for free and compulsory education for all children until they complete the age of fourteen years. Apparently, there was incompatibility between the two provisions of the Constitution.

The Chief Justice, however, tried to reconcile these two conflicting provisions and to give effect to both. The directive principle under Article 45, however, could not override fundamental rights, i.e., under Article 30(1). The Chief Justice referred to the judgment of the Supreme Court in the *State of Madras* v. *Smt. Champakam Dorairajan*[46] in which the Court held, "The directive principles of state policy have to conform to and run as subsidiary to the Chapter on Fundamental Rights."

The Chief Justice interpreted Article 30(1) as giving two rights to the minorities, (i) right, to establish, and (ii) right to administration of educational institutions. The right to administer, however, did not include right to maladminister. The minority could not claim recognition or aid from the State for a maladministered Constitution in unhealthy surroundings without competent teachers and, very low standard of education, and if the State insisted that in order to grant aid, certain reasonable regulations were to be followed, there was no violation of Article 30(1). However, the aid must not be granted in such a way as to take away the right under Article

46. S.C.R. 1951, 525 at p. 531.

30(1). The question, therefore, whether or not the restrictions imposed 'were reasonable. The Chief Justice found provisions under clauses 7, 8 (3), 9, 10, 11, 12 and 13 to be mere regulatory and held that they did not offend Article 30(1). However, clauses: (5), 14 and 15 offended the provisions of Article 30(1).

The last were the institutions which sought recognition only. Clauses 7(2), 4 to 9, 10 and 20 of the Bill applied to category of schools. It was held that leaving aside clause 20, the rest of these clauses was merely regulatory and did not violate Article 30(I). Clause 20 which provided that no fees should be charged for tuition in the primary classes was not merely regulatory. Had there been a provision for making the loss good by the State to the institutions resulting by virtue of clause 20, then the provision might have been 'valid'. Since there was on such provision, Clause 20 was violative of Art. 30(1).

It was also held by the Chief Justice that there was no difficulty in construing Cause 33 as a provision subject to the overriding provisions of Article 226 of the Constitution.

8. Main Points of Opinion

The majority opinion of the Court as regards the four questions in the presidential reference was as follows:

1. The first question was answered in the negative.
2. The second question, so far as Anglo-Indian educational in situations entitled to grant under Article 337 were concerned, was answered in affirmative. As regards other minorities not entitled to grants as of right under any express Provision of the Constitution, but are in receipt of aid or desire, such aid and also as regards Anglo-Indian educational institutions in so for they were receiving aid in excess of what were due to them under Article 337, Clauses 8(5), and 9 to 13 did not offend Article 30(1) but clause 3(5), in so far as it makes such educational institutions subject to clauses 14 and 15 did offend Article 30(1). Further, clause 7 (except sub-cls. (1) and (3) which apply only to aided

schools) and clause 10 in so far as they apply to recognised schools to be established after the said Bill comes into force do not offend Article 30(1) but clause 3(5) in so far as it make the new schools established after the commencement of the Bill subject to clause 20 does offend Article 30(1).

3. The answer to the third question was in the negative.
4. Clause 33 was subject to Article 226 of the Constitution.

(THIRD REFERENCE) IN THE BERUBARI REFERENCE (Special Reference No. 1 of 1959)[47]

9. Main Facts

The Government of India came across a peculiar situation in the year 1958. It had concluded an agreement involving exchange of territorial land with a foreign State. The problem arose as to how the agreement could be implemented. Some constitutional experts opined that it could be done simply by an executive action; others pointed out that not even an ordinary legislation but a constitutional amendment was required for implementing the agreement; still others pointed out that 'there was no provision in the Indian Constitution which empowered the Parliament or any authority of the land to cede its territory to another country and, hence the agreement, they argued, was null and void'. The Government apprehended that any action it took to execute the agreement would be challenged in courts of law and, therefore, it decided to consult the Supreme Court on the matter beforehand. The institution of advisory jurisdiction in this way was found to be useful and expedient for settling a constitution issue.

With the passage of the Indian Independence Act, 1947 there came into existence two independent countries known as India and Pakistan. The Act made provisions for demarcating the boundaries of the two countries. But there arose a number of boundary disputes between the two. This problem of boundary adjustment formed the most crucial subject for

47. A.I.R., 1960 SC 845.

settlement after independence. As to the eastern side Section 3, sub-section (1) of the Indian Independence Act provided that from the appointee day i.e., 15th Aug. 1947, the Province of Bengal as constituted under Government of India Act, 1935 shall cease to exist and there shall be in lieu thereof two new provinces to be known respectively as East Bengal and West Bengal.

The boundaries of the two provinces were, according to the Act, to be determined by the award of a boundary commission to be appointed by the Governor-General in that behalf. The Radcliff Boundary Commission was appointed in June 1947 which made its award on August 12, 1947, i.e., three days before the appointed day under the Independence Act, 1947. The two provinces, i.e., the East and West Bengal, were demarcated in accordance with the Award. It is worth mentioning here that since the date of the Award, Berubari Union No. 12 (one of the territories under Reference[48]) as treated and governed as a part of West Bengal, there having been claim to this territory by the Government of Pakistan.

Further boundary disputes arose subsequently between India and Pakistan and it was agreed between them at the Inter-Dominion Conference held in New Delhi on December 14, 1948 that a tribunal would be set-up without delay for the adjudication and final decision of the boundary disputes. The tribunal which was set-up accordingly, is known as Indo-Pakistan Boundaries Disputes Tribunal and it was presided over by the Hon'ble Lord Justice Algot-Bagge. The Bagge Award was made on January 26, 1950. No issue about the Berubari Union was raised in the proceedings before the tribunal. Two years later, i.e., in 1952, the Government of Pakistan for the first time, raised the issue alleging that under the Award it should really have formed part of East Bengal and it had been wrongly treated as a part of West Bengal.

The background of the events which ultimately led to the proposed exchange of Cooch-Behar Enclaves between India and Pakistan, also deserves a note here. The erstwhile state of Cooch-Behar was merged with the State of West Bengal in 1950.

48. A.I.R., 1960 SC 845.

However, it appears that certain areas which formed part of the erstwhile. Cooch-Behar State and which subsequently became part of the West Bengal State became enclaves in Pakistan after partition. Similarly, certain Pakistani enclaves were found in India. The existence of these enclaves of India in Pakistan and Pakistan's in India worked as constant source of tension of conflict between the two countries.

The Prime Minister of the two countries sought to resolve the dispute about these two areas—Berubari Union and Enclaves, by way of an agreement[49] signed on Sept. 10, 1958. According to the Agreement, Berubari Union was to be divided half and half between the two countries and the enclaves existing between India and Pakistan were to be exchanged[50] respectively.

The implementation of the agreement posed that problem. The issue was how the agreement should be implemented; could it be done by a mere executive action of the Government of India or could it be possible by enacting a legislation under Article 3 of the Constitution or by making an amendment to Article 3 by the procedure prescribed under Article 368 and then to enact legislation under the amended Article?

Some political parties like Bhartiya Jana Sangh, and Jalpaiguri Revolutionary Socialist Party and the State of West Bengal had raised their voice against that part of the

49. Item 3 in Paragraph 2 of the Indo-Pakistan Agreement of 1958, ran as follows:
"(3) Berubari Union No. 12. This will be so divided as to give half of the area to Pakistan, the other half adjacent to India being retained by India. The division of Berubari Union No. 12 will be horizontal starting from the north-east corner of Deviganj Thana. The division should be made in such a manner that the Cooch-Behar Enclaves between Pachagar Thana of East Pakistan and Berubari Union No. 12 of Jalpaiguri Thana of West Bengal will remain connected as at present with Indian territory and will remain with India. The Cooch-Behar Enclaves lower down between Boda Thana of East Pakistan and Berubari Union No. 12 will be exchanged alongwith the general exchange of enclaves and will go to Pakistan".

50. Item 10 of the Agreement ran as follows:
"10. Exchange of old Cooch-Behar Enclaves in Pakistan and Pakistan Enclaves in India without claim to compensation for extra area going to Pakistan is agreed to".

agreement under which some part of the territories of Berubari Union and enclaves were to be transferred to Pakistan.

It was apprehended by the Indian Government that any action taken in pursuance of the agreement might be challenged in Courts of law involving heavy legislation. Under the circumstances, the President was satisfied that the questions of law, which had arisen, were of such nature and of such importance that it was expedient to obtain the opinion of the Supreme Court.

10. Questions Referred

The following questions, therefore, were referred to the Court for its opinion thereon:

1. Is any legislative action necessary for the implementation of the Agreement relating to Berubari Union?
2. If so, a law of Parliament relatable to Article 3 of the Constitution sufficient for the purpose or is an amendment of the Constitution in accordance with Article 368 necessary, in addition to or in the alternative?
3. Is a law of Parliament relatable to Article 3 of the Constitution sufficient for implementation of the Agreement relating to exchange of Enclaves or is an amendment of the Constitution in accordance with Article 368 of the Constitution necessary for the purpose, in addition or in the alternative?"

11. Opinion

The presidential reference was heard by a Constitution Bench consisting of eight judges including the Chief Justice B.P. Sinha. The unanimous opinion of the court was delivered by Justice Gajendragadkar.

The Court first set to consider the question as to what was actually done under the agreement, was it for the purpose of mere ascertaining and delineating the boundaries in the light of the Radcliff award or did it intend to cede a part of the Indian territory to Pakistan. After going in the relevant portion of the agreement, the Court came to the conclusion that the agreement was concluded because it was expedient and reasonable to ensure friendly relations between the parties and to remove causes of tension between them. No trace could be found in the agreement of any attempt to interpret the award or to determine what the award really meant. On the other hand, the agreement really meant that though the whole of the area of Berubari Union No. 12 was within India, it was prepared to give half of it to Pakistan in a spirit of give and take in order to establish friendly relations between the two countries.[51]

The Court concluded that the agreement did not purport to be and had not been reached as result of any interpretation of the award and its terms. It had been reached independently of the award. The court, therefore rejected the Attorney General's contention that the agreement was no more than ascertainment and determination of the boundaries in light of the Redcliff Award. The Court also ruled that the decision[52] of the Australian High Court upon which Attorney General had relied, did not support his contention.

The next question before the Court was whether any part of Indian territory could at all be ceded to another country and if so how it could be done. The political parties had argued that any part of India could not be ceded in any circumstances. Mr. N.C. Chatterjee (Senior Advocate of Political Parties) pointed out that the Preamble to the Constitution had postulated that like the democratic republican form of government, the entire territory of India was beyond the reach of the parliament. The Court held this argument to be without any substance.

The Court was not ready to import any limitation, on the exercise of sovereign powers[53] for ceding of territory as it was an essential attribute of sovereignty that a state could acquire

51. A.I.R. 1960 SC 845.
52. *In re* the State of South Australia *v.* The State of Victoria (1911) 12 CLR 667.
53. Article 1 of the Constitution runs as follows:
    1. India, that is Bharat shall be a Union of States.
    2. The States and the territories thereof shall be as specified in the first schedule.

territory from a foreign country and it could also cede a part of its territory to a foreign state in exercise of its treaty making power. Such acquisition and transfer were always possible subject to the limitations provided under the various provisions of the Constitution. How a treaty regarding acquisition or cession of territory could be implemented depended on the constitutional provisions.

The Court having decided that the agreement involved cession of territory and the sovereign state could cede its territory to another country, now set to consider the way in which cession could be effected. Here the Court proceeded on the assumption that a legislation for the agreement amounted to a cession of Indian territory to Pakistan and its implementation involved the alteration of the Content of Article 1 and of the relevant part of the First Schedule of the Constitution.[54]

Provisions under Article 2 of the constitution provide that Parliament by law admit into the Union or establish new states on such terms and conditions as it thinks fit. This Article establishes that foreign territories which after acquisition would become a part of the territory of India under Article 1 (3)(c) can by law be admitted into the Union under Article 2.

In the light of the provisions contained in Articles 1 and 2 of the Constitution, the court now considered the question whether a legislation under Article 3 of the Constitution was enough for implementing the agreement or was it necessary to legislate under Article 368? *Prima facie* Article 3 postulated only for internal adjustment *'inter se'* of the territories of the constituent States of India.[55]

It was pointed out that clause (a) of Article (3) dealt with the issue of formation of new states and clause (b) of the same Article provided for a law to be enacted to increase the area of any state. It was also pointed out by the Court that Article 3

3. The territory of India shall comprise:
   (a) The territories of the states;
   (b) The Union territories specified in the First Schedule; and
   (c) Such other territories as may be acquired.

54. A.I.R. 1963 S C 1760.
55. *Supra* n. 47 at p. 862

dealt only with the states and did, not at all cover Union Territories and clause and (c) of the Article gave the Parliament powers to by law diminish the area of any State and this was the only one clause which could be relevant for the purpose of the reference. The Court, however, did not accede to the contention advanced by the Attorney General that clause (c) of Article 3 was wide enough to cover even cession of Indian territory to a foreign State which caused diminution of the area of the State in question.

The Court held that when the Constitution did not expressly provide for acquisition of foreign territory, it must not have intended to provide for cession of Indian territory to a foreign country by implementation under Clause (c) of Article 3. The diminution envisaged there should be such that the territory taken out from one State should not cease to be a part of Indian territory. The Court, therefore, opined that Article 3(c) of the Constitution did not cover cession of national territory to a foreign Country.

Resultantly, Article 3 of the Constitution did not cover Union territories at all and if a part of Union territories was to be ceded no Law under Article 3 could serve the purpose and the only way to do that was to enact legislation under Article 368. It was, in the opinion of the Court, unreasonable, illogical and anomalous to suggest that if a law under Article 368 was required for ceding a part of Union territory, an outright legislation under Article 368 would have to be enacted and it could not be done by a legislation under Article 3, alternatively, the Court opined, Parliament could amend Article 3 by legislation under Article 368 so as to cover cases of cession of Indian territory in favour of a foreign country and then to enact a legislation under the amended Article 3 to implement the Agreement in question. However, if the relevant law was enacted under Article 368, that itself could be sufficient to implement the Agreement.

12. Main Point of Opinion

The Supreme Court pronounced its opinion on the questions under reference in the following manner:

1. Yes.

2. (a) A law of Parliament relatable to Article 3 of the Constitution would be incompetent.
   (b) A law of Parliament relatable to Article 368 of the Constitution is competent and necessary.
   (c) A law of Parliament relatable to both Articles 368 and 3 would be necessary only if Parliament chooses first to a law amending Article 3 as indicated above, in that case Parliament may have to pass a law on those. Lines under Article 368 and then follow it up with a law relatable to the amended Article 3 to implement the Agreement.
3. Same as answers (a), (b) and (c) to question 2.

(FOURTH REFERENCE) IN THE SEA CUSTOMS ACT REFERENCE (Special Reference No. 1 of 1962)

13. Main Facts

By this Reference,[56] which the President of India made in exercise of his powers under Article 143(I) of the Constitution, the Supreme Court was called upon to interpret the provisions of Article 289[57] of the Constitution. There arose a dispute between the Centre and some States on the issue of taxation. The Supreme Court by way of its advisory jurisdiction counselled the President on a point of law pertaining to the immunity of States from Union Taxation.

The controversy arose by way of a proposal for the enactment of a parliamentary legislation substituting section 20(2) of the Sea Customs Act, 1878 and section 3(IA) of the Central Excise and Salt Act, 1944.

Under the provisions sec. 20(2) read with its sub-section (1) of the Sea Customs Act. 1878, customs duties were leviable on all goods imported or exported by sea and belonging to the Government of a State and used for the purposes of a trade or

56. AIR 1963 SC 1760.
57. Article 289(1) of the Constitution of India reads thus:
"(1) The property and income of a State shall be exempt from Union Taxation".

business of any kind carried on by or on behalf of that Government or of any operations connected with such trade or business. Similarly, under section 3(1A) read with sub section (1) of the Central Excise and Salt Act 1944 duties of excise were leviable on all excisable goods other than salt produced or manufactured in India and a duty was leviable on salt manufactured in, or imported by land into any part of India by or on behalf of the Government of a State and used for the purposes of a trade or business of any kind earned on by or on behalf of that Government or of any operation connected with, such trade or business.[58]

The point to be noted here is that the customs and excise duties and duty on salt thus levied on the goods of a State Government were levied when such goods were used for any trade or business or for any operations connected with such trade or business and not when they were to be used by the Government for any purposes other than business.[59]

The Central Government decided to go to extend the levying of these duties in respect of all goods belonging to a State Government whether or not these goods were to be used by the Government for purposes of trade or business[60] or for any purpose incidental to such trade or business. With the purpose in view, it proposed to introduce in Parliament a Bill substituting Sections 20(2) of the Act of 1878 and Section 3 (1A) of the Act of 1944. Certain State Governments came out to express the view that the proposed amendments would not be constitutionally valid as the provisions of Article 289 read with the definitions of 'taxation' and 'tax' in clause 28 of Article 366 of the Constitution of India preclude the Union from imposing or authorising the imposition of any tax, including customs duties and excise, on or in relation to any property of a state except to the extent permitted by clause (2) read with clause (3) of Article 289. The Union Government was, however; of the view that the exemption did not exist in case of the proposed levy. Thus, the conflict of views among the different governments had, in the opinion of the President,

58. *Supra* n. 56 at p. 1766.
59. *Supra* n. 56 at p. 1768.
60. *Supra* n. 56 at p. 1771

arisen questions of such a nature and of such public importance that it was expedient to obtain the opinion of the Supreme Court under Article 143(1) of the Constitution.

14. Questions Referred

The following questions, therefore, were referred by the President, to the Supreme Court for its opinion:

1. Do the provisions of Article 289 of the Constitution preclude the Union from imposing, or authorising the imposition of customs duties on the import or export of the property of a State used for purposes other than those specified in clause (2) of that Article?
2. Do the provisions of Article 289 of the Constitution of India preclude the Union from imposing or authorising the imposition of excise duties on the production or manufacture in India of the property of a State used for purposes other than those specified in clause (2) of that Article?
3. Will sub-section (2) of section 20 of the Sea Customs Act, 1878 and sub-section (1A) of section 32 of the Central Excise and Salt Act 1944 as amended by the Bill set out in the Annexure be inconsistent with the provisions Constitution of India?

15. Opinion

A nine Judges Bench heard the Reference and four separate opinion were delivered. The majority view was delivered by the Chief Justice B.P. Sinha who delivered the opinion on behalf of himself and three other judges. Justice Rajgopal Ayyangar while concurring with the opinion delivered by the Chief Justice delivered a separate opinion with a view to dealing with certain issues more comprehensively. Two minority opinions were also delivered by Justice S.K. Das, A.K. Sarkar and K.C. Dasgupta and by Justice Hidayatullah.[61]

61. *Supra* n. 56 at p. 1762

The Chief Justice, before going into the merits of the rival contentions emphasised to bear in mind certain general considerations and the scheme of the constitutional provisions on the powers of the Union to impose the taxes contemplated by the proposed legislation. It was pointed out by the Chief Justice that neither the Union nor the States had unlimited rights of taxation. Their powers were conditioned by their respective duties and liabilities.

On the point, the Chief Justice referred to various provisions of Parts XI and XII of the Constitution which relate to Centre-State relationship regarding legislation, administration and finance. Referring to the provisions contained in Articles 265, 246 and 248 of the Constitution. His Lordship ruled[62] that whereas all taxes on income other than agricultural income were within exclusive powers of the Union, taxes on agricultural income only were reserved for the States, Broadly, taxes on income, duties of customs and excise were within the exclusive legislative powers of Parliament. These exclusive powers of taxation of Parliament, the Chief Justice observed, had to be correlated with the exclusive power of Parliament to legislate on trade and commerce with foreign countries. A reference was made to Entries 41[63] and 42[64] of List I of the Seventh Schedule in the Indian Constitution. The Chief Justice arrived at the conclusion that if Article 289(1) was interpreted so as to completely exempt all property of the States from all taxes, the power of Parliament to regulate foreign trade by the use of its power of taxation might be seriously impaired.

Part XIII of the Indian Constitution has made exhaustive provisions as to the revenues of the Union and of the States and as to how the Union will share the proceeds of duties and taxes imposed by it and collected either by the Union or by the States. It was pointed out that the sources of revenue which

62. *Ibid.* n. 56 at p. 1764
63. List I: Entry 41 runs as thus:
"Trade and commerce with foreign countries, import and export across customs frontiers, definition of customs frontiers".
64. List I: Entry 43 runs as thus:
"Inter-State trade and commerce".

have been allocated to the Union are, not meant entirely for the Union but the revenue collected thus is distributed among the States according to the principles laid down by parliamentary legislation. The question of the distribution of revenue by the Union to the States are matters to be decided by a high powered Finance Commission, which is a responsible body designated to determine those matters in an objective way. These provisions in the opinion of the Chief Justice, establish that the Construction of Article 289 as suggested by the Union would not affect seriously and adversely the revenues of the states.

On the contrary the Chief Justice[65] pointed out the wider interpretation suggested by the states might lead to serious difficulties in the way of the Union. The power of taxation assigned to the Union are more because of the considerations of convenience imposition and collection and not with a view to allocating them solely to the Union. These were not meant solely for the expenses of the Union activities. They would also subsidise the activities of the States in accordance with their needs irrespective of the amounts collected from them. It was concluded by the majority opinion of the Court that the Union and the States together formed one organic whole for the purposes of utilization of the sources of the territories of India as a whole.

Now the scope of the words used in Article 289 and its complementary Article 285 came in for consideration by the Chief Justice. There was no dispute on the point of taxes on income exempted under Article 289; the exemption was in respect of income other than agricultural income as envisaged under Entry 22 of List I. Taxes on 'property' formed the main dispute. While rejecting the contention put forward by the States, the Chief Justice held that though List I did not contain any entry regarding a tax directly on property like List II, the Union could still levy a tax directly on property in exercise of powers under Article 246 (4).[66] This could be done in case of,

65. *Supra* n. 56 at p. 1768.
66. Article 245(4) of the Constitution runs thus:
"Parliament has power to make laws with respect to any matter for any part of the territory of India not included in a State notwithstanding that such matter is matter enumerated in the State List".

for instance, Union territories in which a tax directly on property could be levied by Parliament. Thus it could not be argued that the exemption of the property of the States from the Union taxation directly on property under Article 289(1) would be meaningless as Parliament had no such power. The Chief Justice did not accept the contention of the States that Article 289(1) could not be confined to tax directly on property because there was no such tax provided in List-I.[67]

The Chief Justice now considered that word 'property' in Article 289(1) occurring as the property of a State shall be exempt from Union taxation.[68]

The States then urged that even if Article 289(1) exempted the property of the States from direct taxes only, the levy of excise on goods under Item 84 of List I was a tax on property and therefore no excise duty could be levied on goods belonging to States and manufactured by them. Similarly, customs duties under entry 83 of List I were equally duties on the goods imported or exported and, therefore the property of the State must be exempt under Article 289(1) both from excise and customs duties. These contentions were weighed in the light of the question of the nature of these duties. The Court pointed out that similar issue had come in for consideration[69] before the Supreme Court in which it was held that excise duty was primarily a duty on the production or manufacture of goods produced or manufactured within the country. It was an indirect duty which the manufacturer or producer passed on to the ultimate consumer. Accepting the principle established in that case the Chief Justice ruled that excise duty was not a tax directly on goods and was merely an indirect tax

---

67. *Supra* n. 56 at p. 1774.
68. *Supra* n. 56 at p. 1776.
69. The Province of British Columbia *v.* the Attorney General of the Dominion of Canada, 64 S.C.R. (Can.) 377; Attorney General of British Columbia *v.* Attorney General of Canada, (1924) A.C. 222; Attorney General of New South Wales *v.* the Collector of Customs for New South Wales, (1907-08) S.C.R. 818; Attorney General of British Columbia *v.* Kingston Navigation Co. Ltd., (1934) A.C. 45. *In re* Amalgamated Coalfields Ltd. *v.* Union of India, A.I.R. 1962 S.C. 1281.

distinguishable from direct taxes like taxes on property and in come.

Similar was the case with customs duties including export duties. Although these duties were levied with reference to goods, the taxable event was either the import of goods within customs barriers or export beyond customs barriers. They were also indirect taxes like excise duties. Looking to the nature of an import duty, the Chief Justice observed that it could be levied in a condition which must be fulfilled before goods would be brought in the country, i.e., before they form part of the mass goods within the country. Such condition was imposed by way of excise of the power of the Union to regulate the manner and terms on which goods could be brought into the country from a foreign country. Similarly, export duty was a condition precedent to sending goods out of the country to other lands. Neither of them was a duty on property an envisaged under Article 289(1).

The Chief Justice[70] in this context conceded to cut down the amplitude of the term 'taxation' as defined in Article 366(28) when the context otherwise required. It was pointed out that if the States were made exempt from all taxation in respect of their exports or imports it could happen that a State might import or export all kinds of things and thus nullify the exclusive power of parliament to legislate in that respect. The provisions of Article 289(1) being in the nature of an exception to the exclusive power of Parliament to levy taxes, the exception was to be strictly construed and, therefore, limited to taxes on property and on income of a State. Thus the immunity granted to the States under Article 289(1) was to be restricted to taxes levied directly on property and income. The Chief Justice, therefore, concluded that even though import and export duties or duties of excise had reference to good they were not within the exemption of Article 289(1). Hence, the Chief Justice, speaking on behalf of himself and three other judges, answered all the three questions referred to the court in the negative.

70. *Supra* n. 56 at p. 1776.

16. Main Points of Opinion

1. The Chief Justice did not accept the contention of the states. The Article 289(1) could not be confined to tax directly on property because there was no such tax provided in List I.
2. The opinion of the Chief Justice establishes that the construction of Article 289 as suggested by the union would not affect seriously and adversely the revenues of the states.
3. The Chief Justice arrived at the conclusion that if Article 289(1) was interpreted so as to completely exempt all property of the States from all taxes the power of Parliament to regulate foreign trade by the use of its power of taxation might be seriously impaired.
4. A reading of Articles 285 and 289 together makes clear intention of the constitution makers that Article 285 would exempt all property of the union from all taxes on property levied by a state or by any authority with in the state while Article 289 contemplates that all property of the states would be exempt from all taxes on property which may be leviable by the union.
5. Both the articles are concerned with taxes directly either on income or on property and not with taxes which may indirectly affect income or property. Hence, the Chief Justice gave restricted interpretation to the provisions of the two Articles as suggested by the Union.
6. The immunity to the states under Article 289(1) was to be restricted to taxes levied directly on property and income. The Chief Justice, therefore, concluded that even though import and export duties or duties of excise had reference to goods they were not within the exemption of article 289(1).
7. The opinion nicely explained the word property in Article 285 and 289 to mean property itself, not the various aspects of property, i.e. manufacture, gift and import or export.

8. The majority of the judges propounded the theory that the central government could levy customs duty on goods imported or exported or an excise duty on the goods produced or manufactured by a state government irrespective of whether it was used or not for purposes of trade or business.
9. The majority opinion of the Court held that Article 289 bars imposition of central taxes on property and not those taxes which may indirectly affect or are in respect of income or property. The custom duty is a tax on 'import or export' and excise on production of 'manufacture' and none of these taxes is on property as such.

Hence, the Chief Justice, speaking on behalf of himself and three other judges, answered all the three questions referred to the Court in the negative.

(FIFTH REFERENCE)
IN THE KESHAV SINGH CASE REFERENCE
(Special Reference No. 1 of 1964)[71]

17. Main Facts

March 1964 witnessed an unprecented situation. Two vital organs of Government-legislature and judiciary challenged the authority of one another. It was a situation which the framers of the Constitution could not foresee and therefore, made no provision for dealing with such a delicate situation. The conflict was between the Uttar Pradesh Assembly and, the High Court of the same State. Powers, privileges and immunities of the State Assembly to commit a person for its contempt, which had been committed outside the four walls of the Assembly, came in conflict with the powers of the High Court to entertain a writ petition in exercise of its powers under Article 226. The provision of advisory jurisdiction proved most useful in resolving the tangle.

The contempt and breach of privileges of Shri Narsingh Narain Pandey, a member of the Assembly had arisen because

71. AIR 1965 SC 745.

of a pamphlet, which had been published and bore the signatures of one Keshav Singh of Gorakhpur and of some other person. The Assembly passed a resolution that a reprimand be issued to Keshav Singh who inspite of being repeatedly required to appear before the Assembly to receive the reprimand, failed to do so, alleging inability to procure money to pay the fare for the necessary railway journey. He was ultimately brought under custody of the Marshal of Assembly in execution of a warrant issued by the Speaker and produced at the Bar of the House on March 24, 1964. Keshav Singh refused to answer any questions put to him by the Speaker. He stood there with his back to the speaker showing great disrespect to the House. The reprimand was administered.

Thereafter, the Speaker[72] brought to the notice of the Assembly a letter dated March 11, 1964, written by Keshav Singh to him, in which he had stated that he protested against the sentence of reprimand and had absolutely no hesitation in calling a corrupt man corrupt, adding that the contents of his pamphlets were correct and that a brutal attack had been made on democracy by issuing the 'Nadirshahi Firman' (Warrant) upon him. Keshav Singh admitted, that he had written the letter. The Assembly then resolved for seven days imprisonment to Keshav Singh for its contempt.

The Speaker,[73] by a warrant directed the Marshal of the House and the Superintendent, District Jail, Lucknow that Keshav Singh be detained in District Jail for seven days. Keshav Singh was thereupon taken to the jail and kept imprisoned there. It is worth noting that the warrant did not state the facts which constituted the contempt.

On March 19, 1964, B. Solomon, an Advocate, moved a petition for the issue of a writ of *habeas corpus* for the release of Keshav Singh under Article 226 of the Constitution and Section 49 of the Code of Criminal Procedure, 1898 against the Speaker of the House, the Chief Minister of Uttar Pradesh and the Superintendent of the District Jail at Lucknow. The petition was moved before a division bench at Lucknow which was

72. *Supra* n. 71 at p. 748.
73. *Ibid.* n. 71.

constituted by Mr. Justice Beg and Mr. Justice Sahagal, The Advocate for the petitioner pleaded that the petitioner had been deprived of his personal liberty without any authority of law and that the detention was malafide. It was prayed that pending the disposal of the petition he be ordered to be released on bail.

The learned Judges admitted the petition[74] on the same day and ordered for release of Keshav Singh on bail and issued notices to the respondents. In pursuance of the order, Keshav Singh was promptly released on bail. This order of the Court naturally came into conflict with the sentence of imprisonment awarded by the Assembly as Keshav Singh had to be released before he had served the full term of imprisonment.

On March 21, 1964, the Assembly by the adoption of a resolution, held that the two Judges by passing the release order, Advocate by moving the petition and Keshav Singh by causing the petition moved, committed contempt of the House and directed that Keshav Singh be immediately taken into custody to serve the residue of the sentence, that two Judges and the Advocate be brought in custody before the House and that Keshav Singh be brought before the House after he had served the remaining term of sentence. Necessary warrants were issued for the purpose on March 21, 1964.

The resolution of the Assembly dated 21st March, 1964, caused a number of petitions to be filed before the High Court. The two judges, Advocate B. Soloman, Avadh Bar Association and others prayed in their petitions for the writ of *mandamus* restraining the respondent thereto, namely, the Speaker and Marshal of the House and Superintendent of Police, Lucknow from implementing the Resolution. A full bench of the Allahabad High Court heard the petitions on 23rd March and stayed the operation of the Assembly's resolution of March 21, 1964. On the same day the House clarified its stand.[75]

The Assembly, by the resolution adopted on 25th March 1964, declared that by its earlier resolution of March 21, 1964,

74. *Supra* n. 68 at p. 751.
75. AIR 1965 SC 745

it had not intended to deprive the two Hon'ble Judges, Shri B. Solomon and Shri Keshav Singh of an opportunity of giving their explanations before a final decision about the commission of contempt by them was taken by the Home.[73] Notices were issued on March 26, 1964, to all these persons informing them that they may appear before the Privileges Committee on April 6, 1964 at 10 a.m. to make their submissions. The warrant of March 25, 1964 was withdrawn by the Speaker of the House.

The above circumstances gave rise to a serious conflict between a High Court and a State Assembly involving important complicated questions of law regarding the powers and jurisdiction of the High Court and its Judges in relation to the State Legislature and its officers and regarding the powers, privileges and immunities of the State Legislature and its members in relation to the High Court and its Judges in the discharge of their duties. The President of India, therefore, was satisfied that a substantial question of constitutional importance had arisen and it was expedient to obtain the opinion of the Supreme Court.

18. Questions Referred

The following questions were formulated and referred to the Supreme Court for its opinion:

1. Was it competent for the Lucknow Bench of the High Court to entertain and deal with the petition of Mr. Keshav Singh challenging the legality of the sentence imposed by the Assembly?
2. By acting on such petition and releasing the petitioner, was the High Court guilty of contempt of the Assembly?
3. Could the Assembly direct for production of the Judges of the High Court before it in custody or to call for their explanation for its contempt?
4. Was the full bench of the High Court competent to entertain and deal with the petitions of the two Judges and to pass an interim order restraining the Speaker?
5. Whether a judge of the High Court entertaining such

petition commits contempt of the legislature and whether the legislature was competent to take proceedings against him?

19. Opinion

The reference was heard by seven judges (P.B. Gajendragadkar, C.J., A.K. Sarkar, K. Subba Rao, K.N. Wanchoo, M. Hidayatulla, J.C. Shah and N. Rajagopala Ayyangar J.J.) and two opinion were delivered. The majority opinion was delivered by Chief Justice Gajendragadkar and the descending opinions was given by Justice Sarkar.

Interpretation of the provisions of clause (3) of Article 194 was the crux of the matter. For the purpose, two things were considered. One, what are the privileges of the house of Commons and two, whether these privileges existed on 26th January, 1950. As to the first point, the majority observed that only those powers and privileges of the House of Commons were really to be accepted which were not only claimed by the house but were recognised by the English court. One more question was relevant in this connection. Is a law passed by a State Legislature in pursuance of Clause (3) of Article 194, was the law to be subject to the provisions of Article 13? *Prima facie* the answer to this was in the affirmative as it had been held in *M.S.M. Sharma vs. Sri Krishna Sinha.*[76]

The majority opinion also emphasised the necessity of bearing in mind one fundamental feature of our federal Constitution which does not exist in England. In England Parliament is sovereign which has the right to make or unmake any law and such law can not be questioned by anyone, not even by the courts, and its power or right extends to the whole of the Queen's dominions.[77] Contrary to this, in a federal Constitution, the essential characteristic of the distribution of powers is limited executive, legislative and judicial authority among bodies which are co-ordinate with and independent of each others.

This supremacy of the Constitution is protected by the

76. (1959) Supp. S.C.R. 906.
77. Dicey, The Law of the Constitution, (10th Ed.) pp. 34-35.

authority of an independent judicial body to act as the interpreter of a scheme of distribution of powers. Thus if a law was enacted by legislature violating a fundamental right it could be struck down by the courts. The legislatures, in this way, have plenary powers of legislation in India but they function within the limits prescribed by the Constitution. Hence, the Sovereignty claimed by British Parliament could be claimed by legislatures in India.

Yet another matter was considered to be important by the majority of the judges. It was the fact that whenever there was any challenge to a statute as unconstitutional either on the ground that it violated fundamental rights or otherwise, the judiciary, and not the legislature enacting the legislation, was the sole and exclusive judge of the dispute. Hence it was held that the decision about the construction of Article 194(3) ultimately rested exclusively with the judiciary in this country. Thus the Court overruled Mr. Seervai's arguments that it was the legislature which had to interpret the provisions of Article 194(3).

Their Lordships on the majority side took the view that by virtue of Article 194(3) all the privileges enjoyed by the House of Commons could not be claimed by State legislatures in India. Some of them, the Court enumerated, were the privileges of the freedom of access, to pass acts of attainder, impeachment, privileges of the Constitution of the House itself.

The majority of judges tried to formulate its opinion in the light of the Supreme Court's decision in the *M.S.M. Sharma case*, wherein it was held by the majority that (a) the privileges in question, right to punish for contempt of the House and the Speaker existed in England, and therefore, must be deemed to have been included in Article 194(3). Article 19(1)(a)(b) did not apply because under the rule of harmonious construction in a case like the present one where Article 19(1)(a) was in direct conflict with Article 194(3), the particular provision of the later Article prevailed over the former provision which was general, and (c) though Article 21 applied, it had not contravened.

The minority view[78] held that the privilege had not been established and even if it was presumed to have existed it was controlled by Article 19(1)(a). Both the majority and the minority opinions held that Articles 19(1)(a) and 194(3) have to be reconciled and harmonious construction principle must be adopted. Both the views however accepted the argument that law passed under Article 194(3) was subject to the provisions of Article 13.

The Ganupati case[79] which was discussed in the *Sharma case* was also referred to in the present reference. In this case the Court had to deal with the applicability, of Article 22(2) to a case following under the latter part of 194(3). It was found by the majority that the question of applicability of Article 22(2) *vis-a-vis* Article 194(3) as decided in the *Ganupati case* had not settled the point in question. The majority in the present reference however, agreed with the majority in the *Sharma case* that when a law was enacted under Article 194(3), it was subject to Article 13 of the Constitution because the law, though enacted by virtue of powers conferred under Article 194(3), the legislature will undoubtedly be acting under Article 246 read with Entry 30 of List II of Seventh Schedule. The enactment of such a Law could not be in exercise of constituent power and so such a law will have to be considered as a law within the meaning of Article 13.

Another question considered by the majority was whether the dualism existing in England for three centuries (17th to 19th) was carried over to the Indian Constitution as well. The answer to this question depended on a harmonious construction of the relevant constitutional provisions. After referring to Articles 32 and 226 which give powers to the Supreme Court and High Courts to issue various writs for the enforcement of fundamental rights, the majority referred Articles 208, 211, 212 and 121 as well. Article 208 empowers State Legislature to make rules, subject to the provisions of the Constitution, for regulating procedure and conduct of its business.

Thus when legislatures make rules under Article 194(3), those rules must be subject to fundamental rights. Article

78. *Supra* n. 71 at p. 745.
79. G. Keshavram Reddy *v.* Nafisul Hussain and the State of U.P., A.I.R. 1954 SC 639.

212(1) lays down that the proceedings of a State Legislature shall not be called in question on the ground of any irregularity of procedure. Under Article 211, the conduct of a High Court or Supreme Court Judge can not be discussed in a State Legislature and, therefore, the conduct of a judge in the discharge of his duties could never be the subject matter of any action taken by the House in exercise of its powers and privileges conferred under latter part of Article 194(3). Even in Parliament, the conduct of a High Court or Supreme Court Judge could be discussed only under Article 121 while presenting an address to the President praying for the removal of a judge.

Mr. Seetalwad[80] argued before the Court that in view of these provisions, if the judicial conduct of a judge could not be discussed in the House, it was inconceivable that the same conduct could legitimately be made the subject matter of action by the House in exercise of its power under Article 194(3). The majority agreed with the argument and it held that Articles 211 and 121 be read together. The conduct which could not be discussed under Article 211, could not be discussed under Article 194 (3) least the provisions of power should become meaningless.

Mr. Seervai,[81] however, contended that inspite of all the above arguments, it was not disputed that a Court could not go behind the reasons of a general or unspeaking warrant of the House of Commons which power is available to the State Legislature under Article 194(3). That took the majority to consider the powers and privileges of the House of Commons in England.

Their Lordships on the majority side found *Sir Erskine May's*[82] traeatise as the most authoritative work for ascertaining the privilege of the Commons Sir May has pointed out in his book that except in one respect, the surviving privileges of the House of Lords and House of the Commons were justifiable. This exception was in case of power to punish for contempt. The historical origin of the right

80. *Supra* n. 68 at p. 1781
81. *Supra* n. 68 at p. 1783.
82. May, Sir T.F. : *Parliamentry Practice,* (London, Butterworths Co., p. 1957.

to punish for contempt exercised by, the House of Commons was examined by the majority. In early times, privileges were available only to the House of Lords, which was not only an organ of Parliament but also a judicial organ. Thus the origin of the modern Parliament consisted in its judicial functions and privileges exercised by the House of Commons thus descended by the virtue of this judicial function of the Parliament.

The majority of the judges noted Sir Erskine May's[83] views on the divergence of the stands of the Parliament and the Courts. However, in due course the two extreme views were reconciled in practice. The solution appears to be that the Courts insist on their right in principle to decide all questions of privileges coming in litigation before them with exceptions in which the House was the sole judge. These were regulations of its internal proceedings and the right to commit and punish for contempt. Sir Erskine May concluded that as question about the existence and extent of privileges was generally treated as justiciable in Courts, it became relevant for adjudication of any dispute brought before the Courts.

In this matter the dualism was treated by the majority on the basis of May's observations. The ultimate result had been, according to May that the House of Common had not for hundred years refused to submit its privileges to the decisions of Courts and thus practically Courts' jurisdiction had been recognised over the existence and extent of its privileges. On the other hand, courts have also refused to interfere in the application of the recognised privileges of the House.[84]

Their Lordships on the majority side discussed a large number of cases[85] decided by the British Courts regarding punishment of persons committing contempt of House of Commons. An analysis of these cases showed that the right

83. May, Sir T.F. : *Parliamentry Practice,* (London, Butterworths Co., p. 1957.

84. *Supra* no. 82.

85. Some of the important among them were, The Earl of Sheftsbury's cases. (1677) 86 E.R. 782; Burdett *v.* Abbot (1811) 104 C R 504; Stock deals V. Hausford (1839) 112 E R 1112: 9 Ad and KI.L.: In case of Shreiff of Middle (1840) 113 E R 419: Murray's Case (1751) 95 E R 629: Howard *v.* Sir William Gossett (1845) 116 E R 139:

claimed by the House of Commons not to have its general warrant examined in *habeas corpus* proceedings was based on the consideration that the House of Commons was in the position of a superior court of record and had the right, like other superior courts of record, to issue a general warrant for commitment of persons found guilty of contempt.

It was on this ground that general warrants issued by the House of Commons were treated beyond the scrutiny of the courts. However, even while recognising the validity of such general warrants, the English Courts had frequently observed that if they were satisfied that such general warrants were issued for frivolous or extravagant reasons it was open to them to examine their validity.

The majority[86] considered the point that the relevant right of the House of Commons was based either on the ground that as a part of the High Court of Parliament, the House was a superior court of record and as such a general warrant issued for commitment by it for its contempt was treated by English Courts as conclusive or in course of time the right to claim a conclusive character for such a general warrant became incidental and included in the latter part of Article 194(3).

Looking to the Indian constitutional history, it was clear, according to the majority that the legislature in India was never treated as a superior court of record nor this status was conferred under Article 194(3) of the present Constitution Further, in England, the House of Commons had to fight a long battle for the recognition of its privileges against the House of Lords, the King and the Courts. No such battle was ever fought by Indian Legislatures.

After making a reference to Article 32, the majority observed that the Article was absolute in its terms and no exception was made there in favour of Article 194(3), and therefore it was illogical to suggest that a citizen could not move Supreme Court under Article 32 even if the right claimed by the House may contravene his fundamental right.

86. *Supra* n. 68 at p. 1787.

Similarly, the right of an advocate, by the virtue of the Advocates Act, 1961, to assist the Court and the enforcement of that right is also uncontrolled by Article 194(3). Therefore, the majority concluded[83] that the particular right which the house claimed to be an integral part of its power or privilege was inconsistent with the material provisions of the Constitution and could not be deemed to have been included under the latter part of Article 194(3).

Thus, the majority ruled[87] that the particular power claimed to be conclusive by the House to issue general warrant should not be deemed to be the subject matter of the latter part of Article 194(3). Further, it was opined that the power to commit by general warrant was not essential for the effective functioning of a House of Legislature. The American Congress, having no such power, had been functioning effectively. Looking to the numerical strength of State Legislatures in India, the majority also held that if the power claimed by the U.P. Legislative Assembly was conceded, it might lead to anomalous situation when a member of one Legislature was committed for contempt by a general warrant issued by another legislature on account of a speech made by him in his own legislature.

On the basis of the facts of the case, the majority upheld[88] the power of the High Court to entertain the petition of Keshav Singh and to grant his bail pending disposal of his petition. No contempt of the U.P. Assembly was committed by Keshav Singh, and his advocate in moving the writ petition or the judges of the High Court who entertained the petition and passed order for his release on bail.

20. Main Points of Opinion

On consideration of all facts and circumstances, constitutional provisions and judicial pronouncements, the majority answered the questions as follows:

---

87. *Supra* n. 71 at p. 1789.
88. *Supra* n. 71 at p. 1789.

1. It was competent for the Lucknow Bench of the High Court of Uttar Pradesh to entertain and deal with the Petition of Keshav Singh.
2. Keshav Singh by causing the petition to be presented on his behalf to the High Court, Mr. B. Solomon, advocate by presenting the said petition, and the two Hon'ble Judges by entertaining and dealing with the said petition and ordering the release of Keshav Singh on bail did not commit contempt of the Legislative Assembly of Uttar Pradesh.
3. It was not competent for the Assembly to direct the production of the two Hon'ble Judges and Mr. B. Solmon before it in custody or to call for their explanations for its contempt.
4. It was competent for the full Bench of the Allahabad High Court to entertain and deal with the petitions of the two judges and Mr. B. Solomon and to pass interim orders restraining the Speaker and other respondents from implementing the aforesaid direction of the said Assembly.
5. A Judge of a High Court who entertains or deals with a petition challenging any order or decision of a legislature imposing any penalty on the petitioner or issuing any process against the petitioner for its contempt, or for infringement of its privileges and immunities, or who passed any order on such petition, does not commit contempt of the said legislature; and the said legislature is not competent to take proceedings against such a judge in the exercise and enforcement of its powers, privilegee and immunities. It was made clear by the majority opinion that the answer was confined to cases in relation to contempt alleged to have been committed by a citizen who is not a member of the House outside the four walls of the Legislative chamber.

(SIXTH REFERENCE) IN THE PRESIDENTIAL POLL REFERENCE (Special Reference No. 1 of 1974, Decided on June 5, 1974)[89]

21. Main Facts

The Supreme Court, this time came forward to counsel the President on a purely constitutional issue. It related with the election to the office of the President. The term of the office of the president was coming to amend on August 24, 1974. The State of Gujarat was at this time under the Presidential rule and its legislature has been dissolved.

Article 56(1) of the constitution of India says that the President is to hold office for a term of five years from the date on which he enters upon his office. Now, the term of office to be President expires on 24th August, 1974. Under article 62(1) an election to fill a vacancy caused by the expiration of the term of office of President shall be completed before the expiration of the term. Under Article 54 the President is to be elected by the members of an electoral college consisting of:

(a) The elected members of both houses of Parliament.
(b) The elected members of the legislative assemblies of the States.

But the Gujarat State legislative assembly was dissolved on the 15th of March, 1974. A general election for constituting a new legislative Assembly for the State of Gujarat can be held only after the assembly constituencies have been delimited of fresh on the basis of the 1971 census under Article 170 of the constitution and the provisions of the Delimitation Act, 1972, it was impossible to complete the general election to the legislative assembly of the State of Gujarat before the expiration of the term of office of the President as aforesaid date.

89. AIR 1974 SC 168 : (1974) 2 SCC 33.

So doubts had arisen as to the true interpretation of the provisions contained in Articles 54, 55, 56, 62 and 71 of the Constitution of India.[90]

22. Questions Referred

1. Whether on a true and correct interpretation of Articles 54, 55, 56, 62 and 71 of the constitution of India the electoral college mentioned in Article 54 is to consist only of the elected members of such of the Legislative Assemblies of the states as are in existence at or before the expiration of the term of office of President under Article 56 of the Constitution.
2. Whether on a true and correct interpretation of the provisions of Article 71(4) of the Constitution of India, when the Legislative Assembly or Assemblies of any State or States is or are dissolved it will amount to a vacancy or vacancies having occurred in the electoral college within the meaning of the said article.
3. Whether in view of the provisions contained in, inter alia, Articles 54, 62(1) and 71(4) of the Constitution of India election to the office of President must be held before the expiration of the term of the outgoing President notwithstanding the fact that at the time of such election the Legislative Assembly or Assemblies of any State or States is or are dissolved.
4. Whether the dissolution of the Legislative Assembly or Assemblies of any State or States precludes the holding of election to the office of President.
5. Where are Legislative Assembly or Assemblies of any State or States is or are dissolved before the expiration of the term of office of the outgoing President under Article 56(1) of the Constitution of India, how and when is the election to fill the vacancy in the office of President to be held and

90. *Supra* n. 89 at p. 171.

completed on a correct interpretation of the relevant provisions of the Constitution of India to make the Constitution of India workable regarding the office of President.

6. Whether in the event of the election to the office of President not being completed before the expiration of the term of office of President under Article 62(1) of the Constitution, the President can, notwithstanding the expiration of the term, continue to hold office under clause (c) of the proviso to Article 36(1) of the Constitution of India.

23. Opinion

The entire controversy was centered around the interpretation of article 54, 55, 62 and 71(4) of the constitution of India with the supplementary provisions of the Presidential and vice Presidential elections Act, 1962.

The full constitutional bench of seven judges including the Chief Justice A.N. Ray, after hearing the arguments for five days gave a unanimous opinion within four days of the conclusion of arguments.[91]

1. The court held that article 56(1) and 62(1) were mandatory in character. The time limit put under Article 62(1) did not provide for extension of time. Article 56(1) was held to be complementary to Article 62(1).
2. The Court held[92] that the word 'otherwise' in Article 62(1), unsound and ruled that the word 'otherwise' did not cover a vacancy which occurred by reason of expiration of term of office of the President and hence the contention of interveners that the elections could be held within six months of the date of occurrence of vacancy as provided under clause (2) of Article 62 was not accepted by the Court.

3 The court ruled[93] that neither of the Articles 54 and

91. *Supra* n. 89 at p. 187.
92. *Ibid* at p. 189.
93. Id at p. 191.

55 had anything to do either with the time of the election to fill the vacancy before the expiration of the term of the President or to prevent the holding of the election before the expiration of the term by dissolution of the legislative assembly of a state.

4. Article 71(4) also came in for interpretation. The constitutional declaration under Article 71(4) manifests that the existence of any vacancy for any reason whatever (including due to the dissolution of a State Assembly) among members of the Electoral College could not be a ground for questioning the presidential election.

5. The Court ruled[94] that it would be not only undemocratic but also unconstitutional to deny the elected members of both houses of Parliament as well as elected members of State Legislative assemblies the right to elect the President in accordance with the provisions of the constitution only because the legislative assembly of a state is dissolved.

6 The impossibility of the completion of the election to fill the vacancy in the office of the President before the expiration of the term of office in the case of death of a candidate as may appear from Section 7 of the 1952 Act does not rob Article 62(1) of its mandatory character. The Observation of the Supreme Court in *N.B. Khare's case*[95] regarding the mandatory nature of Article 62 was not obiter. It is possible that the successor cannot enter upon his office on the day following the expiration of the term of office of the outgoing President for unavidable reasons. That is why Articles 56(1), 56 (1)(C) and 62(1) are to be read together to give effect to the constitutional intent and content that the election to fill the vacancy caused by the expiration of the term

94. *Supra* n. 86 at p. 190.

95. Narayan Bhaskar Khare *v.* Election Commission of India, 1957 SCR 1081.

of the President is to be completed before the expiration of the term.

7. If as a result of dissolution of a Legislative Assembly of a State, there are no elected members of the Legislative Assembly of a state, a state will not have any elected member of a state legislative assembly to qualify for the Electoral College. It may be said that there are vacancies in the Electoral College by reason of the fact that there are no elected members of the Legislative Assembly of a State where the Legislative Assembly is dissolved, that matter will not be a ground either for preventing the holding of the election on the expiry of the term of the President or suggesting that the election to fill the vacancy caused by the expiry of the term of the office of the President could be held only after the election to the Legislative Assembly of a State where the Legislative Assembly is dissolved is held.

24. Main Points of Opinion

The Court thus answered the questions in the reference as follows:

(1) Only such persons who are elected members of the both Houses of Parliament and the Legislative Assemblies of the States on the date of the election to fill the vacancy caused by the expiration of the term of office of the President will be entitled to cast their votes at the election.

(2) The vacancies caused by the dissolution of Assemblies will be covered by Article 71(4).

(3) The election to the office of the President must be held before the expiration of the term of the President notwithstanding the fact that at the time of such election the Legislative Assembly of a State is dissolved. The election to fill the vacancy in the office of the President is to be held and completed having regard to Articles 62(1), 54, 55 and the Presidential and Vice-Presidential Elections Act, 1952.

(4) Article 56(1)(c) applies to a case where a successor as explained in the foregoing reasons has not entered on his office and only in such circumstances can a President whose term has expired continue.

(SEVENTH REFERENCE) IN THE SPECIAL COURTS BILL REFERENCE (Special Reference No. 1 of 1978)[96]

25. Main Facts

This was a reference which was made in face of deep political controversy. The Janta Party had won the 1977 elections on the promise that it will bring the emergency offenders to the book. It needed some speedy trial which was hardly possible under the ordinary procedure of law. Mr. Ram Jethmalani, a member of Parliament gave notice of a Special Courts Bill. It was thought proper to obtain the opinion of the Supreme court before going ahead with the proposal of creating Special Courts.

July 1977 saw the first non-Congress Government installed at the Centre. The Janta Party, newly formed coalition of political parties which were anti-Congress, made the 'Emergency' an important issue in their election campaign. The people were told about the excesses committed by persons holding high political offices during the 'dark era'. All freedoms and rights were ruthlessly crushed. Censorship on press was imposed. Powers of the judiciary were also curtailed through constitutional amendment. The administration came into the hands of a Caucus. This all was done, they alleged, with the purpose of keeping their chairs intact.

The leaders of the Janta Party, in their speeches during the election campaign, promised to the people that, if they came to power, those responsible for the excesses against the people would be brought to book. Hence, a mandate on the point was sought. Eventually, they were voted to power. The Janta Cabinet was installed at the Centre. It was an amalgam of persons holding different ideologies, i.e., Jansanghis and

96. AIR 1979 SC 478 : (1979) 1 SCC 380.

Socialists. Soon the differences began to come to the surface. There was a wide diversity of views on the best course of action in regard to the emergency trial. In the meantime, a number of Commissions under the Commissions of Inquiry Act, 1952 were appointed by the Government. The reports of the various inquiry commissions revealed that there was reason to believe that various offences were committed by high ranking political and public offices during the period of emergency and the period immediately preceding it. Now the question was what should be done?[97]

The demand was for a speedy trial by a special machinery set-up for the purpose. As the persons concerned held high positions, they would adopt delaying tactics. Keeping in view this fact, setting up of special courts was suggested. It was amidst these circumstances that Ram Jethmalani a Member of Parliament gave notices of the Special Courts Bill.[98] The Government had to make up mind over the issue. It feared criticism from the Opposition who was labelling the charge of being vindictive against them. Under the situation, the Government thought it proper to get seal of the highest judiciary on any course to be adopted to deal with the matter. Hence, the Reference to the Supreme Court, the President in exercise of his powers under clause (1) of Article 143 referred the following questions to the Supreme Court for its opinion:

26. Questions Referred

1. Whether the bill or any of the provisions thereof, if enacted, would be constitutionally valid?
   During the hearing of the reference before the court, the following several significant questions were raised regarding the scope of Article 143(1) and the maintainability of the reference.
2. If the Parliament is to be conceded the power to enlarge the jurisdiction of Supreme Court, then what were the objects and purposes behind provisions like

97. *Supra* n. 96, at p. 381.
98. *Ibid.*

Article 133(3), 134(2), 138(1), 139 and 140?

3. Whether the Bill violates the guarantee of equality contained in Article 14 of the Constitution?
4. Whether the procedure prescribed by the Bill was violative of any other provisions of the constitution?
5. Whether the Parliament has power to make a law by which an appeal shall lie from any judgment or order of a special court only to the Supreme Court?
6. The reference was hypothetical and speculative because the bill was yet to come on Act.
7. The reference was vague, general and of an omnibus in nature.
8. Since the parliament was seized of the bill, it was its exclusive function to decide upon the constitutionality of the bill?

27. Opinion

The main judgment of the Court was delivered by the Chief Justice on behalf of himself and Mr. Justice R.S. Sarkaria and Mr. Justice S. Murtaza Fazal Ali, Justices V.R. Krishna Iyer and N.L. Untwalia, in their separate judgments, fully concurred with the conclusions in the main judgment. However, Mr. Justice Krishna lyer made it clear that he was concurring with the judgment but for divergent, reasons given by him in his judgment. Concurring with the other members of the Bench that the Bill was bad on account of the defects pointed out by the Court in its main judgment Mr. Justice P.N. Shinghal gave his note of dissent and held that clauses 5 and 7 were constitutionally invalid.

(A) Answer of Question 1

The majority opinion of the Court is to be studied first. The question upon which the Court had to deliver its opinion first was regarding the validity of clauses 2, 10(1) and 6 of the Bill. The main challenge to the validity of these clauses came from Sri Shiv Shankar (Advocate on the behalf of Andhra Pradesh). The challenge to the legislative competence of Parliament to provide for the creation of special courts, the Court ruled was devoid of any substance. Entry 11A of the Concurrent List relates "administration of justice, constitution and organisation of all courts, except the Supreme Court and the High Court". By virtue of Article 246(2) the parliament has clearly the power to make laws with respect to the Constitution and organisation, that is to say the creation and setting up of the special courts. Clause 2 of the Bill was therefore, the Court ruled, within the competence of the Parliament.

The Chief Justice held that the very foundation of the argument against the validity of clauses 6 and 10(1) of the Bill was fallacious. The argument rested on the plea that the provisions of Chapter IV, Part V of the Constitution were exhaustive and, therefore, no more and no greater jurisdiction could be conferred on the Supreme Court than the provisions of that Chapter authorised. The contention, if allowed, would result in the virtual abrogation of the legislative power conferred on the Parliament by Article 246(1) and (2) of the Constitution.

(B) Answer of Question 2

This question was raised by Shri Shiv Shankar he asked that if the Parliament is to be concluded the power to enlarge the jurisdiction of the Supreme Court in the manner impugned, herein what were the objects and purposes behind provisions like those contained in Articles 133(3), 134(2), 138(1), 139 and 140? In other words, the argument was that specific provision of the Constitution under which the jurisdiction of the Supreme Court can be enlarged must override the general provisions under which Parliament can pass laws in respect of matters enumerated in Lists I and III of the Seventh Schedule.

Their Lordships found it difficult to accept the argument that conferment of power to pass laws on specific matters limits the parliament power to pass laws to those matters only and takes away its power to pass laws on matters which are otherwise within its legislative competence. The language of Article 206(1) and (2) is clear and explicit and admits of no doubt or difficulty. It must, therefore, be given its due effect. In the first place, therefore, no implications can be read into the provisions of Chapter IV, Part V of the Constitution which their language does not warrant, and secondly, the attempt has to harmonise the various provisions of the Constitution and not to treat any part of it as otiose or superfluous.

The Parliament, therefore, the Court in its majority opinion ruled, had the competence to pass laws in respect of matters enumerated in List I and II notwithstanding the fact that by such laws, the jurisdiction of the Supreme Court is enlarged in a manner not contemplated by or beyond what is contemplated by the various articles in Chapter IV, Part V. It is to be noted that Entry 77[99] of the Union List covers the subject matter of the jurisdiction of the Supreme Court.

(C) Answer of Question 3

Another question which came before the Court for its opinion was whether the Bill violates the guarantee of equality contained in Article 14 of the Constitution. The court, in appreciation of the arguments on the point, discussed a number of cases.[100] After going through the different cases, the Court found the following propositions which were relevant to the point in question.

1. The first Part of Article 14 is a declaration of equality of the civil rights of all persons within the territories of India. The second part enjoins that equal protection shall be secured to all such persons in the enjoyment of their rights and liberties without discrimination or favouritism.
2. The State, in the exercise of its governmental power has of necessity, to make laws operating differently on different groups or classes of persons to attain particular ends.

---

99. Entry 77 of the Union List reads thus:
Constitution, organisation, jurisdiction and powers of the Supreme Court (including contempt of such court) and the fees taken therein; persons entitled to practice before the Supreme Court.

100. Budhan Chaudhary *v.* State of Bihar (1955) 1 SCR 1045: (AIR 1955 SC 191); State of West Bengal *v.* Anwar Ali Sarkar, 1952 SCR 284 (AIR 1952 SC 75); Kathi Raning Rawat *v.* State of Saurashtra, 1952 SCR 435 (AIR 1953 SC 123); Lachmandas Kewalram Ahuja *v.* State of Bombay, 1953 SCR 710 (AIR 1952 SC 235).

3. The principles of equality means that all persons similarly circumstances shall be treated alike both in privileges conferred and liabilities imposed.
4. By the process of classification the State has the power of determining who should be regarded as a class for purposes of legislation. It postulates a rational basis and does not mean holding together of certain persons and classes arbitrarily.
5. The law can make and set apart the classes according to the needs and exigencies of the society.
6. The classification must be rational and not arbitrary. In order to pass the test two conditions must be fulfilled, namely, (a) that classification must be founded on an intelligible differentia which distinguishes those that are grouped together from others, and (b) that, differentia must have rational relation with the object sought to be achieved by the Act.
7. While Article 14 forbids class discrimination, it does not forbid classification for the purpose of legislation, provided such classification is not arbitrary in the sense above mentioned.
8. If the legislative policy is clear and definite and as an effective method of carrying out that policy a discretion is vested by the Statute upon a body of administrators or officers to make selective application on the law to certain classes or groups of persons the statute itself can not be condemned as piece of discriminatory legislation.

By applying these tests, the Court concluded that the classification provided for by the Special Courts Bill was valid. The classification which Section 4(1) made was both of offences and offenders, the former in relation to the period mentioned in the preamble, that is to say, from Feb. 27, 1975 until the expiry of the proclamation of emergency and in relation to the objective mentioned in the 6th paragraph of the preamble that it is imperative for the functioning of parliamentary democracy and the institutions created by or under the Constitution of India that the commission of such offences should be judicially determined with the utmost dispatch, and the latter in relation to their status, that is to say, in relation to the high public or political office held by them in India. It was only if both of the factors co-existed that the prosecution in respect of the offences committed by the particular offenders could be instituted in the Special Court.

(D) Answer of Question 4

The next point which the Court considered was whether the procedure prescribed by the Bill was violative of any other provision of the Constitution. Article 21 of the Constitution was examined in this context. After giving due consideration to the grievances and apprehensions posed before the Court, their Lordships held that there was no substance in them, except to the extent to be indicated later. Clause 9 of the Bill provided, for trial before the Special Court; the procedure prescribed by the 'Code' for the trial of warrant cases before a magistrate. In *Syed Quasim Razvi case,*[101] it was held by this Court that the warrant procedure was in no sense prejudicial to the interests of an accused. As regards bail, the Court ruled, it was open to the accused to ask for that and in appropriate cases, the Special Courts would be justified in enlarging the accused on bail. As regards the status of trial, it was unfair to make an assumption of malafides and say that an inconvenient forum would be chosen deliberately.

Though, this is so, the Chief Justice pointed out three infirmities in the Bill. In the *first place,* there was no provision in the Bill for the transfer of cases from one Special court to another. The manner in which a judge conducts himself may disclose a bias or a judge may not in fact be biased and yet the accused may entertain reasonable apprehension on account of attendant circumstances that he will not get a fair trial. In such cases interests of justice would require that the trial of the case is withdrawn from him. To compel an accused to submit to the jurisdiction of a court which, in fact, is biased or is reasonably apprehended to be biased is a violation of the fundamental principles of natural justice and a denial of fairplay.

101. 1953 SCR 589 at p. 600 (A.I.R. 1953 SC 155 at pp. 159-60).

The second infirmity from which the procedural part of the Bill suffered was regarding the presiding officers of the Court. Under clause 7 of the Bill it was provided that the Special Courts would be presided over either by a sitting or a retired judge of a High Court to be nominated by the Central Government in consultation with the Chief Justice of India. It was to the alternate provision that their Lordships objected. While expressing highest respect for retired judges, the Court pointed out that whereas by Article 217, a sitting judge of a High Court enjoyed security of tenure until he got a particular age, the retired judge would hold his office as a judge of the Special Court during the pleasure of the Government. He may be forward upon by the Government. The pleasure doctrine is subversive of judicial independence.

There was yet another infirmity[102] in the procedural part of the Bill. The only obligation which clause 7 of the Bill imposed on the Central Government while nominating a judge to the Special Court was to consult the Chief Justice of India. Although as a matter of convention, it was in the rarest of rare cases that the advice of the Chief Justice of India was not honoured by the Government. But the right of an accused to life and liberty could not be made to depend upon pious expressions of hope.

Hence, the Chief Justice ruled that the three infirmities pointed out above were violative of Article 21 of the Constitution, in the sense that they made the procedure prescribed by the Bill unjust and unfair to the accused. It was, therefore, ruled that so long as the Bill contained the three

102. During the course of arguments, these points were highlighted by the judges. The Government responded promptly. On 25th Sept., 1978 Sri S.N. Kacker, Solicitor General of India, made the following statement before the Court: "That after careful consideration the Government accepts the suggestion that only a sitting judge of the High Court would be appointed to preside over a Special Court and that the appointment will be made with the concurrence of the Chief Justice of India.

That the Government also agrees to the suggestion that the Supreme Court will be specifically empowered to transfer a case from one Special Court to another notwithstanding any other provisions in the Bill," (AIR 1979 SC 478 at p. 518).

offending provisions, the procedure would be violative of Article 21.

(E) Answer of Question 5

Once the argument regarding the exhaustiveness provisions of Chapter IV of Part V is rejected. Parliament clearly had the competence to provide by clause 10(1) of the Bill that notwithstanding anything contained in the Cr. P. C. an appeal shall lie as of right from any judgment or order of a Special Court to the Supreme Court both on fact and on law. A law which confers additional powers on the Supreme Court by enlarging its jurisdiction is evidently a law with respect to the "jurisdiction and powers" of that court. If there is power in the Parliament to establish a new court, as undoubtedly there is it would be strange that the Parliament should not possess the wholesome power to provide for an appeal to the Supreme Court from the decision of that Court.

It must follow as a logical corollary that Parliament also possesses the legislative competence to provide by clause 6 of the Bill that if on the date of the declaration in respect of any offence, an appeal or revision against any judgment or order in prosecution in respect of such offence is pending in any court of appeal or revision, the same shall stand transferred to the Supreme Court. In this way, the Court held that the clauses 2, 6 and 10(1) of the Bill were within the legislative competence of the Parliament.

(F) Answer of Question 6

Rejecting the contention, the Court argued that it was a fact that the Bill was pending before Parliament. There was nothing speculative about the existence of the Bill and there was nothing hypothetical about its contents. The Bill could undergo changes in course of time but that would not make it speculative. The Court observed in this connection.[103]

> 'The Special Courts Bill is there in flesh and blood for anyone to see and examine. That sustains the reference, which is founded upon the satisfaction of the President

103. AIR 1979 SC at 491.

that a question as regards the constitutional validity of the Bill is likely to arise and that the question is of such a nature and of such public importance that it is expedient to obtain the opinion of this Court upon it."

In the past also references had been made in regard to contemplated legislation and not in regard to Acts which had been enacted.[104]

(G) Answer of Question 7

The only question referred was whether the Bill was constitutional. This was a very broad question. The whole Bill had been referred without mentioning specifically which of the provisions of the Bill could be open to attack under the Constitution and on what grounds. Those specific points on which Court's advice was sought had not been mentioned.

The Court agreed that a reference in such broad and general terms would be difficult to answer because it gave no indication of the specific points on which the opinion of the Court was sought. "It is not proper or desirable that this Court should be called upon to embark upon a roving inquiry into the constitutionality of a Bill or on Act". It ought not to be expected of the Court that it would examine each constitutional provision to find out under which of these provisions could the validity of the Bill be challenged.

The Court said that in the beginning it was "so much exercised over the undefined breadth of the reference" that it was contemplating to return the reference to the President. But, then, after perusing the briefs presented to the Court by the lawyers of the various parties, and after listening to the oral arguments advanced by them, it was possible to narrow down the legal controversies surrounding the Bill, to crystallise the issues arising for the consideration of the Court, and to ascertain the points of dispute needing the opinion of the Court. The Court emphasized.[105]

---

104. *In the Estate Duty case,* AIR 1944 SC 73; *In the Kerala Education Bill case,* AIR 1958 SC 956; *supra; In the Sea Customs Bill,* AIR 1963 SC 1760.
105. AIR 1979 SC at 493.

"We hope that in future whenever a reference is made to this Court under Art. 143 of the Constitution, care will be taken to frame specific questions for the opinion of the Court the risk that a vague and general reference may be returned unanswered in real..."

(H) Answer of Question 8

Since Parliament was seized of the Bill, it was its exclusive function to decide upon the constitutionality of the Bill.

The Court rejected this argument saying that under the Indian Constitution the power of reviewing the constitutionality of legislation was vested in the Supreme Court and the High Courts. The Court observed on this point:

> *"The right of the Indian judiciary to pronounce a legislation void if it conflicts with the Constitution is not merely a tacit assumption but is an express avowal of our Constitution. The principle is firmly and wisely embedded in our Constitution that the policy of law and the expediency of passing it are matters for the legislature to decide while interpretation of laws and questions regarding their validity fall within exclusive advisory or adjudicatory functions of courts."*

28. Main Points of Opinion

The Chief Justice through the main judgment, delivered the opinion of the Court on the Presidential Reference[106] as under:

(1) The Parliament has the legislative competence to create Special Courts and to provide that an appeal shall lie as of right from any judgment or order of a Special Court to the Supreme Court, Clause 2 and 10 (1) of the Bill are, therefore, within the Parliament's legislative competence.

106. AIR 1979 SC at 498.

(2) The classification provided for in clause 4(1) of the Bill is valid to the extent to which the Central Government is empowered to make a declaration in respect of offences alleged to have been committed during the period of Emergency by persons who held high public or political offices in India. Persons who are alleged to have committed offences prior to the declaration of Emergency can not validly be grouped along with those who are alleged to have committed offences during the period of Emergency. It is, therefore, not competent to the Central Government to make a declaration under clause 4(1) of the Bill in respect of persons who are alleged to have committed offences between Feb. 27, 1975 and June 25, 1975.

(3) The procedure prescribed by the Bill for the trial of offences in respect of which a declaration can be validly made by the Central Government under clause 4(1) of the Bill is just and fair except in regard to the following matter:

   (a) the provision in clause 7 under which a retired judge of the High Court can be appointed as a judge of the Special Court;
   (b) the provision in clause 7, under which the appointment of a judge to the Special Court can be made by the Central Government in consultation with but without the concurrence of the Chief Justice of India; and
   (c) the absence of a provision for transfer of a case from one Special Court to another.

(4) The Bill is valid and constitutional in all other respects.

(EIGHTH REFERENCE) REFERENCE ON JAMMU & KASHMIR RESETTLEMENT ACT (Special Reference No. 1 of 1982)[107]

29. Related Cases

1. *Bachan Lal Kalgotra Vs. State of Jammu & Kashmir.*[108]
2. Two Writ Petitions filed by *Panther's Party President Dr. Bhim Singh and Others* in 2002.

30. Main Facts

On Sept. 30, 1982 the President of India made yet another use of the provision of advisory jurisdiction. The controversial Bill called the Jammu & Kashmir Grant of permit for Resettlement in the State Bill was passed by the J&K Assembly on March 30, 1982 with the entire opposition bycotting the session. It was, thereafter, sent to the Governor for assent. The Governor, having considered with great care the provisions of the Bill, the views of the State Government, as explained to him by the Law Minister and the best constitutional and legal advice that, he could get, returned the Bill to the Assembly with the suggestion that the Legislative Assembly should make changes in the Bill to make it consistent with the correct constitutional position.

The controversial Bill provides for the return to the State of anyone who voluntarily migrated from there to Pakistan in the past 35 years provided he can establish that he was a Kashmiri citizen before May 1954. The Bill also permits the wives and even descendants to return and settle in the State.

The Governor, while returning the Bill under section 78 of the Constitution of Jammu & Kashmir to the Assembly, said that granting admission to and conferring citizenship rights to an outsider under the Seventh Schedule of the Constitution of India, lies in the exclusive domain of Parliament, and J. and K. Assembly had no power to make legislation on these subjects. Mr. B.K. Nehru, the Governor pointed out that the legislature,

107. Opinion delivered on November 2001.
108. 1987 (2) S.C.C. at p. 223.

'perhaps without intending it' has not considered that the Bill will give legal right to return and settle down permanently persons, who may have deliberately and voluntarily migrated to Pakistan settled, there, taken Pakistani citizenship, appropriated evacuee property, served in the Pakistani civil or armed services, fought against India or committed other treasonable acts against the country at any time of their choosing.

The Governor said that he understands that the real reasons for the proposed legislation is that there are many cases of hardship of permanent residents of the State, who is their old age or for other family reasons, wish to return permanently to the State, 'who are not security risk.' For such cases, the Governor said, the existing laws under Section 51 (A) for the Indian Citizenship Act, 1955 can easily be employed.

But in disregard of the view of the Governor to remove the legal lacunae in the controversial Resettlement Bill, the J. and K. Assembly on Oct., 4, 1982 passed it again in its original form with over whelming support. The Bill came in for severe criticism from Congress I, BJP, and Janta Party members. They wanted the Bill 'which could be dangerous for the security of the country',[109] referred to the Supreme Court to ascertain its legality.

The Chief Minister, Dr. Farooq Abdullah, described the Bill as necessity because of the human factor involved. "Think of a family whose members have not been able to meet for years. My father would weep when such pathetic cases were placed before him and found himself helpless," Mr. Abdullah said. He pleaded that the opponents of the Bill must know that it was ultimately the Central Government and its embassy in Pakistan that would give visas to any subject of Jammu & Kashmir living in Pakistan and wanting to return here. Nobody should say that those who return were spies, saboteurs, etc. "Muslims alone can not be spies or anti-national. Hindus can also be. Were the people involved in the famous Sabma spy case Muslims?" Mr. Abdullah asked loudly.

109. *Indian Express*, Oct. 5, 1982, p. 1, Col. 1.

In a compromise move the Centre decided to refer to the Supreme Court the controversial Bill while the Chief Minister, Mr. Farooq Abdullah, declared the Bill would not be implemented. Unless the Court pronounced it valid. The move averted what had seemed to be a developing confrontation between the Centre and the State over the Bill which had been returned to the legislature.[110]

31. Question Referred

The President on Sept. 30, 1982, referred the following question to the Supreme Court for advice:

> Whether the Bill or any of the provisions thereof, if enacted, "would be constitutionally valid?[111]

Hence, once again the highest Court has been called for settling an issue of great constitutional importance. In reality the Provision has already helped in providing a face-saving formula to both the Governments before the opinion was delivered by the Supreme Court, the civil writ petition of Bachan Lal was decided on 20th Feb. 1987, first of all we have to discuss this case.

32. Facts of Writ Petition

The petitioner is the Chairman of the Action Committee of West Pakistani Refugees. He migrated from West Pakistan to the State of Jammu & Kashmir in India in 1947 in the wake of the partition of the country. He claims to speak on behalf of the refugees from West Pakistan who migrated and settled in the State of Jammu & Kashmir He contends that notwithstanding the fact that it is almost four decades since they migrated and settled down in the State of Jammu & Kashmir, they are denied many basic rights which other Indian citizens have in other parts of the country.

Such as, the right to acquire any immovable property in the State, the right to employment under the State, the right to start an industry, the right to purchase transport vehicles, the

110. *Indian Express*, Oct. 5, 1982, p. 1, col. 3.
111. *Indian Express*, Oct. 5, 1982, p. 1, col. 6.

right to higher technical education, the right to be elected to the State Assembly or a local body, etc. He complains that while refugees from West Pakistan who migrated into the State of Jammu & Kashmir in 1947 and have settled down in the State are denied these rights, recently the Jammu & Kashmir legislature has enacted the Resettlement Act, 1982 by which all these rights are given to erstwhile residents of Jammu & Kashmir who had voluntarily migrated to West Pakistan at the time of the partition of the country in 1947 and their children, who may now choose to return to Jammu & Kashmir.

The present writ petition was initially filed challenging the vires of the Resettlement Act, 1982. The vires of the Act is already awaiting the decision of this Court in Special Reference No. 1 of 1982. The petitioner, therefore, gave up the challenge to the vires of the Act in this petition leaving the question to be decided in Special Reference No. 1 of 1982. For the purposes of this petition, he now proceeds on the basis that the Act is valid but claims that he and other persons situated like him should at least be given the same rights as are given to those who voluntarily migrated to West Pakistan at the time of the partition in 1947.

It is true that the persons in the position of the petitioner who migrated from West Pakistan to the State of Jammu & Kashmir in the wake of the 1947 partition and have settled down in the State of Jammu & Kashmir and who are citizens of India and who also have the right to participate in elections to Parliament, have very anomalous rights within the State. For example, they are not entitled to be included in the electoral roll of the State Assembly, they are not entitled to be elected to a village panchayat, they are not entitled to purchase any land and they are also not entitled to be appointed to any service under the State Government. All these denials and deprivations are the consequence of the definition of a 'permanent resident' under section 6 of the Jammu & Kashmir Constitution. Section 6 is as follows:

> *Permanent residents*—(1) Every person who is, or is deemed to be, a citizen of India under the provisions of the Constitution of India shall be a permanent resident of the State, if on the fourteenth day of May, 1954—

(a) he was a State subject of Class I or of Class II; or

(b) Having lawfully acquired immovable property in the State, he has been ordinarily resident in the State for not less than ten years prior to that date.

(2) Any person who, before the fourteenth day of May, 1954, was a State subject of Class I or of Class II and who having migrated after the first day of March, 1947, to the territory now included in Pakistan, returns to the State under a permit for resettlement in the State or for permanent return issued by or under the authority of any law made by the State legislature shall on such return be a permanent resident of the State.

(3) In this section, the expression "State subject of Class I or of Class II" shall have the same meaning as in State Notification No. 1-L/84 dated the twentieth April, 1927, read with State Notification No. 13/L dated the twenty-seventh June, 1932.

The 1927 Notification defining State subject is as follows:

The term State subject means and includes :

Class-I – All persons born and residing within the State before the commencement of the reign of His Highness the late Maharaja Ghulab Singh Sahib Bahadur, and also persons who settled therein before the commencement of Samvat year 1942, and have since been permanently residing therein.

Class-II – All persons other than those belonging to Class I who settled within the State before the close of Samvat year 1968, and have since permanently resided and acquired immovable property therein.

Class-III– All persons, other than those belonging to

Classes I and II permanently residing within the State, who have acquired under a rayatnama any immovable property therein or who may hereafter acquire such property under an ijazatnama and may executed a rayatnama after ten years continuous residence therein.

Class-IV– Companies which have been registered as such within the State and which, being companies in which the government are financially interested or as to the economic benefit to the State or to the financial stability of which the government are satisfied, have by a special order of His Highness been declared to be State subjects.

33. Judgment

The judgment of the court was delivered by O. Chinnappa Reddy and S. Natrajan, J.J.[112]

There is no dispute that the petitioner and others like him are not 'permanent resident's of Jammu & Kashmir within the meaning of Section 6 of the Jammu & Kashmir Constitution. It is because they are not permanent residence as defined by section 6 of the Jammu & Kashmir Constitution.[113]

They do not have the rights and privileges mentioned earlier. Section 12 (b) of the Jammu & Kashmir Representation of the People Act provides that a person shall be disqualified for registration in an electoral roll if he is not a permanent resident of the State as defined in Part III of the Constitution, Section 8(a) of the Village Panchayat Act provides that a person shall be disqualified for being chosen as or for being a member of a Panchayat if he is not permanent resident of the State, Section 4 of the Land Alienation Act, 1995 JK provides that transfer of land in favour of any person who is not a State subject is prohibited and Rule 17(a) of the Jammu & Kashmir Civil Services, Classification of Control and Appeal Rules

112. *Supra* note n. 108.
113. *Supra* note n. 108.

provides that no person shall be eligible for appointment to any service by direct recruitment unless he is a hereditary State subject to be known hereafter as a permanent resident.

It is to be noticed here that these provisions are not open to challenge as inconsistent with the rights guaranteed by Part III of the Constitution of India because of "the Constitution (Application of Jammu & Kashmir) Order, 1954" issued by the President of India under Article 370(1)(d) of the Constitution by which Article 35-A was added to the Constitution in relation to the State of Jammu & Kashmir. This article states;

35-A. Notwithstanding anything contained in this Constitution, no existing law in force in the State of Jammu & Kashmir, and no law hereafter enacted by the legislature of the State:

(a) defining the classes of persons who are, or shall be, permanent residents of the State of Jammu & Kashmir; or

(b) conferring on such permanent residents any special rights and privileges or imposing upon other persons any restrictions as respects:

(i) employment under the State Government;
(ii) acquisition of immovable property in the state;
(iii) settlement in the State; or
(iv) right to scholarship and such other forms of aid as the State Government may provide,

shall be void on the ground that it is inconsistent with or takes away or abridges any rights conferred on the other citizens of India by any provisions of this part. The net result is that persons in the position of the petitioner through citizens of India and entitled to the various fundamental rights guaranteed by the constitution are not in a position to enjoy many of those rights within the state of Jammu & Kashmir through they are domiciled in that state for nearly 40 years.

On the other hand, those who had migrated to West

Pakistan in 1947 and who may choose to return to the State of Jammu & Kashmir now, appear to stand in a better position. But that is apparently because of the special position secured to them in the Jammu & Kashmir Constitution itself. Section 6(2) of the Jammu & Kashmir Constitution which has already been extracted by us, expressly provides that such persons if they were previously State subjects of Class I and Class II shall be permanent residents of the state on their return to the State of Jammu & Kashmir from West Pakistan under a permit for resettlement in the State or for permanent return issued by or under the authority of any law made by the State legislature. It is pursuant to this provision that the Resettlement Act has been enacted.

In the circumstances, in view of the peculiar constitutional position obtaining in the State of Jammu & Kashmir, Court do not see what possible relief it can give to the petitioner and those situate like him. All that it can say is that the position of the petitioner and those like him is anomalous and it is up to the legislature of the State of Jammu & Kashmir to take action to amend legislations, such as, the Jammu & Kashmir Representation of the People Act, the Land Alienation Act, the Village Panchayat Act, etc. so as to make persons like the petitioner who have migrated from West Pakistan in 1947 and who have settled down in the State of Jammu & Kashmir since then, eligible to be included in the electoral roll, to acquire land, to be elected to the Panchayat, etc.

This can be done by suitably amending the legislations without having to amend the Jammu & Kashmir Constitution. In regard to providing employment opportunities under the State Government, it can be done by the government by amending the Jammu & Kashmir Civil Services, Classification, Control and Appeal Rules.

In regard to admission to higher technical educational institutions also, the government may make these persons eligible by issuing appropriate executive directions without even having to introduce any legislation. The petitioners have justifiable grievances. Court told that they constitute nearly seven to eight per cent of the population of the State of Jammu & Kashmir. Surely they are entitled to expect to be protected by the State of Jammu & Kashmir. In the peculiar context of the State of Jammu & Kashmir, the Union of India also owes an obligation to make some provision for the advancement of the cultural, economic and educational rights of these persons. Court do hope that the claims of persons like the petitioner and others to exercise greater rights of citizenship will receive due consideration from the Union of India and the State of Jammu & Kashmir. Court, however, unable to give any relief to the petitioners.

34. Order

Writ petition dismissed.

35. Opinion on Special Reference No. 1 of 1982

After 19 long years in October, 2001 the constitution bench of the Supreme Court returned without comment on the reference. The lordships at the apex court have said they have no comments to offer on the act which justifies our stand that the bill is in order and with in the ambit of country's constitution. The five judge constitution bench of the Supreme Court headed by Chief Justice S.P. Bharucha said the bill cannot be struck down as it had already become an act.

36. Writ Petitions of Dr. Bhim Singh[114]

A 60 years old Gani, who had come on a tourist permit through Karvan-e-Aman bus from Muzaffarabad to Srinagar staked claim to her ancestral property in Srinagar left in 1948, before Evacuees Department of Jammu & Kashmir.

A writ petition was filed by Dr. Bhim Singh.[115] Writ petition had raised two main points stating that the reunion of Jammu & Kashmir, thousands of Militants shall enter into India to Sabotage national security, which could being more than 2 lakh persons descendants of those who were born in Pakistan and many more trained under the Taliban.

Secondly, deliberately and voluntarily migrated to Pakistan, settled there and taken Pakistani citizenship and Pakistan civil or armed services or fought against India or committed other treasonable acts against any time of their

114. *Supra* n. 108
115. Chairman, Jammu & Kashmir National Panthers Party.

choice return to India and settle here with legal rights. Petitioners sought declaration that the act was illegal and *ultra vires* the basic structure of the constitution and prayed for quashing of the same.

The petitioners argued that the 1982 Act was being challenged, as, after the Constitution Bench of the apex court "returned unanswered" the 'President reference' of the related Bill in this regard, the Chief Minister, Farooq Abdullah, had announced that the State would implement the Act. They submitted that the Chief Minister's announcement had caused apprehensions in the minds of the people of the State that this Act would be misused by militants and terrorists to settle here permanently.

On behalf of the Union Government it was submitted that implementation of the Act would result in large number of aliens returning to India which was not permissible under the Citizenship Act.

37. Supreme Court Interim Order

On Feb. 2002, the Supreme Court stayed the implementation of the Jammu & Kashmir Resettlement Act, 1982, providing for the resettlement of all those persons who had migrated to Pakistan after March 1947, if they returned to Kshmir on a permanent basis. A Bench comprising Justice G.B. Pattanaik and Justice S.N. Phukan, granted interim stay of the Act on two writ petitions filed by the Panther's Party president, Bhim Singh and another, challenging the Constitutional validity of the Act, on the ground that if the Act was implemented it would result in "chaos and pose a threat to country's defence and security.[116]

The Bench granted two weeks time to the J&K Government to file a reply after the Centre supported the stand of the petitioners that the Act would facilitate the entry of terrorists into J&K where over 50,000 people had fallen victims to militant activities and *prima facie* the Act was *ultra vires* the Constitution.

116. "J&K Resettlement Act Stayed". *The Hindu*, (New Delhi Ed.) Vol. 125, 02 Feb., 2002, p. 1, C-1.

On May 13, 2005 a division bench of Supreme Court comprising Chief Justice R. Lahoti, Justice Santosh G. Mathur, directed the Union of India to file a counter affidavit in the case. Although the special reference of 1982 was returned without any comment but the apex court is going to deliver the judgment on the related petitions, which are subjudices before the court.

(NINTH REFERENCE) THE CAUVERY WATER DISPUTES TRIBUNAL REFERENCE (Special Reference No. 1 of 1991)[117]

38. Main Facts

The river Cauvery is an inter state river and is one of the major rivers of the Southern Peninsula. The basis area of the river and its tributaries has substantial spread over with in the territory of three states of Karnataka, Tamilnadu, Kerala and Union Territory of Pondicherry. The total length of the river from its head to its outflow into the Bay of Bengal is about 802 kms. There were two agreements of 1892 and 1924 for sharing the water of the river between the areas which are predominantly today comprised it the states of Karnataka and Tamilnadu. The present state of Tamilnadu has an area of about 43868 sq. kms. of the Cauvery river basin, reducing the basin area which at the time of the agreement was about 49136 sq. kms. as against this the basin area of the said river which was about 28887 sq. kms. in the state of Mysore has increased to about 34273 sq. kms. in the present State of Karnataka.

In 1956 the Parliament enacted The River Board Act, 1956 for the purpose of regulation and development of inter-state rivers and river valleys and also The Inter-state Water Disputes Act, 1956 for adjudication of disputes with regard to the use distribution or control etc. of the said waters. In 1970 Tamilnadu invoked the provisions of Sec. 3 of the Inter-state Water Disputes Act, 1956 and requested the central government for reference of the dispute between the two states—Tamilnadu and Karnataka to a Tribunal under the Act.

117. AIR 1992 SC 522 : 1993 Supp. (1) SCC 96(2): (1993) 4 SCC 441.

The central government initiated negotiations between the two states. Simultaneously, Tamilnadu moves to the Supreme Court by means of a suit under Article 131 seeking a direction to the union government to constitute a tribunal and to refer the dispute to it, but the Court dismissed the application for interim relief.[118]

In July 1986 the State of Tamil Nadu lodged a letter of request under sec. 3 of the act with the Central Government for the constitution of a Tribunal and for reference of the water dispute for adjudication on to it at the hearing of the writ petition filed by the Tamilnadu the Central Government left the matter to the Supreme Court. Court taking into consideration the course of negotiations and the length of the time which has passed, by its judgment dated May 4, 1990 held that the negotiations between the two states has failed and directed the union government to constitute a tribunal under Sec. 4 of the act.

In pursuance of the directions given by this court, the union government by its notification dated June 2, 1990 constituted. The Couvery Water Disputes Tribunal and by another notification of even date referred on it. Tamilnadu submitted a letter before tribunal seeking interim relief. The interim relief claimed by Tamilnadu was that Karnataka be directed not to impound or utilise water of Couvery river beyond the extent impounded or utilised by them on May 31, 1972 as agreed to by the parties, besides contesting the application on merits both Karnataka and Kerala raised a preliminary objection to the jurisdiction of the tribunal to entertain the said application and to grant any interim relief. The preliminary objection was that the Tribunal constituted under the act has a limited jurisdiction, it had no inherent powers as an ordinary civil court has, and there was no provision of law which authorised or conferred jurisdiction on the tribunal to grant any interim relief. The tribunal heard the parties both on the preliminary objection as well as on merits and by its order held that state of Karnataka must release water from its reservoirs in Karnataka so as to ensure that 205 TMC water is available to Tamilnadu. The tribunal further

118. *Supra* n. 117, p. 542.

directed Karnataka to regulate the release of water every year in the manner stated in the order. The tribunal then observed that its said order would remain operative till the final adjudication of the dispute was referred to it.[119]

Only July 25, 1991 the governor of Karnataka issued an ordinance named "The Karnataka Cauvery basin irrigation protection ordinance, 1991, it is in the context of these developments that the president has made reference on July 27, 1991 the president under Article 143 of the constitution referred to this court for its opinion.

39. Question Referred

The reference reads as follows:

> In existence of the powers conferred by Sec. 4 of the Inter-state Water Disputes Act, 1956; the central government constituted a water disputes tribunal called "The Cauvery water disputes tribunal" on June 25, 1991, the tribunal passed an interim order, but differences have arisen with regard to certain aspects of the order on July 25, 1991, the governor of Karnataka promulgated The Karnataka Cauvery Basin Irrigation Protection Ordinance, 1991. Doubts have been expressed with regard to the constitutional validity of the ordinance and its provisions. The differences and doubts have given rise to a public controversy which may lead to undesirable consequences.

Therefore in exercise of the powers conferred upon by clause (1) of article 143 of the constitution president refer the following question to the Supreme Court of India for consideration:

(i) Whether the ordinance (Karnataka Cauvery basis irrigation Protection, 1991) and the provisions there of are in accordance with the provisions of the constitution.

(ii) Whether the order passed by the tribunal constitutes

119. *Supra* n. 117 at p. 548.

a report and a decision with in the meaning of sec. 5 (2) of Inter-state water disputes act, 1956.

(iii) Whether the order of the tribunal is required to be published by the central government in order to make it effective.

(iv) Whether water disputes tribunal constituted under the act is competent to grant any interim relief to the parties to the dispute.

40. Opinion

Opinion was decided on November 22, 1991 by a full bench consisting of five judges (before Ranganath Mishra C.J. and K.N. Singh, A.M. Ahamadi, Kuldip Singh and P.B. Sawant, J.J.). The opinion was delivered by the P.B. Sawant J.)[120]

(A) Answer of the first Question

Dominant provisions, among others, of the Inter State Water Disputes Act, 1956 clearly show that apart from its title, the Act is made by the Parliament pursuant to the provisions of Article 262 of the Constitution specifically for the adjudication of the disputes between the riparian States with regard to the use, distribution or control of the waters of the inter-state rivers or river valleys. Art. 262 has given an exclusive power to the Parliament to enact a law providing for the adjudication of such disputes.

The disputes or complaints for which adjudication may be provided relate to the "use, distribution or control" of the waters of, or in any inter-state river or river valley. The words "use", "distribution" and "control" are of wide import and may include regulation and development of the said waters. The provisions clearly indicate the amplitude of the scope of adjudication in as much as it would take within its sweep the determination of the extent, and the manner, of the use of the said waters, and the power to give directions in respect of the same.

Since the subject of adjudication of the said disputes is taken care of specifically and exclusively by Article 262, by

120. *Supra* n. 117 at p. 540.

necessary implication the subject stands excluded from the field covered by Entry 56 of List I and Entry 17 of List II.

It is not, therefore, permissible either for the Parliament under Entry 56 or for a State legislature under Entry 17 to enact a legislation providing for adjudication of the said disputes or in any manner affecting or interfering with the adjudication or adjudicatory process of the machinery for adjudication established by law under Article 262. This is apart from the fact that the State legislature would even otherwise be incompetent to provide for adjudication or to affect in any manner the adjudicatory process or the adjudication made in respect of the inter-state river waters beyond its territory or with regard to disputes between itself and another State relating to the use, distribution or control of such waters. Any such act on its part will be extra-territorial in nature and, therefore, beyond its competence.[121]

Though the water of an inter-State river pass through the territories of the riparian States such water cannot be said to be located in any one State. They are in a state of flow and no State can claim exclusive ownership of such waters so as to deprive the other State of their equitable share.[122]

Hence in respect of such waters, no state can effectively legislate for the use of such waters since its legislative power does not extend beyond its territories. It is further an acknowledged principle of distribution and allocation of waters between the riparian States that the same has to be done on the basis of the equitable share of such States.[123]

Further, the State of Karnataka has assumed the role of a judge in its own cause. Thus, apart from the fact that the Ordinance directly nullifies the decision of the Tribunal dated June 25, 1991, it also challenges the decision dated April 26, 1991 of the Supreme Court which has ruled that the Tribunal had power to consider the question of granting interim relief since it was specifically referred to it. To the extent that the Ordinance interferes with the decision of the Supreme Court and of the Tribunal appointed under the Central Legislation, it

121. *Supra* n. 117 at p. 452.

122. *Ibid.*

123. State of Kansas *v.* State of Colorado, 51-52 L Ed. 956: (206) US 46.

is clearly unconstitutional being not only in direct conflict with Article 262 under which the said enactment is made by being also in conflict with the judicial power of the State.

Further, the effect of the Ordinance is to affect the flow of the waters of the river Cauvery into the territory of Tamil Nadu and Pondicherry which are the lower riparian States. The Ordinance has, therefore, an extra-territorial operation. Hence the Ordinance is on that account beyond the legislative competence of the State and is *ultra vires* the provisions of Article 245(1).

The Ordinance is also against the basic tenets of the rule of law in as much as the State of Karnataka by issuing the Ordinance has sought to take law in its own hand and to be above the law. Such an act is an invitation to lawlessness and anarchy, in as much as the Ordinance is a manifestation of a desire on the part of the State to be a judge in its own cause and to defy the decision of the judicial authorities. The action forebodes evil consequence to the federal structure under the Constitution and opens doors for each State to act in the way it desires disregarding not only the rights of the other States, the orders passed by instrumentalities constituted under an Act of Parliament but also the provision of the Constitution. If the power of a state to issue such an ordinance is upheld it will lead to the breakdown of the constitutional mechanism and affect the unity and integrity of the nation.[124]

(B) Answer of the Second Question

Sub-section (1) of Section 5 expressly empowers the Central Government to refer to the Tribunal not only the main water dispute but any matter appearing to be connected with or relevant to it. A request for an interim relief whether in the nature of mandatory direction or prohibitory order, whether for the maintenance of *status quo* or for the grant of urgent relief or to prevent the final relief being rendered infrustuous, would be a matter connected with or relevant to the main dispute.

---

124. Tamil Nadu Cauvery Neerppasana Vilaiporugal Vivasayigal Nala Urimai Padhugappu Sangam *v.* Union of India (1990) 3 SCC 440. Union of India *v.* Paras Laminators (P) Ltd., (1990) 4 SCC 453 : 1991 SCC (L&S) 208: (1990) 14 ATC 798.

The interm orders passed or relief's granted by the Tribunal when they are not of purely procedural nature and have to be implemented by the parties to make them effective, are deemed to be a report and a decision within the meaning of Sections 5(2) and 6 of the Act. The present order of the Tribunal is not meant to be merely declaratory in nature but is meant to be implemented and given effect to by the parties. Hence, the order in question constitutes a report and a decision within the meaning of Section 5(2) and is required to be published by the Central Government under Section 6 of the Act in order to be binding on the parties and to make it effective.

The connection that since the order does not say that it is a report and decision it is not so under Section 5(2) of the Act is facetious. Either the order is such a report and decision because of its contents or not so at all. If the contents do not show that it is such a report, it will not become one because the order states so. On facts, the contents of the order clearly show that it is a report and a decision within the meaning of Section 5(2).

(C) Answer of the Third Question

The Supreme court by its decision dated April 26, 1991 had held that the Central Government had made a reference to the Tribunal for the consideration of the claim for interim relief prayed for by the State of Tamil Nadu and hence the Tribunal had jurisdiction to consider the said request being a part of the Reference itself. Implicit in the said decision is the finding that the subject of interim relief is a matter connected with or relevant to the water dispute within the meaning of Section 5(1) of the Act. Hence the Central Government could refer the matter of granting interim relief to the Tribunal for adjudication. Thus the decision has in terms concluded that the Tribunal is competent to grant interim relief when such reference is made to it. However, the Court by the said decision has kept open the question, viz., whether the Tribunal has incidental, ancillary, inherent or implied power to grant the interim relief when no reference for grant of such relief is made to it.

41. MAIN POINTS OF OPINION

For Question No. 1: The Karnataka Cauvery Basin Irrigation Protection Ordinance, 1991 passed by the Government of Karnataka on July 25, 1991 (now the Act) is beyond the legislative competence of the State and is, therefore, *ultra vires* the Constitution.

For Question No. 2 : (i) The order of the Tribunal dated June 25, 1991 constitutes report and decision within the meaning of Section 5(2) of the Inter-State Water Disputes Act, 1956.

(ii) The said Order is, therefore, required to be published by the Central Government in the official Gazette under Section 6 of the Act in order to make it effective.

For Question No. 3: (i) A Water Dispute Tribunal constitute under the Act is competent to grant any interim relief to the parties to the dispute when a reference for such relief is made by the Central Government.

(ii) Whether the Tribunal has power to grant interim relief when no reference is made by the Central Government for such relief is a question which does not arise in the facts and circumstances under which the Reference is made. Hence we do not deem it necessary to answer the same.

42. New Development

The Cauvery Water Disputes Tribunal announced its final verdict on February 5, 2007. According to its verdicts, Tamil Nadu gets 419 billion ft^3 (12 km^3) of Cauvery water while Karnataka gets 270 billion ft^3 (7.6 km^3). The actual release of water by Karnataka to Tamil Nadu is to be 192 billion ft^3 (5.4 km^3) annually. Further, Kerala will get 30 billion ft^3 and Puducherry 7 billion ft^3. The government of Karnataka, unhappy with the decision, filed a revision petition before the tribunal seeking a review. Following the final award of the tribunal, violence against Tamil population was anticipated in parts of Karnataka and consequently the city of Bangalore was put on high alert.[125]

125. Subramanian, T.S. : "An award in Sight" available at www.hinduonnet.com accessed on 26.07.2007.

(TENTH REFERENCE)
IN THE MATTER OF RAM JANMABHOOMI REFERENCE
(Special Reference No. 1 of 1993)[126]

43. Related Cases

1. *Dr. M. Ismail Faruqui and Others* v. *Union of India and Others*[127]
2. *Mohd. Aslam* v. *Union of India and others*
3. *Hargyan Singh* v. *State of U.P. & Others*
4. *Thakur Vijay Ragho Bhagwan Birajman Mandir and Others* v. *Union of India and Other.*

44. Main Facts

Ayodhya situated in the north of India is a township in District Faizabad of Uttar Pradesh. It has long been a place of holy pilgrimage because of its mention in the epic Ramayana as the place of birth of Sri Ram. The structure commonly known as Ram Janmabhoomi-Babri Masjid was erected as a mosque by one Mir Baqi in Ayodhya in 1528 AD, it is claimed by some sections that it was built at the site believed to be the birthspot of Sri Ram where a temple had stood earlier. This resulted in a long-standing dispute.

The controversy entered a new phase with the placing of idols in the disputed structure in December 1949. The premises were attached under Section 145 of the Code of Criminal Procedure, Civil suits were filed shortly thereafter. Interim orders in these civil suits restrained the parties from removing the idols or interfering with their worship effect, therefore, from December 1949 till 6-12-1992 the structure had not been used as a mosque.

The movement to construct a Ram Temple at the site of disputed structure gathered momentum in recent years which became a matter of great controversy and a source of tension. This led to several parleys the details of which are not very material for the present purpose. These parleys involving the Vishwa Hindu Parishad (VHP) and the All India Babri Masjid

126. (1993) SCC 642.
127. AIR 1995 SC 605.

Action Committee (AIBMAC), however, failed to resolve the dispute.[128]

The focus of the temple construction movement from October 1991 was to start construction of the temple by way of *kar sewa* on the land acquired by the Government of Uttar Pradesh while leaving the disputed structure intact. This attempt did not succeed and there was litigation in the Allahabad High Court as well as in this Court. There was a call for resumption of *kar sewa* from 6-12-1992 and the announcement made by the organisers was for a symbolic *kar sewa* without violation of the court orders including those made in the proceedings pending in this Court. In spite of initial reports from Ayodhya on 6-12-1992 indicating an air of normalcy, around mid-day a crowd addressed by leaders of BJP, VHP, etc., climbed the Ram Janmabhumi-Babri Masjid (RJM-BM) structure and started damaging the domes. Within a short time, the entire structure was demolished and razed to the ground.

A brief reference to certain suits in this connection may now be made. In 1950, two suits were filed by some Hindus; in one of these suits in January 1950, the trial court passed interim orders whereby the idols remained at the place where they were installed in December 1949 and their puja by the Hindus contained. The Interim order was confirmed by the High Court in April 1955. On 1-2-1986, the District Judge ordered the opening of the lock placed on a grill leading to the sanctum sanctorum of the shrine in the disputed structure and permitted puja by the Hindu divotees.[129]

In 1959, a suit was filed by the Nirmohi Akhara claiming title to the disputed structure. In 1981, another suit was filed claiming title to the disputed structure by the Sunni Central Wakf Board. In 1989, Deoki Nandan Agarwal, as the next friend of the Deity filed a title suit in respect of the disputed structure. In 1989, the aforementioned suits were transferred to the Allahabad High Court and were ordered to be heard together. On 14-8-1989, the High Court ordered the

128. *Supra* n. 126 at p. 644.
129. *Supra* n. 126 at p. 648.

maintenance of status quo in respect of the disputed structure.[130]

As a result of the incidents at Ayodhya on 6-12-1992, the President of India issued a proclamation under Article 356 of the Constitution of India assuming to himself all the functions of the Government of Uttar Pradesh, dissolving the U.P. Vidhan Sabha.

The Government has decided to acquire all areas in dispute in the suits pending in the Allahabad High Court. It has also been decided to acquire suitable adjacent area. The acquired area excluding the area on which the disputed structure stood would be made available to two Trusts which would be set-up for construction of a Ram Temple and a Mosque respectively and for planned development of the area.

In pursuance of these decisions an ordinance named 'Acquisition of Certain Area at Ayodhya Ordinance' was issued on 7-1-1993 for acquisition of 67.703 acres of land in the Ram Janmabhoomi-Babri Masjid complex.

The Acquisition of Certain Area at Ayodhya Ordinance, 1993 has been replaced by the Acquisition of Certain Area at Ayodhya Act, 1993 the constitutional validity of which has to be examined.

The said Ordinance, later replaced by Act No. 33 of 1993 and the Special Reference under Article 143(1) of the Constitution of India were made simultaneously of same day on 7-1-1993.

45. Questions Referred

The President of India on 7th January, 1993 sent a special reference under article 143(1). In special reference, following questions were asked[131] —

(1) Whereas a dispute has arisen whether a Hindu temple or any Hindu religious structure existed prior to the construction of the structure (including the premises of the inner and outer courtyards of such

130. *Ibid.*

131. (1993) 1 SCC 642 also Ismail Faruqui M. (Dr.) *v.* Union of India, A.I.R. 1995 SC 605.

structure) commonly known as the Ram Janmabhumi-Babri Masjid in the area in which the structure stood in village Kot Ramachandra in Ayodhya in Pargana Haveli Avadh in Tehsil Faizabad Sadar, in the district of Faizabad of the state of Uttar Pradesh.

(2) And whereas the said area is located in Revenue Plot Nos. 159 and 160 in the said village Kot Ramchandra.

(3) And whereas the said dispute has affected the maintenance of public order and harmony between different communities in the country.

(4) Now, therefore, in exercise of the powers conferred upon me by clause (1) of Article 143 of the Constitution of India, President of India, hereby refer the following questions to the Supreme Court of India for consideration and opinion thereon, namely.

(5) Whether a Hindu temple or any Hindu religious structure existed prior to the construction of the Ram Jamabhumi-Babri Masjid (including the premises of the inner and outer courtyards of such structure) in the area on which the structure stood.

46. Opinion

The opinion of the Supreme Court was delivered by a five judge bench.[132] The judges of the Supreme Court differed in their views. The majority view is taken by M.N. Venkatachaliah CJI, J.S. Verma, G.N. Roy J.J. and the minority view by A.M. Ahmadi, S.P. Bharucha J.J. The main point of the opinion may be divided into following heads.

(A) Answer of Question Referred

The *Special Reference No. 1 of 1993* made by the President of India under Article 143(1) of the Constitution of India is superfluous and unnecessary and does not require to be answered and therefore, the same is returned. The question relating to the constitutional validity of the said Act and

132. *Supra* n. 126, 648.

maintainability of the Special Reference are decided in these terms.

The Supreme Court is entitled to decline to answer a question posed to it under Article 143 if it considers that it is not proper or possible to do so, but it must indicate its reasons. The Reference must not be answered for the following reason:

The Act and the Reference favour one religious community and disfavour another; the purpose of the Reference is, therefore, opposed to secularism and is unconstitutional. Besides, the Reference does not serve a constitutional purpose.

Secondly, the fifth recital to the Reference states that "the Central Government purposes to settle the said dispute after obtaining the opinion of the Supreme Court of India and in terms of the said opinion". It is clear that the Central Government does not purpose to settle the dispute in terms of the Court's opinion. It purposes to use the Court's opinion as a springboard for negotiations. Resolution of the dispute as a result of such negotiations cannot be said to be a resolution of the dispute "in terms of the said opinion". Even in the circumstance that the Supreme Court opines that no Hindu temple or Hindu religious structure existed on the disputed site before the disputed structure was built thereon, there is no certainty that the mosque will be rebuilt.

Thirdly, there is the aspect of evidence in relation to the question referred. It cannot be said that a court of law is not competent to decide such a question. It can be done if expert evidence of archaeologists and historians is led, and is tested in cross-examination. The principal protagonists of the two stands are not appearing in the Reference; they will neither lead evidence nor cross-examine. The learned Solicitor General stated that the Central Government would lead no evidence, but it would place before the Court the material that it had collected from the two sides during the course of earlier negotiations.

The court being ill-equipped to examine and evaluate such material, it would have to appoint experts in the field to do so, and their evaluation would go unchallenged. Apart from the inherent inadvisability of rendering a judicial opinion on such evaluation, the opinion would be liable to the criticism of one or both sides that it was rendered without hearing them or their evidence. This would ordinarily be of no significance for they had chosen to stay away, but this opinion is intended to create a public climate for negotiations and the criticism would find the public ear, to say nothing of the fact that it would impair the Supreme Court's credibility. Ayodhya is a storm that will pass. The dignity and honour of the Supreme Court cannot be compromised because of it.

(B) Acquistion of Certain Area by Ayodhya Act, 1993

Section 3 provides for acquisition of Rights in relation to the 'area' defined in Section 2(a). It does not suffer from any invalidity.

Since the Central Government purposes to resort to a process of negotiation between the rival claimants after getting the answer to the question referred, and if the negotiations fail, then to adopt such course as it may find appropriate in the circumstances, the Special Reference made under Article 143(1) of the Constitution cannot be construed as an effect alternate dispute-resolution mechanism to permit substitution of the pending suits and legal proceedings by the mode adopted of making this reference. Therefore, the abatement of pending suits amounts to denial of the judicial remedy. This fact alone is sufficient to invalidate sub-section (3) of Section 4 of the Act. However, its invalidity is not an impediment to the remaining status being upheld as valid.[133]

Section 8 is meant only for the property acquired absolutely, other than the disputed area, being adjacent to, and in the vicinity of the disputed area. The disputed area being taken over by the Central Government only as a statutory receiver, there is no question of payment of compensation for the same as it is meant to be handed over to the successful party in the suits, in terms of the ultimate judicial verdict therein, for the faithful implementation of the judicial decision.

The exercise of the power under Section 8, by the Central Government is to be made only then in respect of the disputed area, in accordance with the final judicial decision, preserving status quo therein terms of Section 7(2) till then.

---

133. *Union of India* v. *Paras Laminators (P) Ltd.*, (1990) 4 SCC 453: 1991 SCC (L&S) 208: (1990) 14 ATC 798.

The legislative competent is traceable to Entry 42, List III and the State of Uttar Pradesh being under President's rule at the relevant time, the legislative competence of Parliament, in the circumstances, cannot be doubted. That apart the pith and substance of the legislation is "acquisition of property" and not 'public order' under Entry 1 of List III of Seventh Schedule to the Constitution. The comprehensive Entry 42 in List III as a result of the Constitution (Seventh Amendment) Act leaves no doubt that an acquisition Act of this kind falls clearly within the ambit of this entry and, therefore, Parliament has the legislative competence to enact this legislation.[134]

(C) Secularism is a Basic Feature of the Constitution

It is clear from the constitutional scheme that it guarantees quality in the matter of religion to all individuals and groups irrespective of their faith emphasising that there is no religion of the State itself. The preamble of the Constitution read in particular with Articles 25 to 28 emphasises this aspect and indicates that it is in this manner the concept of secularism embodied in the constitutional scheme as a creed adopted by the Indian people has to be understood while examining the constitutional validity of any legislation on the touchstone of the constitution.

The concept of secularism is one facet of the right to equality woven as the central golden thread in the fabric depicting the pattern of the scheme in our Constitution. "The purpose of law in plural societies is not the progressive assimilation of the minorities in the majoritarian milieu. This would not solve the problem; but would vainly seek to dissolve it." The true concept of secularism, and the role of judiciary in a pluralistic society, as also the duty of the court in interpreting such a law, has to be kept in mind.[135]

---

134. *State of Bihar* v. *Maharajadhiraja Sir Kameshwar Singh of Darbhanga,* 1952 SCR 889: AIR 1952 SC 252; *Deputy Commissioner and Collector* v. *Durga Nath Sharma,* (1968) 1 SCR 561 : AIR 1968 SC 394.
135. *"Law in Pluralist Society"* by M.N. Venkatachaliah, J., *relied on. S.R. Bommai* v. *Union of India, (1994)* 3 SCC 1, *Kesavananda Bharti* v. *State of Kerala,* (1973) 4 SCC 225: 1973 Supp SCR 1: *Indira Nehru Gandhi* v. *Raj Narain,* 1975 Supp SCC 1 : 1976) 2 SCR 347; *S.P. Mittal* v. *Union of India,* (1983) 1 SCC 51: (1983) 1 SCR 729.

Article 25 does not contain any reference to property unlike Article 26 of the Constitution. The right to practice, profess and propagate religion guaranteed under Article 25 of the Constitution does not necessarily include the right to acquire or own or possess property. Similarly, this right does not extend to the right of worship at any and every place of worship so that any hindrance to worship at a particular place *per se* may infringe the religious freedom guaranteed under Articles 25 and 26 of the Constitution. The protection under Articles 25 and 26 is to religious practice which forms an essential and integral part of the religion.

A practice may be a religious practice but not an essential and integral part of practice of that religion. While offer of prayer or worship is a religious practice, its offering at every location where such prayers can be offered would not be an essential or integral part of such religious practice unless the place has a particular significance for that religion so as to form as essential or integral part thereof. Places of worship of any religion having particular significance for that religion, to make it an essential or integral part of the religion, stand on a different footing and have to be treated differently and more reverentially.[136]

Subject to the protection under Articles 25 and 26, places of religious worship like mosques, churches, temples, etc. can be acquired under the State's sovereign power of acquisition. Such acquisition *per se* does not violate either Article 25 or Article 26. The decisions relating to taking over of the management have no bearing on the sovereign power of the State to acquire property. The power of acquisition is the sovereign or prerogative power of the State to acquire property. Such power exists independent of Article 300-A or the earlier Article 31 of the Constitution which merely indicate the limitations on the power of acquisition by the State.[137]

136. *Acharya Maharajshri Narendra Prasadji Anandprasadji Maharaj* v. *State of Gujarat*, (1975) 1 SCC 11: (1975) 2 SCR 317. *Raja Suryapalsingh* v. *U.P. Govt.*, AIR 1951 All 674: 1951 All LJ 365 : 1951 AWR (HC) 317.

137. *Chiranjit Lal Chowdhuri* v. *Union of India*, 1950 SCR 869: AIR 1951 SC 41; *State of W.B.* v. *Subodh Gopal Bose*, 1954 SCR 587: AIR 1954 SC 92; *Khajamian Wakf Estates* v. *State of Madras*, (1970) 3 SCC 894; (1971) 2 SCR 790.

Section 3(26) of the General Clause Act comprehends the categories of properties known to Indian Law. Article 367 adopts this secular concept of property for purposes of our Constitution. A temple, church or mosques etc. are essentially immovable properties and subject to protection under Articles 25 and 26. Every immovable property is liable to be acquired. Viewed in the proper perspective, a mosque does not enjoy any additional protection, unique or special status, higher than that of the places of worship of other religions in secular India to make it immune for acquisition by exercise of the sovereign or prerogative power of the State. A mosque is not an essential part of the practice of the religion of Islam and *namaz* (prayer) by Muslims can be offered anywhere, even in open.

Accordingly, its acquisition is not prohibited by the provisions in the Constitution of India. Irrespective of the status of a mosque in an Islamic country for the purpose of immunity from acquisition by the State in exercise of the sovereign power, its status and immunity from acquisition in the secular ethos of India under the Constitution is the same and equal to that of the places of worship of the other religions, namely, church, temple, etc. It is neither more nor less than that of the places of worship of the other religions.

Obviously, the acquisition of any religious place is to be made only in unusual and extraordinary situations for a larger national purpose keeping in view that such acquisition should not result in extinction of the right to practice the religion, if the significance of that place be such. Subject to this condition, the power of acquisition is available for a mosque like any other place of worship of any religion. The right to worship is not at any and every place, so long as it can be practised effectively, unless the right to worship at a particular place is itself an integral part of that right. Under the Mahomedan Law applicable in India, title to a mosque can be lost by adverse possession.[138]

138. *Mulla's Principles of Mahomedan Law*, 19th Edn., by M. Hidayatullah—Section 217, *Muthialu Cheti* v. *Bapun Saib*, ILR (1883) 6 Mad 203: 2 Weir 77 (FB); *Mosque known as Masjid Shahid Ganj* v. *Shiromani Gurdwara Prabandhak Committee, Amritsar*, AIR 1938 Lah 369:40 PLR 319; *Mosque known as Masjid Shahid Ganj* v. *Shiromani Gurdwara Prabhandhak Committee, Amritsar*, AIR 1940 PC 116: 44 CWN 957: 67 IA 251.

Secularism is a part of the basic features of the Constitution. Article 25(1) protects the rights of Individuals. Exercise of the right of the individual to profess, practice and propagate religion is subject to public order.

Secularism is absolute; the State may not treat religions differently on the ground that public order requires it. The principle of secularism illumines the provisions of Articles 15 and 16.[139] (Per Ahmadi and Bharucha, J.J., in concurring).

47. Main Points of Opinion

1. Presidential reference seeking the Supreme Court's opinion on whether a temple originally existed on the site where the Babri Masjid subsequently stood was superfluous and unnecessary and opposed to secularism and favoured one religious community and therefore, does not require to be answered.
2. The Court upheld the validity of the acquisition of 67 acres of land in Ayodhya. But it allowed revival of the title suit pertaining to the disputed site.
3. Till the disposal of the dispute regarding the ownership of the land on which the Babri Masjid stood the government would act as a receiver of this portion of the land. It cannot transfer this part of the acquired land to any third party and would return it to whoever was found to be the original owner by the Allahabad High Court. As regards undisputed land the acquisition is absolute and the government can transfer it to any organization or trust.
4. Even though, *prima facie* the acquisition of the adjacent area in respect of which there is no dispute of title and which belongs to Hindus may appear to

139. *Commissioner, Hindu Religious Endowments, Madras* v. *Sri Lakshmindra Thirtha Swamiar of Sri Shirur Mutt.*, 1954 SCR 1005; AIR 1954 SC 282; *S.R. Bommai* v. *Union of India, (1994)* 3 SCC 1; *Kesavananda Bharti* v. *State of Kerala,* (1973) 4 SCC 225: 1973 Supp. SCR 1, *Indira-Nehru-Gandhi* v. *Raj Narain,* 1975 Supp. SCC 1: (1976) 2 SCR 347.

be a slant against the Hindus, yet on closer scrutiny it is not so since it is for the larger national purpose of maintaining and promoting communal harmony and in consonance with the creed of secularism.[140]

5. The right to practice, profess and propagate religion guaranteed under Article 25 of the Constitution does not necessarily include the right to acquire or own or possess property. Similarly, this right does not extend to the right of worship at any and every place of worship so that any hindrance to worship at a particular place *per se* may infringe the religious freedom guaranteed under Articles 25 and 26 of the Constitution.
6. While offer of prayer or worship is a religious practice, its offering at every location where such prayers can be offered would not be an essential or integral part of such religions unless the place has a particular significance.
7. A mosque does not have a unique or special status higher than that of the places of worship of other religions in secular India to make it immune from acquisition by exercise of the sovereign or prerogative Power of the State. A mosque is not an essential part of the practice of the region of Islam and Namaaz (Prayer) by Muslims can be offered any where even in open.
8. The Court, therefore, is entitled to decline to answer a question posed to it under Article 143 if it considers that it is not proper or possible to do so but it must indicate its reasons.

Majority held that reference must not be answered for the following reasons:

Firstly, The act and the reference as stated herein above favour one religious community and disfavour another, the

140. "Ram Janmabhoomi and the Courts" available at www.bharatvgani.org accessed on 26 July, 2007.

purpose of the reference is, therefore, opposed to secularism and is unconstitutional.

Secondly, there is the aspect of evidence in relation to the question referred. It is suggested that a court of law is not competent to decide such a question. It can be done if expert evidence of archaeologists and historian is led and is tested in cross-examination.

The main features of the judgment are as follows :

(i) The Presidential reference is not maintainable.

(ii) Pooja to continue at the make shift Ram Lala temple that had been erected on disputed site following demolition of Babri Masjid structure on December 6, 1992.

(iii) The judgment is no reflection on the President of India.

(iv) The title suits regarding disputed structure pending in Allahabad High Court revived.

(v) Land of disputed structure cannot be transferred to a third party.

(vi) The Center is permitted to settle dispute through negotiation.

(vii) Acquisition of 67 acres of land upheld except disputed area.

(viii) The Center under duty to handover land to the real owner after final verdict by Allahabad High Court.

(ix) Surplus land must be restored to the undisputed owners.

(x) Land other than disputed structure can be transferred to trust or to a third party.

(xi) Mosque does not enjoy a special position as a place of worship in Muslim law and can be acquired and shifted like every immovable property.

(xii) A mosque is not an essential part of the practice of religion of Islam and Namaz can be offered any where even in open. Accordingly, its acquisition is not prohibited under Constitution of India.

(ELEVENTH REFERENCE) REFERENCE ON THE PRINCIPLES AND PROCEDURE REGARDING APPOINTMENT OF SUPREME COURT AND HIGH COURT JUDGES (Special Reference No. 1 of 1998)[141]

48. Main Facts

The Supreme Court of India has laid down principles and prescribed procedural norms in regard to the appointment of judges of the Supreme Court (Article 124(2) of the Constitution), Chief justices and judges of the High Court (Article 127(1)), and transfer of judges from one High Court to another (Article 222(1)). In the case of *Supreme Court Advocates on Record Association* v. *Union of India*.[142] The decision was rendered by a bench of judges and five judgments were delivered. As doubts arose about the interpretation of the law laid down by the Supreme Court and it is in public interest that the said doubts relating to the appointment and transfer of judges be resolved.

49. Questions Referred

In exercise of the powers conferred upon by clause (1) of Article 143 in the Constitution of India, President of India hereby refer the following questions to the Supreme Court of India for consideration and to reports its opinion thereon.

1. Whether the expression "consultation with the CJI in Articles 217(1) and 222(1) requires consultation with a plurality of judges in the formation of the opinion of the CJI or does the sole individual opinion of the CJI constitute consultation within the meaning of the said articles.
2. Whether the transfer of judges is judicially review able in the light of the observation of the Supreme Court in the aforesaid judgment that such transfer is not justifiable on any ground (and its further

141. AIR 1999 SC 1.
142. (1993) 4 SCC 441.

observation that limited judicial review is available in matters of transfer and the extent and scope of judicial review).

3. Whether Article 124 (2) as interpreted in the said judgment requires the Chief Justice of India to consult only the two senior most judges or whether there should be wider consultation according to past practice.
4. Whether the Chief Justice of India is entitled to act solely in his individual capacity without consultation with other judges of the Supreme Court in respect of all materials and information conveyed by the Government of India for non appointment of a judge recommended for appointment.
5. Whether the Government is entitled to require that the opinions of the other consulted judges be in writing in accordance with the aforesaid Supreme Court judgment and that the same be transmitted to the Government of India by the CJI along with his views.
6. Whether any recommendations made by the Chief Justice of India without complying with the norms and consultation process are binding upon the Govt. of India.
7. Whether the CJI is obliged to comply with the norms and the requirement of the consultation process in making his recommendation to the Government of India.
8. Whether in the light of the legitimate expectation of senior judges of the High Court in regard to their appointment to the Supreme Court referred to in the said judgment the 'strong cogent reason' required to justify the departure from the order of the seniority has to be recorded in respect of each such senior judge, who is over looked, while making recommendation of a judge junior to him or her.
9. Whether the government is not entitled to require that the opinions of the order consulted judges be in writing in accordance with the aforesaid Supreme

> Court judgment and that the same be transmitted to the government of India by the Chief Justice of India.

The majority view in the *Second Judges case*[143] is that in the matter of appointment to the Supreme Court and the High Courts, the opinion of the Chief Justice of India has primacy. The opinion of the Chief Justice of India is "reflective of the opinion of the Judiciary, which means that it must necessarily have the element of plurality in its formation." It is to be formed after taking into account the view of some other Judges who are traditionally associated with this function.

The opinion of the Chief Justice of India which has primacy in the matter of recommendations for appointment to the Supreme Court has to be formed in consultation with a collegium of Judges. Presently, and for a long time now, that collegium consists of the two senior most Puisne judges of the Supreme Court. In making a decision as to whom that collegium should recommend, it takes account the vies that are elicited by the Chief Justice of India from the Senior most Judge of the Supreme Court who comes from the same High Court as the person proposed to be recommended. It also takes into account the views of other Judges of the Supreme Court or the Chief Justice or Judges of the High Courts or, indeed, members of the Bar who may also have been asked by the Chief Justice of India or on his behalf.

Necessarily, the opinion of all members of the collegium in respect of each recommendation should be in writing. The ascertainment of the views of the senior most Supreme Court Judges who hail from the High Courts from where the persons to be recommended come must also be in writing. These must be conveyed by the Chief Justice of India to the Government of India along with the recommendation. The other views that the Chief Justice of India or the other members of the collegium may elicit, particularly if they are from non-Judges, need not be in writing, but it seems to us advisable that he who elicits the opinion should make a memorandum thereof, and the

143. (1993) 4 SCC 411.

substance thereof in general terms, should be conveyed to the Government of India.[144]

The expression "consultation with the Chief Justice of India" in Articles 217(1) and 222(1) of the Constitution of India requires consultation with a plurality of Judges in the formation of the opinion of the Chief Justice of India. The sole individual opinion of the Chief Justice of India with regard to a person to be recommended for appointment to a High Court does not constitute "consultation" within the meaning of the said articles.

The Chief Justice of India should from his opinion in the same manner as he forms it in regard to a recommendation for appointment to the Supreme Court, that is to say, in consultation with his senior most puisne Judges. Having regarding to the fact that information about a proposed appointee to a High Court would best come from the Chief Justice and Judges of that High Court and from Supreme Court Judges conversant with it, the strength of the decision-making collegium's size; where appointments to the High Courts are concerned, should remain as it is, constituted of the Chief Justice of India and the two senior most puisne Judges of the Supreme Court.

The members of the collegium in making their decision should take into account the opinion of the Chief Justice of the High Court which "would be entitled to the greatest weight", the views of other Judges of the High Court who may have been consulted and the views of colleagues on the Supreme Court Bench who are conversant with the affairs of the High Court concerned into that last category would fall Judges of the Supreme Court who were puisne Judges of the High Court or Chief Justices thereof, and it is of no consequence that the High Court is not their parent High Court and they were transferred.

50. Opinion

Opinion was decided on October 28, 1998 by a full bench

144. *Supreme Court Advocates-on-Records Assn.* v. *Union of India*, (1993) 4 SCC 441: AIR 1994 SC 268 : 1993 Supp. (2) SCR 659, *explained*. *S.P. Gupta* v. *Union of India*, 1981 Supp. SCC 87 : (1982) 2 SCR 365.

consisting of five judges (before S.P. Bharucha, M.K. Mukharjee, S.B. Majumdar, Sujata V. Manohar, G.T. Nanavati, S. Sagir Ahmad, K. Venkatswami, B.N. Kripal and G.B. Pattanaik J.J.) The opinion was delivered by S.P. Bharucha, J.J. The reference related to four aspects:

1. Consultation between the Chief Justice of India and his brother judges in the matter of appointments of Supreme Court and High Court judges of the latter.
2. Judicial review of transfers of Judges.
3. The relevance of seniority in making appointments to the Supreme Court.
4. Transfer of High Court Judges.

(A) Consultation Between CJI and his Brother Judges

(i) The majority view in the *Second Judges case* is that in the matter of appointments to the Supreme Court and the High Courts, the opinion of the Chief Justice of India has primacy. The opinion of the Chief Justice of India is reflective of the opinion of the judiciary, which means that it must necessarily have the element of plurality in its formation. The opinion of the Chief Justice of India "so given has primacy in the matter of all appointments".

(ii) The expression 'consultation' with the Chief Justice of India in Article 217(1) and 222(1) of the constitution of India requires consultation with the plurality of judges in the formation of the opinion of the Chief Justice of India. The sole individual opinion of the Chief Justice of India does not constitute "consultation" within the meaning of the said Articles. The Chief Justice of India is obliged to comply with the norms and the requirement of the consultation process in making his recommendations to the Government of India. Recommendations made by the Chief Justice of India without complying with the norms and requirements of the consultation process are not binding upon the Government of India.

(iii) Primacy given to opinion of Chief Justice of India is to that opinion of Chief Justice of India which is reflective of opinion of Judiciary, i.e. having an element of plurality in its formation-opinion formed in any other manner not binding on Government.

(iv) Opinion of the CJI to be in consultation with the collegiums of judges-collegiums to consist of CJI and four senior most judges of Supreme Court.

(v) Successor CJI to be included in collegiums senior most judge of Supreme Court coming from High Court to which person proposed to be recommended belongs not to be included in collegiums.

(vi) Opinion of all members of collegiums and of senior most Supreme Court judge who hails from same High Court as of the persons to be recommended must be in writing to be conveyed by CJI to Government with recommendations.

(vii) Merit is the predominant consideration observation in *Second Judges case* that *inter se* seniority of judges to be given due weight. Explained strong cogent reasons required to be recorded in case of departure from order of seniority means recording of good reasons for appointing a particular judge.

(B) Judicial Reveiw of Transfer of Judges

Judicial review in the case of an appointment or a recommended appointment, to the Supreme Court or a High Court is available if the recommendation concerned is not a decision of the Chief Justice of India and his senior most colleagues, which is constitutionally requisite. They number four in the case of a recommendation for appointment to a High Court.

Judicial review is also available if, in making the decision, the views of the senior most Supreme Court Judge who comes from the High Court of the proposed appointee to the Supreme Court have not been taken into account. Similarly, if in connection with an appointment or a recommended appointment to a High Court, the views of the Chief Justice and Senior Judges of the High Court, as aforestated, and of Supreme Court Judges knowledgeable about that High Court have not been sought or considered by the Chief Justice of India and his two senior most puisne Judges, judicial review is available. Judicial review is also available when the appointee is found to lack eligibility.[145]

(C) The Relevance of Seniority in Appointment to S.C.

The majority judgment in the *Second Judges case*[146] said *"inter se seniority amongst Judges in their High Court and their combined seniority on all-India basis should be kept in view and given due weight while making appointments from amongst High Court Judges to the Supreme Court. Unless there be any strong cogent reason to justify a departure, that order of seniority must be maintained between them while making their appointment to the Supreme Court."*

It also said that the legitimate expectation of the High Court Judges to be considered for appointment to the Supreme Court, according to their seniority must be duly considered. It was thereafter observed, obviously, this factor applies only to those considered, suitable and at lease equally meritorious by the Chief Justice of India for appointment to the Supreme Court. Merit, therefore is the predominant consideration for the purposes of appointment to the Supreme Court.

Where, therefore, there is outstanding merit, the possessor thereof deserves to be appointed regardless of the fact that he may not stand high in the all-India seniority list or in his own High Court. All that then needs to be recorded when recommending him for appointment is that he has outstanding merit. When the contenders for appointment to the Supreme Court do not possess such outstanding merit but have, nevertheless, the required merit in more or less equal degree, there may be reason to recommend one among them because, for example, the particular region of the country in which his parent High Court is situated is not represented on the Supreme Court Bench. All that then needs to be recorded when making the recommendation for appointment in this factor. The strong cogent reasons that the majority judgment in

145. *Supreme Court Advocates-on-Record Assn.* v. *Union of India,* (1993) 4 SCC 441: AIR 1994 SC 268 : 1993 Supp. (2) SCR 659.
146. SCC p. 702 para 478.

the *Second Judges Case* speaks of are good reasons for appointing to the Supreme Court a particular High Court Judge, not for not appointing other High Court Judges senior to him.

It is not unusual that Judge who has once been passed over for appointment to the Supreme Court might still find favour on the occasion of another selection and there is no reason to bolt his copybook by recording what might be construed to be an adverse comment about him. It is only when, for very strong reasons, a collegium finds that whatever his seniority, some High Court Judges should never be appointed to the Supreme Court that it should so record. This would then be justified and would afford guidance on subsequent occasions of considering who to recommend.[147]

(D) Transfer of High Court Judges

Regarding transfer of High Court Judges the Chief Justice of India should obtain the views of the Chief Justice of the High Court from which the proposed transfer is to be effected as also the Chief Justice of the High Court to which the transfer is to be affected. This is in accord with the majority judgment in the *Second Judges case* which postulates consultation with the Chief Justice of another High Court.

The Chief Justice of India should also take into account the views of one or more Supreme Court Judges who are in a position to provide material which would assist in the process of deciding whether or not a proposed transfer should take place. These views should be expressed in writing and should be considered by the Chief Justice of India and the four senior most puisne Judges of the Supreme Court. These views and those of each of the four senior most puisne Judges should be conveyed to the Government of India along with the proposal of transfer. Unless the decision to transfer has been taken in the manner aforestated, it is not decisive and does not bind the Government of India.[148]

---

147. *Supreme Court Advocates-on-Record Assn.* v. *Union of India,* (1993) 4 SCC 441: AIR 1994 SC 268 : 1993 Supp (2) SCR 659.
148. *K. Ashok Reddy* v. *Govt. of India,* (1994) 2 SCC 303.

What applies to the transfer of a puisne Judge of a High Court applies as well to the transfer of the Chief Justice of a High Court as Chief Justice of another High Court except that, in this case, only the views of one or more knowledgeable Supreme Court Judges need to be taken into account.

The transfer of puisne Judges is judicially reviewable only to this extent: that the recommendation that has been made by the Chief Justice of India in this behalf has not been made in consultation with the four senior most puisne Judges of the reliable information about the proposed appointee, such Supreme Court Judge as may be in a position to give it should be asked to do so. All these views should be expressed in writing and conveyed to the Government of India along with the recommendation.

The Chief Justice of India is obliged to comply with the norms and the requirement of the consultation process, as aforesaid, in making his recommendations to the Government of India. Recommendations made by the Chief Justice of India without complying with the norms and requirements of the consultation process, as aforestated, are not binding upon the Government of India.[149]

51. Main Points of Opinion

The questions posed by the Reference are now answered, but we should emphasise that the answers should be read in conjunction with the body of this opinion:

1. The expression "consultation with the Chief Justice of India" in Articles 217(1) and 222(1) of the Constitution of India requires consultation with a plurality of Judges in the formation of the opinion of the Chief Justice of India. The sole individual opinion of the Chief Justice of India does not constitute "consultation" within the meaning of the said articles.
2. The transfer of puisne Judges is judicially reviewable only to this extent: that the recommendation that has

149. *Supreme Court Advocates-on-Record Assn.* v. *Union of India,* (1993) 4 SCC 441 : AIR 1994 SC 268 : 1993 Supp (2) SCR 659.

been made by the Chief Justice of India in this behalf has not been made in consultation with the four senior most puisne Judges of the Supreme Court and/or that the views of the Chief Justice of the High Court from which the transfer is to be effected have not been obtained.

3. The Chief Justice of India must make a recommendation to appoint a Judge of the Supreme Court and to transfer a Chief Justice or punise judge of a High Court in consultation with the four senior most puisne Judges of the Supreme Court. Insofar as an appointment to the High Court is concerned, the recommendation must be made in consultation with the two senior most puisne Judges of the Supreme Court.
4. The Chief Justice of India is not entitled to act solely in his individual capacity, without consultation with other Judges of the Supreme Court, in respect of materials and information conveyed by the Government of India for non-appointment of a Judge recommended for appointment.
5. The requirement of consultation by the Chief Justice of India with his colleagues who are likely to be conversant with the affairs of the High Court concerned does not refer only to those Judges who have that High Court as a parent High Court. It does not exclude Judges who have occupied the office of a Judge or Chief Justice of that High Court on transfer.
6. "Strong cogent reasons" do not have to be recorded as justification for a departure from the order of seniority in respect of each senior Judge who has been passed over. What has to be recorded is the positive reason for the recommendation.
7. The views of the other Judges consulted should be in writing and should be conveyed to the Government of India by the Chief Justice of India along with his views to the extent set out in the body of this opinion.

8. The Chief Justice of India is obliged to comply with the norms and the requirement of the consultation process, as aforestated, in making his recommendations to the Government of India.
9. Recommendations made by the Chief Justice of India without complying with the norms and requirements of the consultation process, as aforestated, are not binding upon the Government of India.

(TWELTH REFERENCE) IN GUJARAT GAS ACT REFERENCE (Special Reference No. 1 of 2001)[150]

52. Related Cases

(a) *Association of Natural Gas and Others* v. *Union of India and Others.*[151]

(b) *Association of Natural Gas Consuming Industries of Gujarat and Others* v. *ONGC & Others.*[152]

(c) *Ram Lal Maganlal Kapadia* v. *Oil and Natural Gas Commission and Others.*[153]

53. Main Facts

The Gujarat State Legislature passed an Act by name The Gujarat Gas (Regulation of Transmission, Supply and Distribution) Act, 2001, which came into force w.e.f. 19.12.2000. The object of the enactment is to provide for regulation of transmission, supply and distribution of gas, in the interests of the general public and to promote gas industry in the state, and for that purpose, to establish the Gujarat gas regulatory authority and for that matters connected herewith and incidental thereto. The term 'gas' has been defined in the Gujarat Act under Sec. 2(h) as follows gas means a matter in gaseous state which predominantly consists of methane.

---

150. SCC (2004), at p. 489 (Opinion delivered on March 25, 2004).
151. Writ Petition (c) No. 852 of 1991.
152. Civil Appeal No. 3575 of 1991.
153. Civil Appeal No. 3576 of 1991.

The state legislature passed the said enactment by tracing its legislative competence under entry 25 of list II of the seventh schedule of the constitution; parliament has passed various enactments under entry 53 of list-1 dealing with the matters of petroleum and petroleum products. Entry 53 of list 1 of the seventh schedule reads as follows: "53 Regulation and development of oil fields and mineral oil resources, petroleum and petroleum products; other liquids and substances declared by parliament by law to be dangerously inflammable. Entry 25 of list II reads as follows—"25 Gas and gas works".

Article 246 of the constitution lays down the principle that parliament alone has exclusive powers to make Laws with respect to any of the matters enumerated in list 1 of the Seventh schedule. As regards entries in list-II, the legislature of the state has exclusive power to make laws subject of course, to clauses (i) and (ii) of Article 246.

When the state of Gujarat passed the Gujarat Act, the question arose whether the state government can pass an enactment in respect of gas, including natural gas in all its forms by virtue of the legislative competence passed on entry 25 of list of the Seventh schedule. The federal legislature passed the petroleum Act, 1934. The Union of India, *inter alia*, enacted various legislations, namely the Oil Fields (Regulation and Development) Act, 1948; the oil industry (Development) Act, 1974; the Petroleum and Minerals Pipelines (Acquisition of Right of User in Land) Act 1962; and the Oil Industry Development Act, 1974. All these legislations have been passed by the Union of India on the basis of the legislative competence under entry 53 of List 1 of the seventh schedule. The oil and natural gas commission increased the price of natural gas supplied by them. The association of natural gas consuming industries of Gujarat and others filed civil writ petition before the High Court of Gujarat wherein they challenged the legislative competence of the Union to make laws on "gas and gas works". Therefore, the question arose whether natural gas is a Union subject or state subject and whether the state of Gujarat and the other states have the legislative competence to make laws on the subject of natural gas. It is in this background, the following questions were referred to this court under clause (1) of Article 143 of the constitution of India.

54. Questions Referred

(1) Whether natural gas in whatever physical from including liquefied natural gas (LNG) is a Union subject covered by Entry 53 of List 1 and the Union has exclusive legislative competence to enact laws on natural gas.

(2) Whether States have legislative competence to make laws on the subject of Natural gas and liquefied natural gas under Entry 25 of List II of the Seventh Schedule to the Constitution.

(3) Whether the State of Gujarat had legislative competence to enact the Gujarat Gas (Regulation of Transmission, Supply and Distribution) Act, 2001.

55. Opinion

A Constitutional bench of the Supreme Court consisting of Five Judges (before S. Rajendra Babu, K.G. Balakrishnan, P. Venkatarama Reddi., B.N. Sri Krishna and G.P. Mathur, J.J.). The Unanimous opinion was delivered by the Justice K.G. Balakrishnan on behalf of himself and five other judges.

(A) Answer of the First Question

The word petroleum literally means "rock oil". It originated from the Latin terms *petra* and *oleum*.[154] Petroleum is an oily, inflammable liquid made up mostly of hydrocarbons—compounds containing only hydrogen and carbon. The hydrogen content of petroleum ranges from 50 per cent to 98 per cent. The rest is made up chiefly of organic compounds containing oxygen, nitrogen or sulphur. Thus, natural gas could very well be comprehended within the expression "petroleum" or "petroleum product". In various legislations covering the field of petroleum and petroleum products, either the word "petroleum" or "petroleum products" has been

154. *Petra* means rock or stone and *oleum* means oil.

defined in an inclusive way, so as to include natural gas. It is important to consider the legislative practice in interpreting the various words used in the Constitution.[155]

Under Entry 53 of List 1, Parliament has got power to make legislation for regulation and development of oilfields, mineral oil resources; petroleum, petroleum products, other liquid and substances declared by Parliament by law to be dangerously inflammable. Natural gas product extracted from oil wells predominantly comprises of methane. Production of natural gas is not independent of the production of other petroleum products; though from some wells natural gas alone would emanate, other products may emanate from subterranean chambers of earth. But all oil fields are explored for their potential hydro carbons. Therefore, the regulation as well as development of natural gas for free and smooth flow of trade, commerce and industry throughout the length and breath of the country, natural gas and other petroleum products play a vital role.

The people of the entire country have a stake in natural gas and its benefit has to be shared by the whole country. There should be just and reasonable use of natural gas for national development. If one State alone is allowed to extract and use natural gas, then other States will be deprived of its equitable share. This position goes on to fortify the stand adopted by the Union and will be a pointer to the conclusion that natural gas in raw and liquefied form is petroleum products and part of mineral oil resources, which needs to be regulated by the Union.[156]

(B) Answer of the Second Question

Going by the definition of gas is Section 2(*g*) of the Gujarat Act wherein "gas" has been defined as "a matter of

155. *State of Madras* v. *Gannon Dunkerley & Co. (Madras) Ltd.*, AIR 1958 SC 560 : 1959 SCR 379. *The New Book of Popular Science*, Vol. 2. *Croft* v. *Dunphy*, 1933 AC 156 : AIR 1933 PC 16; *Wellace Bros. & Co. Ltd.* v. *CIT*, AIR 1948 PC 118 : 75 IA 86.
156. Cauvery Water Disputes Tribunal, *Re* 1993 Supp (1) SCC 96 (11).

gaseous state which predominantly consists of methane", it would certainly include natural gas also. Under Entry 25 List II of the Seventh Schedule, the State would be competent to pass legislation only in respect of gas and gasworks. Entry 25 of List II will have to be read as a whole. The expressions therein cannot be compartmentally interpreted. The word "gas" in the entry will take colour from the other word "gasworks".

The meaning of the term "gas work" is well understood in the sense of the place where the gas is manufactured. In *Ballantine's Law Dictionary*, [157] "gasworks" is defined as "a plant for the manufacture of artificial gas".

Similarly in *Webster's New 20th Century Dictionary*, it is defined as "an establishment in which gas for heating and lighting is manufactured". In *www.freedictionary.com* "gasworks" is explained as "a manufactory of gas, with all the machinery and appurtenances; a place where gas is generated".

Having regard to collocation of words "gas and gasworks", this entry would mean any work or industry relating to manufactured gas which is often used for industrial, medical or other similar purposes. So it is difficult to accept the proposition that "gas" in Entry 25 of List II includes natural gas, which is fundamentally different from manufactured gas in gasworks. Therefore, Entry 25 of List II could only cover manufactured gas and does not cover natural gas within its ambit. This will negative the argument of States that only they have exclusive powers to make laws dealing with natural gas and liquefied natural gas.

This regarding will in no way make that entry a "useless lumber" as feared by the States, because natural gas was never intended to be covered by the entry. It is also difficult to accept the argument of States that all "gas" could be categorized as dangerously inflammable and thus arriving at the conclusion that natural gas is also covered in the State List because this differentiation is based not on the characteristics of gas, but on

157. 3rd Ed., 1969.

the manner of its origin. Entry 25 of List II covers the gas manufactured and used in gasworks. In view of this specific Entry 53, for any petroleum and petroleum products, the State Legislature has no legislative competence to pass any legislation in respect of natural gas.[158]

(C) Answer of the Third Question

The Gujarat Gas (Regulation of Transmission, Supply and Distribution) Act, 2001, so far as the provisions contained therein relating to natural gas or liquefied natural gas (LNG) are concerned, is without any legislative competence and the Act is to the extent *ultra vires* the Constitution.

The Constitution of India delineates the contours of the powers enjoyed by the State Legislature and Parliament in respect of various subjects enumerated in the Seventh Schedule. The rules relating to distribution of powers are to be gathered from the various provision contained in Part XI and the legislative heads mentioned in the three lists of the Schedule. The legislative powers of both the Union and State Legislatures are given in precise terms. Entries in the lists are themselves not powers of legislation, but fields of legislation. However, an entry in one list cannot be so interpreted as to make it cancel or obliterate another entry or make another entry meaningless.

In case of apparent conflict, it is the duty of the court to iron out the crease and avoid conflict by reconciling the conflict. If any entry overlaps or is in apparent conflict with another entry, every attempt shall be made to harmonise the same.

Although Parliament cannot legislate on any of the entries in the State List, it may do so incidentally dealing with the subject coming within the purview of the entry in the Union List. Conversely, the State Legislature also while making

---

158. *Central Provinces and Berar Act No. XIV of 1938, In re.* 1939 FCR 18: AIR 1939 FC 1: *Prafulla Kumar Mukherjee* v. *Bank of Commerce Ltd.*, (1946-47) 741 A 23 : AIR 1947 PC 60; *Subrahmanyan Chettiar* v. *Mutuswami Goundan*, 1940 FCR 188 : AIR 1941 FC 47, *Sir Byramji Jeejibhai* v. *Province of Bombay*, (1939) 3 FLJ 25 : AIR 1940 Bom 65 (HC) (FB).

legislation may incidentally trench upon the subject covered in the Union List. Such incidental encroachment in either event need not make the legislation *ultra vires* the Constitution. The doctrine of pith and substance is sometimes invoked to find out the nature and content of the legislation. However, when there is an irreconcilable conflict between the two legislations. However, when there is an irreconcilable conflict between the two legislations, the Central legislation shall prevail. However, every attempt would be made to reconcile the conflict.

56. Main Points of Opinion

In the result, the reference is answered in the following terms:

Q.1. Whether natural gas in whatever physical form including liquefied natural gas (LNG) is a Union subject covered by Entry 53 of List I and the Union has exclusive legislative competence to enact.

A.1. Natural gas including liquefied natural gas (LNG) is a Union subject covered by Entry 53 of List I and the Union has exclusive legislative competence to enact laws on natural gas.

Q.2. Whether States have legislative competence to make laws on the subject of natural gas liquefied natural gas under Entry 25 of List II the Seventh Schedule to the Constitution.

A.2. The States have no legislative competence to make laws on the subject of natural gas and liquefied natural gas under Entry 25 of List II of the Seventh Schedule to the Constitution.

Q.3. Whether the State of Guajrat had legislative competence to enact the Gujarat Gas (Regulation of Transmission, Supply and Distribution) Act, 2001.

A.3. The Gujarat Gas (Regulation of Transmission, Supply and Distribution) Act, 2001, so far as the provisions contained therein relating to natural gas or liquefied natural gas (LNG) are concerned, is without any legislative competence and the Act is to the extent *ultra vires* the Constitution.

57. Order

In the light of the opinion rendered in Special Reference No. 1 of 2001 Under Article 143(1) of the Constitution of India the writ petition and the civil appeals are dismissed.

(THIRTEENTH REFERENCE) IN GUJARAT ASSEMBLY ELECTION REFERENCE (Special Reference No. 1 of 2001)[159]

58. Main Facts

In the last week of February 2002 a spate of communal violence erupted in various parts of Gujarat and many victims of the riots had to be put in relief camps. The Gujarat Legislative Assembly met on 3.4.2002 and thereafter it was dissolved by the Governor of Gujarat on 19.7.2002 in exercise of the powers conferred on him under Article 174(2)(b) of the Constitution.

The full term of the Legislative Assembly was to expire on 18.3.2003. After the dissolution of the Assembly, the ruling party in the State of Gujarat requested the Election Commissioner to conduct fresh general election urgently so that the new legislative Assembly would be able to have its first session on or before 3.10.2002. The ruling party of the State of Gujarat made this demand on the basis of the premise that under Article 174(1), there shall not be more than six months' period in between the last session of the dissolved Assembly and the first meeting of the next session of the Assembly to be newly constituted.[160]

Certain other political parties, public-spirited citizens and organizations urged the Election Commission not to hold the general election to the Gujarat State Legislative Assembly but to wait for some more time until the people who were affected by the communal riots and violence returned to their houses from the various relief camps where they were staying. The Election Commission visited Gujarat. By its order dated 16.8.2002, while acknowledging that Article 174(1) is

159. (2002) 8 SCC 237 : (2002) 8 JT 389.
160. Dhavan Rajeev, "The Supreme Court Reference". *The Hindu*, Vol. 25, (Aug. 23, 2002) at p. 12.

mandatory and applicable to an Assembly which is dissolved, that the elections for constituting new Legislative Assembly must be held within six months of the last session of the dissolved Assembly and that Article 324 postulates "free and fair election" and when it is not possible to hold it, the provisions contained in Article 174 have to yield, the Election Commission expressed its view that it was not in a position to conduct free and fair election immediately after the dissolution of the Assembly and after the electoral roll is revised it would be in a position to conduct election to the General Assembly in the month of November/December 2002.[161]

It is in this context that the President of India in exercise of powers under Article 143(1) of the Constitution referred three questions for the Opinion of the Supreme Court.[162]

59. Questions Referred

(i) Is Article 174 subject to the decision of the Election Commission of India under Article 324 as to the schedule of elections of the Assembly?

(ii) Can the Election Commission of India frame a schedule for the elections to an Assembly on the premise that any infraction of the Mandate of Article 174 would be remedied by a resort to Article 356 by the President?

(iii) Is the Election Commission of India under a duty to carry out the mandate of Article 174 of the Constitution, by drawing upon all the requisite resources of the Union and the State to ensure free and fair elections?

60. Opinion

The majority opinion was rendered by Khare, J. on behalf of Kirpal, C.J., himself and Ashok Bhan, J. with which Balakrishnan, J. and Arijit Pasayat, J. concurred, but rendered their separate opinions.[163]

161. *Supra* n. 159

162. (2002) 8 SCC 237 : (2002) 8 JT389.

163. Opinion delivered on October 28, 2002.

(A) Answer to Question No. 1

Article 174(1) of the Constitution relates to an existing, live and functional Legislative Assembly and not to a dissolved Assembly.

A plain reading of Article 174 shows that it stipulates that six months shall not intervene between the last sitting in one session and the date appointed for its first sitting in the next session. It does not provide for any period of limitation for holding fresh election in the event a Legislative Assembly is prematurely dissolved. It is true that after commencement of the Constitution, the practice has been that whenever either Parliament or Legislative Assembly were prematurely dissolved, the elections for constituting fresh Assembly or Parliament, as the case may be, were held with in six months from the date of the last sitting of the dissolved Parliament or Assembly.

Articles 85(1) and 174(1) which were physically borrowed from the Government of India Act, 1935 were only for the purposes of providing the frequencies of sessions of existing Houses of Parliament and State Legislature, and they do not relate to dissolved Houses.

Having regard to the Constituent Assembly Debates with regard to Articles 85 and 174 also, it is clear that the intention of the framers of the Constitution was that the provisions contained in Article 174 were meant for a living and existing Legislative Assembly and not for a dissolved Legislative Assembly. So Article 174(1) is in applicable to a dissolved Assembly.[164]

Article 174(1) uses expressions i.e., "its last sitting in one session", "first sitting in the next session". None of these expressions suggests that the sitting and the session would include an altogether different Assembly, i.e. a previous Assembly which has been dissolved and its successor Assembly that has come into being after elections. Again, Article 174 also employs and the word "summon" not "constitute". The act of summoning, sitting, adjoining, proroguing or dissolving of the legislature is necessarily

164. Noorani, A.G., "A historic document", *Frontline*, Vol. 20, No. 18 (Sept. 13, 2002) at pp. (10-14).

referable to an assembly in present, i.e. as existing, functional legislature and has nothing to do with the Legislative Assembly which is not in existence. Since a dissolved House is incapable of being summoned or prorogues, Article 174 (1) has no application to a dissolved Legislative Assembly, as nothing survives after dissolution.

Again, Article 174 contemplates a session, i.e. sitting of an existing Assembly and not a new Assembly after dissolution and this can be appreciated from the expression "its last sitting in one session and its first sitting in the next session". When the term "session or sessions" is used, it is employed in the context of a particular Assembly or a particular House of the People and not the legislative body whose life is terminated after dissolution. Dissolution ends the life of the legislature and brings an end to all business.

The entire chain of sittings and sessions gets broken and there is no next session or the first sitting of the next session after the House itself has ceased to exist. Dissolution of the Legislative Assembly ends the representative capacity of legislators and terminates the responsibility of the Cabinet to the Members of the Lok Sabha or the Legislative Assembly, as the case may be.[165]

Conceptually, Article 174 deals with a live legislature. The purpose and object of the said provision is to ensure that an existing legislature meets at least every six months, as it is only an existing legislature that can be prorogued or dissolved. Thus Article 174 which is a complete code in itself deals only with a live legislature. Further, a perusal of Articles 172 and 174 would show that there is a distinction between the frequency of meetings of an existing Assembly and periodicity of elections in respect of a dissolved Assembly which are governed by the aforesaid provisions. As far as frequency of meetings of the Assembly is concerned, the six months' rule is mandatory, which as far as periodicity of the election is concerned, there is no six months' rule either expressly or impliedly in Article 174.

165. Venkatesan, V., "In the Supreme Court", *Frontline,* Vol. 12, No. 19 (Sept. 27, 2002) at p. 31.

The provision in Article 174(1) that six months shall not intervene between its last sitting in one session and the date appointed for its sitting in the next session is mandatory and relates to the frequencies of the sessions of a live and existing Legislative Assembly and does not provide for any period of limitation for holding fresh elections for constituting Legislative Assembly on premature dissolution of the Assembly.

Neither under the Constitution nor under the Representation of the People Act, any period of limitation has been prescribed for holding election for constituting legislative Assembly after premature dissolution of the existing one.[166] Since the entire matter relating to the elections was entrusted to the Election Commission, it was found to be a matter of no consequence to provide any period of limitation for holding fresh election for constituting a new Legislative Assembly in the event of premature dissolution. This was a deliberate and conscious decision. However, care was taken not to leave the entire matter in the hands of the Election Commission.

However, the employment of words "on an expiration" occurring in Sections 14 and 15 of the Representation of the People Act, 1951 respectively shows that the Election Commission is required to take steps for holding election immediately on expiration of the term of the Assembly or its dissolution, although no period has been provided for. Yet, there is another indication in Sections 14 and 15 of the Representation of the People Act that the election process can be set in motion by issuing notification prior to the expiry of six months of the normal term of the House of the People or Legislative Assembly.[167]

The provisions of Article 172(1): Articles 123 and 213; and Articles 109, 110 and 111 and analogous articles for the State Assembly indicate that on the premature dissolution of the Legislative Assembly, the Election Commission is required to initiate immediate steps for holding election for constituting

166. Singh, Prof. M.P., "Conducting elections", *The Hindu*, Vol. 25, (Aug. 29, 2002) at p. 12.
167. Tandon Bishan, "Laxman Rekha Khan Lang Raha Hai". *Hindustan*, (Aug. 31, 2002).

legislative Assembly on the first occasion and in any case within six months from the date of premature dissolution of the Legislative Assembly.

(B) E.C. Power in Article 324

The General power of superintendence, direction, control and conduct of the election although vested in the Election Commission under Article 324(1), yet it is subject to any law either made by Parliament or the State Legislature, as the case may be, provided the same does not encroach upon the plenary powers of the Election Commission under Article 324. Article 324 operates in the area left unoccupied by legislation and the words "Superintendence", "control", "direction" as well as "conduct of all elections" are the broadest of the terms.[168]

The superintendence, direction and control of the conduct of elections referred to in Article 324(1) of the Constitution are entrusted to the Commission.[169] The words "superintendence", "direction" and "control" are wide enough to include all powers necessary for the smooth conduct of elections. The general powers of superintendence, direction and control of the elections vested in the Commission under Article 324(1) naturally are subject to any law made either under Article 327 or under Article 328 of the of the Constitution.

The word "election" in Article 324 is used in a wide sense so as to include the entire process of election which consists of several stages and it embraces many steps, some of which may have an important bearing on the result of the process. Article 324 operates in areas left unoccupied by legislation and the words "superintendence", "direction" and "control" as well as "conduct of all elections" are the broadest terms which would include the power to make all such provisions.

168. Krishna Iyer, V.B., "Gujarat Imbroglio : Some Reflections". *The Hindu*, Vol. 25, (Aug. 24, 2002) at p. 11.

169. Mohinder Singh Gill *v.* Chief Election Commr. (1978) 1 SCC 405; AIR 1978 SC 851; Kanhiaya Lal Omar *v.* R.K. Trivedi, (1985) 4 SCC 628: AIR 1986 SC 111.

(C) Articles 324 and 174

Article 174(1) and Article 324 operate in different fields and neither Article 174(1) is subject to Article 324 nor Article 324 is subject to Article 174(1) of the Constitution.

Fixing schedule for elections either for the House of the People or the Legislative Assembly is in the exclusive domain of the Election Commission and it is not subject to any law framed by Parliament. Parliament is empowered to frame law as regards conduct of elections but conducting elections is the sole responsibility of the Election Commission. As a matter of law, the plenary powers of the Election Commission cannot be taken away by law framed by Parliament. If Parliament makes any such law, it would be repugnant to Article 324. Holding periodic, free and fair elections by the Election Commission are part of the basic structure of the Constitution.[170]

(D) Answer of Question 2

This question also proceeds on the assumption that Article 174 (1) is also applicable to a dissolved House. Since Article 174 (1) is inapplicable to a dissolved Legislative Assembly, there is no infraction of the mandate of Article 174(1) in preparing a schedule for elections to an Assembly by the Election Commission. The Election Commission in its written submissions stated :

> *"The decision, contained in the Election Commission's order dated 16.8.2002, was taken without reference to Article 356. However, it was merely pointed out that there need be no apprehension that there would be constitutional impasse as Article 356 could provide a solution in such a situation."*

In view of the matter, the question of applicability of Article 356 on the infraction of the provisions of Article 174 looses much of its substance and, therefore, application of Article 356 is not required to be gone into.

170. Indira-Nehru-Gandhi *v.* Raj Narain, 1975 Supp. SCC 1.

(E) Answer of Question No. 3

This question proceeds on the assumption that the provisions of Article 174(1) also apply to a dissolved Assembly. Since Article 174(1) neither applies to a prematurely dissolved Legislative Assembly nor does it deal with elections. The question that the Election Commission is required to carry out the mandate of Article 174(1) of the Constitution does not arise. Under Article 324, it is the duty and responsibility of the Election Commission to hold free and fair elections at the earliest.

No efforts should be spared by the Election Commission to hold timely elections. Ordinarily law and order or public disorder should not be occasion for postponing the elections and it would be the duty and responsibility of all concerned to render all assistance, cooperation and aid to the Election Commission for holding free and fair elections.[171]

The Election Commission is under a constitutional duty to conduct the election at the earliest on completion of the term of the Legislative Assembly on dissolution or otherwise. If there is any impediment in conducting free and fair election as per the schedule envisaged by Election Commission, it can draw upon all the requisite resources of the Union and the State within its command to ensure free and fair election, though Article 174 has no application in the discharge of such constitutional obligation by the Election Commission. It is the duty of the Election Commission to see that the election is done in a free and fair manner to keep the democratic form of government vibrant and active.

As Article 174 does not deal with election, the question of the Election Commissioner taking the aid, assistance or cooperation of the Centre or the State Governments or to draw upon their resources to hold the election does not arise. On the contrary for effective operation of Article 324 the Election Commission can do so to ensure holding of free and fair election. The question whether free and fair election is possible to be held or not has to be objectively assessed by the Election

171. Venkatesan, V., "Care taker by default", *Frontline*, Vol. 20, No. 18 (Sept. 13, 2002) at pp. 17-18.

Commission by taking into consideration all relevant aspects. Efforts should be to hold the election and not to defer holding of election.[172]

Timely election which is not free and fair subverts democracy and frustrates the ultimate responsibility to assess objectively whether free and fair election is possible. Any man-made attempt to obstruct free and fair election is antithesis to democratic norms and should be overcome by garnering resources from the intended sources and by holding the elections within the six months' period.[173]

Democracy is a basic feature of the Constitution. Whether any particular brand or system of government by itself, has this attribute of a basic feature, as long as the essential characteristics that entitle a system of government to be called democratic are otherwise satisfied is not necessary to be gone into. Election conducted at regular, prescribed intervals is essential to the democratic system envisaged in the Constitution. So is the need to protect and sustain the purity of the electoral process. That may take within it the quality, efficacy and adequacy of the machinery for resolution of electoral disputes.

61. Main Points of Opinion

1. The provisions of Article 174 are mandatory in character so far as the time period between two sessions is concerned, in respect of live Assemblies and not dissolved Assemblies. Article 174 and Article 324 operate in different fields. Article 174 does not deal with elections which is the primary function of the Election Commission under Article 324. Therefore, the question of one yielding to the other does not arise. There is scope of harmonizing both in a manner indicated supra.

172. Election Commission of India *v.* State of Haryana, 1984 Supp. SCC 104 : (1984) 3 SCR, 554; Election Commission of India *v.* Union of India, 1955 Supp. (3) SCC 643; Election Commission of India *v.* State of T.N., 1995 Supp. (3) SCC 379.

173. S.R. Chaudhuri *v.* State of Punjab (2001) SCC 126.

2. Article 174 is not relatable to a dissolved Assembly. Similar is the position under Article 85 *vis-à-vis* House of the People. Merely because the time schedule fixed under Article 174 cannot be adhered to, that *per se* cannot be a ground for bringing into operation Article 356.
3. As Article 174 does not deal with election, the question of the Election Commissioner taking the aid, assistance or cooperation of the Centre or the State Governments or to draw upon their resources to hold the election does not arise. On the contrary for effective operation of Article 324 the Election Commission can do so to ensure holding of free and fair election. The question whether free and fair election is possible to be held or not has to be objectively assessed by the Election Commission by taking into consideration all relevant aspect. Efforts should be to hold the election and not to defer holding of election.

(FOURTEENTH REFERENCE)
IN THE SATLUJ-YAMUNA LINK CANAL REFERENCE
(Special Reference No. 1 of 2004)

62. Related Cases

1. *State of Haryana* vs. *State of Punjab and others.*[174]
2. *J.K. Dhir* vs. *State of Punjab and Others.*[175]
3. *State of Punjab and Others* vs. *Khushal Singh and others.*[176]

63. Main Facts

If the Satluj-Yamuna Link (SYL) canal were a Hollywood epic, its producers would without doubt have advertised it as the most expensive and useless ditch ever built. Upwards of

174. Supreme Court of India, 15 June, 2002.
175. Supreme Court of India, 5 June, 1987.
176. Supreme Court of India, 31 June, 1989.

Rs. 850 crores have been spent building the 306-kilometer-long canal. But because Punjab refuses to build the small section of the project that has yet to be completed, it carries no water. The 1,700 strong staff that Punjab employs to build the canal has not had a day's serious work for the past two decades. The project even claimed two lives in July 1990, when terrorists shot dead two of its top engineers and succeeded in bringing work to a grinding halt. If the polemic emanating from Punjab and Haryana is any indication it might just claim a few more lives before it is finally built or, of course, simply filled in.

History, however, suggests that Punjab in fact has some ground to feel hard done by. The problem began in November, 1966, when Punjab was divided and two new States were formed—Haryana and Himachal Pradesh. The Reorganisation Act of 1966 made it mandatory for the Union government to divide the waters of the Satluj and Beas systems if Punjab and Haryana were unable to arrive at a mutually acceptable solution. A decade later, since no agreement could be hammered out, New Delhi divided unutilized water of the Ravi and Beas systems between the two States. Punjab found the order unacceptable. For one, it apportioned the waters of the Ravi, excluded from the 1966 Act. Secondly, Punjab argued that the 1976 order mandated the sharing of water on the basis of its utilisation in 1960 not that which was actually used in 1976, by which time approved projects on the river systems had been completed. Punjab moved the Supreme Court, but in 1981 withdrew its legal intervention. It instead arrived at an agreement with Haryana and Rajasthan. New flow data was used to give both Punjab and Haryana an increase in their share of water.[177]

Unsurprisingly, the agreement created a furore in Punjab. Many people in Punjab believed that the accord was arrived at under political pressure. Experts argued that the new flow data were unreliable, and that the agreement gave the State water that did not exist. Discontent simmered on. At one point the Punjab Assembly even declared the inter-State agreement invalid. Then, in 1985 Prime Minister Rajiv Gandhi and

177. Praveen Swami, "A battle for water" (2003), Issue 03, *Frontline*, 1-3 at 2.

Shirmani Akali Dal chief Longowal arrived at a broad agreement on the Punjab problem, intended to end the terrorist violence in the State. The agreement mandated that Chandigarh was to be made the capital of Punjab and that both Haryana and Punjab would swap Hindi and Punjabi-speaking areas on their borders. In turn, Punjab would build the SYL link canal to carry water to Haryana, but with the caveat that neither State's current use of the Ravi-Beas systems would be affected. Justice V. Balakrishna Eradi was appointed to head the Ravi-Beas Waters Tribunal, which was to find out just how much water Punjab and Haryana in fact used, and to then apportion the surplus.

The Ravi-Beas Tribunal eventually handed out a please-all interim award in January, 1987, even as terrorism in the State was escalating and the government of Surjit Singh Barnala, formed as a consequence of the Rajiv-Longowal accord, was about to fall. Eradi found that the usage of Ravi-Beas waters by formers in the three States totalled 9.711 MAF. Haryana accounted for 1.620 MAF, and Rajasthan 4.985 MAF. Punjab farmers took 3.106 MAF, including about 0.352 MAF that Rajasthan could not utilize. This let some 6.6 MAF of surplus water to be divided between the two warring States.

Justice Eradi made an interim award giving Punjab 5.00 MAF, and Haryana 3.83 MAF. The Problem? The numbers did not add up. The difference between the 6.6 MAF actually available, and the 8.83 MAF of water they were given, was simply ingenious fiction. Water below the rim stations of the Ravi and Beas, the lowest points at which flow data were recorded, made up the difference. Punjab correctly pointed out that this water was useless, for the simple reason that no dams or barrages could be built along the Pakistan border to store it. Moreover, Punjab claimed the utilisation of water by its farmers was understated.

Eradi wound up work soon afterwards, citing escalation of violence in Punjab as the reason. Work on the canal, too, came to a halt. The coming of peace in 1993 did not, however, help matters. Two Congress (I) backed Chief Ministers, Beant Singh and Bhajan Lal, failed to reach any kind of agreement. In 1997, two Bhartiya Janta Party-backed Chief Ministers, Prakash

Singh Badal and Bansi Lal, again exchanged invective on the issue.

Meanwhile, in 1994, Punjab added another grievance to its growing portfolio of complaints. In May, 1994, Haryana, Uttar Pradesh, Rajasthan, Himachal Pradesh and Delhi arrived at an agreement on the use of the Yamuna system. Use of the Yamuna was earlier governed by a 1954 inter-State agreement that gave united Punjab two-thirds of its water, and Uttar Pradesh the rest. The agreement was to have been binding until 2000, and Punjab's request to be included in the 1994 agreement was shot down outright. The State however, pointed out that if the successor-State of Haryana could be given a share of the Ravi-Beas systems, neither of which fell in its territory, Punjab ought to get a share of the Yamuna.

64. Legal Development

The renewed bickering over the SYL canal in December illustrates just how often history can repeat itself, the farce deepening each time around. On January 15, 2002, the Supreme Court ordered Punjab to finish work on the canal within a year. Failing this, it said, the Union government would have to undertake the work. Justice G.B. Pattanaik noted that "the Union government is feeling embarrassed to take any positive decision, which, in our view, is not in the interest of the nation." The core problem, he argued, was "lack of political will at the Central level to deal with the problem with determination". The Centre was also ordered to find a Judge to head the Ravi-Beas Waters Tribunal, which had for all practical purposes ceased to function in 1987. True to form, neither the Punjab government nor the Centre did anything, January 15, 2003, was the seventh deadline for the completion of the canal, after the ones in December 1983, August, 1986, December 1987, March 1988, June 1989 and January 1991. Like the previous ones, this was also ignored.

Central officials seem reluctant to intervene in this protracted Punjab-Haryana feud. At a meeting with delegates from all major political parties in Haryana on January 14, Prime Minister Atal Behari Vajpayee refused to commit to Central intervention. When Haryana Chief Minister Om Prakash Chautala argued that the failure to build the canal was costing Haryana Rs. 1,000 crores a year, Vajpayee is believed to have replied that there was nothing new or urgent about this fact, that warranted immediate action.

Efforts to resolve issues between Punjab and Haryana too have gone nowhere. A letter from Punjab Chief Minister Amarinder Singh to Chautala asking for negotiations met with a stinging riposte. Chautala described Punjab's basis for negotiations as "totally irrelevant". "I also do not feel it necessary," the letter stated, "to give my viewpoint on issues such as the transfer of Chandigarh to Punjab or Hindi-speaking areas of Punjab to Haryana in lieu thereof, or the proposed Yamuna basin allocations or Sharda-Yamuna link, as in my opinion, these issues are absolutely out of context in reference to the legal mandatory obligation caused upon Punjab for implementing the apex court judgment." As things stand, matters seem headed to exactly the same place they have been for the past decade—the Supreme Court.

A fresh legal intervention by Punjab is now awaiting hearing. Punjab, in essence, argues that it has no surplus water to release. While 17.17 million acre-feet (MAF) was earlier believed to have been available in the Ravi-Beas systems, Punjab says, the 1981-2002 flow data show only 14.37 MAF is in fact on hand. As a result, the transfer of water to Haryana would affect 9 lakh acres of irrigated land in Ferozepore, Muktsar, Moga and Faridkot. The recharge of Punjab's depleted groundwater reserves would also be hit hard, the State government claims. Punjab argues that the release of water through the SYL canal is contingent on other key components of the 1985 Rajiv Gandhi-H.S. Longowal Accord, including the handling over of Chandigarh to Punjab, and the transfer of Punjabi-speaking areas of Haryana. Finally, Punjab claims that Haryana has no claims to the water of rivers that do not flow through its territory—that is, the Ravi and the Beas.

Both States have now hired legal top-guns to argue the issue afresh: Punjab has engaged the services of Fali S. Nariman, while Haryana will be represented by Harish Salve and P.P. Rao. Sources in the Punjab government told that the legal battle would cost both side some Rs. 50 lakhs apiece.

Many experts, however, believe the chances of Punjab achieving a breakthrough in the courts are poor.

Most of the issues it has now raised were argued earlier, in a review petition Punjab had filed after the Supreme Court judgment of January 2002. In March that year, the Supreme Court rejected Punjab's arguments out of hand. Haryana, for its part, has asked the Supreme Court to set a deadline by which the Centre must complete work on the canal.

65. Special Reference No. 1 of 2004

On July 22, 2004 President referred Punjab's controversial Terminations of Agreement Act to the Supreme Court, starting what could prove to be the last legal round in India's longest-running and most complex water dispute. In the coming months, the Supreme Court will consider whether the Act is constitutional and whether Punjab must obey a 2002 order mandating that the SYL Canal be completed in a year. The Act is unprecedented. It is the first time a State government has sought to overturn a Supreme Court order through legislative means. Even the Karnataka Assembly, which passed legislation on how much water it would release to Tamil Nadu from reservoirs on the Cauvery, sought to overturn only an award of a water disputes tribunal, not a judicial fiat.[178]

The president has sought the advise of the apex court by way of reference whether a state assembly can pass a legislation in interrogation of the central legislation as well as in violation of the Supreme Court directions?

66. Argument of the Parties

Punjab's move has sparked off a furore in neighbouring Haryana, which has threatened to retaliate by abrogating the Yamuna Waters Treaty, crucial to meeting the water needs of New Delhi. The State has witnessed massive protests and its Congress MLAs have threatened to resign en bloc if those form other parties will joint them.

By contrast, almost everyone in Punjab is standing behind the Act. It is not hard, however, to spot the many ironies glossed over by the extraordinary support. Chief Minister

178. Praveen Swami, "Acaral Crisis", (2004), Issue 16, *Frontline*, 1-4 at 1.

Amarinder Singh's course of action has won him in Punjab. Shiromani Akali Dal (SAD) leader and former Chief Minister Prakash Singh Badal, at Amarinder Singh's throat until recently because of the Chief Minister's anti-corruption campaign, has thrown his weight behind the Act. Yet, it was during Badal's term as Chief Minister that work on the canal first began, in 1978. Three Congress Chief Ministers—Punjab's Darbara Singh, Haryana's Bhajan Lal and Rajasthan's S.C. Mathur—along with Prime Minister Indira Gandhi signed the 1981 agreement Punjab now seeks to repudiate.

Punjab as has said not actually intend to tenege on the quantity of river water it has been releasing to other States in past years, but no hard commitments have been made on just how much will be given and when. Just as important, it is obvious that Punjab's course of action takes Indian federalism into uncharted waters. No one is quite certain just how the SYL, Çanal saga will play out—and what it will mean for emerging and existing water disputes across the country.

For all the opprobrium the Act has earned him, it is hard to flaw Amarinder Singh's political survival instincts. Starting work on the SYL Canal would have given a political handle to the SAD, something the Punjab Congress can ill afford. At once, the fact that the Chief Minister chose the path of confrontation with the Supreme Court casts instructive light on the state of the Central Congress apparatus. In this case, the interests of the Punjab unit of the party clearly prevailed over its national interests, since the Act is likely to damage the Congress' chances in the elections to the Haryana Assembly. Politicians close to the Chief Minister say that the central leadership was only told that the Punjab Congress was considering a dramatic tactic to avoid starting work on the SYL Canal, but its advice was not sought. Some analysis point to the unusually rapid gubernatorial assent given to the Act as evidence that the Union government preferred to duck a bruising confrontation with the Punjab government. If true, it would suggest that some kind of dramatic shift in the structure of power within the Congress apparatus is under way.

Advocates of Punjab's new law have not, however, put forward a particularly compelling case on the actual issues so far. In full-page advertisements put out in newspapers across

India, the Punjab government has argued that the latest flow data shows the amount of water in the Satluj has declined from an average of 17.17 million acre-feet (MAF) a year, on which the 1981 agreement was based, to just 14.37 MAF now. But the significance of this data has not been made clear. The average amount of water available in a river will always fluctuate over the years, depending on several factors, notably rainfall. The latest data include several bad monsoon years; a succession of good monsoon years would raise the average amount of water available to the 1981 levels or higher. The data is at best an argument for a clear distress formula, which would divide the burden of a bad monsoon among all the users. This, however, would have to be hammered out in the Eradi Tribunal or in multilateral dialogue, and does not *per se* constitute an argument against agreements signed in the past.

Punjab's argument that the 1981 agreement constitutes unreasonable Union intervention in a State subject is also somewhat perplexing. The Union's rights to the waters of the Satluj, the Ravi and the Beas were the outcome of the Indus Waters Treaty, which gave Pakistan exclusive rights to the waters of the Indus, the Jhelum and the Chenab and India the use of the three southern rivers. Interestingly, some politicians in Jammu & Kashmir have argued against the Indus Waters Treaty, claiming it robbed the State of rights to rivers that flow through its territory. In this case, Union mediation compelled all States—Punjab, Haryana and Himachal Pradesh to make sacrifices and sought to protect all their interests.

Should all agreements be abrogated, Himachal Pradesh could in principle start demanding royalties for the water and power it releases to Punjab and the Union government could, in turn, ask the reimbursement of the funds it pumped into the construction of the dams at Bhakra-Nagal, Ranjit Sagar, Pong and Chimera. It could also begin to unilaterally sell water, to which Punjab is currently entitled, to other States. Himachal Pradesh residents could argue that they bore the burnt of the submergence caused by the dams and ask for recurring compensation.

What none of the States seems to be addressing is the most basic question of all: how much water do the farmers of Punjab and Haryana actually need? According to former

Haryana government Chief Engineer Ram Niwas Malik, the command area of the Sirhand Canal, which feeds water released from the right-hand power houses of the Bhakra-Nangal Dam, simply cannot absorb all of the 7.0 MAF diverted to it from the Beas. Therefore, he says, the 3.85 MAF Haryana was granted for use through the SYL Canal would have been diverted without fuss had the division of Punjab not occurred. In other words, Malik seems to believe that chauvinistic concerns, not actual need, have shaped Punjab's move—it simply does not need the water that is Haryana's due.

Others, such as agricultural economist S.S. Johl, believe that any reduction in the canal water available to Punjab will lead to massive problems. In fact, Johl argued in a recent article that even the existing levels of irrigation in Punjab were not enough to stave off a crisis. The "water-table is receding at the rate of 36 to 42 inches per year in most parts of the central districts", he wrote. "If this trend continues, Punjab will be a barren State in less than a decade."

If nothing else, these irreconcilable views point to the need for a much more careful and nuanced debate on the use of water in both States, one that transcends any kind of parochialism. Some of the hysteria in Haryana on the SYL Canal issue is particularly hard to comprehend, since the lack of irrigation in its southern districts has not stopped the State from registering impressive growth in agriculture and industry. In Punjab, for its part, agricultural scientists and economists have for decades been calling both for massive investments in irrigation systems, to reduce seepage looses that exceed 30 per cent, as well as measures to contain the irrational use of water on soils that are less than ideal for flood irrigation. The massive rise in land committed to growing water hungry paddy and sugarcane in both States is a large part of the problem and has caused considerable depletion of the water table. Neither State government, however, seems willing to even discuss the possibility that the right kind of public investment and usage policies could be more important to their long-term water security than the loss or gain of water through the SYL Canal.

Underlying the desperation, particularly in Punjab, is a larger crisis that confronts the farming community one that has nothing to do with the SYL Canal debate. As the Punjab University academic Dr. H.S. Shergill pointed out: The falling water level and environmental degradation are, no doubt, serious problems; but are certainly not the central issue. The core of Punjab's agrarian crisis is the stagnation of farm incomes for the past many years, and farmer's fears of imminent fall in their incomes if the World Trade Organisation agenda is implemented thoughtlessly.

In several scholarly papers, Shergill noted that efforts to push farmers out of the wheat-rice cycle imposed punitive costs on them and exposed them to dangerous price fluctuations seen in new high-value crops. Instead, he argued, the answer to the agrarian impasses lies in improving the efficiency of cultivation techniques the increased mechanisation of farming and a real effort to rebuild the public distribution system, bearing in mind that by some estimates, the slow growth of food grain production will mean that India will face a deficit by 2020.

As things stand, then Punjab will face serious problems even if it does not lose water through the SYL Canal. "The scope of further expansion of irrigated areas is very limited," Shergill noted. "Most of the areas; options for increasing canal irrigation have already been exploited. Ground water in dry areas has been tapped so heavily that the water table has fallen precipitously and there is little scope of further expansion of tubewell irrigation." Punjab, then, needs to be talking seriously about reducing its usage of water in its own long-term interests.

Haryana, too, need to seriously consider if the arid southern districts will be well served by massive canal irrigation, or whether other, more cost-effective and sustainable options exist. India's experiments with water imports through canals have not always been happy, and the sad fact is that there is simply not an adequate body of scholarly work on the potential impacts the SYL Canal would have on southern Haryana soils. In both States, however, emotive mass mobilization on river water issues has been a way for politicians to deflect attention away from the very real agrarian crisis they face and the need for serious, constructive reform.

Similarly, Punjab's riparian rights argument is problematic on several counts. Legal convention and discourse on the issue has, worldwide, rejected narrow riparian rights claims and privileges the need for water over territorial rights. Punjab claims that Haryana ought not to have been granted waters from the Satluj since it is not a riparian state, or, alternatively, that it should have received a share of the Yamuna waters, which pass through Haryana. This line of argument is specious on a first-principles basis. Until the 1966 division of Punjab, the residents of what is now Haryana had riparian rights, and cannot have lost them simply because of a redrawing of State borders a redrawing, moreover, demanded by political parties in what is now Punjab, not Haryana. Equally important, Punjab has pressed its own claims to a share of Yamuna waters through the courts. In 1995, after the Yamuna basin States signed an agreement on the use of its waters, Punjab moved a legal challenge to its exclusion from the process. If Punjab believes it deserves a share of the Yamuna waters, it needs to mount a credible legal campaign not abrogate agreements.

67. Conclusion

The saddest part of the saga, however, is that the SYL canal issue is in essence a straw man. The real problems facing farmers in both Punjab and Haryana have to do with their colossally inefficient irrigation policies, and the indiscriminate proliferation of water-hungry, crops such as paddy and sugarcane. At a recent conference, top irrigation engineer G.S. Dhillon pointed out that Punjab faced a crisis even though it had access to all the water that would be ceded if the canal was built.

In 1955, Punjab had 34.8 MAF of water in all forms, but was today left with a reserve of only 12.8 MAF. While groundwater levels had been falling precipitately in areas such as Malerkotla and Sangrur owing to the excessive use to aquifers, areas on the State's borders were waterlogged because of seepage from poorly maintained canals, and the intensive watering of soils not suited for flood irrigation. Haryana has similar problems, but neither State appears to take the need for water conservation seriously.

Punjab wants to now litigation the issue afresh, arguing

that political pressures skewed the whole course of events since the creation of Haryana. "We want a *de novo* examination of the entire issue," says Amarinder Singh. "The fact is that Punjab has just not received a fair hearing of its position over all these years." As Chautala's recent letters make clear, that is not a position Haryana is willing to accept.

While both States spend lakhs slugging it out in court, they might consider doing their farmers a real favour. Union government-backed plans for subsidies for farmers introducing sprinklers and drip irrigation seem to have been forgotten by the NDA at the Centre. Even they, by stopping early sowing in May and June, both States could save enormous quantities of water. Moving away from paddy and sugarcane to a welter of crops that need less water would also help curb both State's almost alcoholic thirst. Punjab at last seems to be making some conservation efforts, by encouraging crop diversification and introducing user charges for canal users. If these efforts take root, the outcome of the SYL battle might just prove irrelevant.

Where might events go from here? The decision to refer the Punjab legislation to the Supreme Court means that all parties have some breathing space. Judging by past experience in politically sensitive and complex issues, it could be several years before the Supreme Court hands down a final verdict.

Most legal experts seem to believe Punjab has a less than fighting chance of securing judicial redress, should its challenge to the 1981 agreement fail, the State will have little option other than to construct the remaining portion of the canal. Others believe Punjab will use the nuisance value of its legislation to attempt to secure a softer deal, perhaps involving the loss of less water to Haryana, or a face-saving share of the waters of the Yamuna.[179]

Whatever happens, it is unlikely farmers in either State will actually benefit a great deal. It is certain, however, that the ugly regional chauvinism unleashed in recent weeks will gather momentum, spurred on by the patronage it has received from politicians in both Punjab and Haryana. So far, there has been little violence on the issue, but it seems possible that the SYL Canal will claim more lives before it is finally built.

179. Ajay Bharadwaj, "No need for SYL canal : Punjab" available at www.The Times of India.indiatimes.com. accessed on 07.19.2007.

5

New Dimensions in Consultative Jurisdiction

India has had a specific provision for advisory opinions since 1937; under the government of India Act, 1935. There is no doubt that the Federal Court and the Supreme Court have always attempted to assist in the Constitutional governance of the country by giving guidance to the executive and legislatures to act in accordance with the constitution. After every opinion the honourable court has added some new dimensions in the field of law. On the whole, the institution of advisory opinions has functioned very innovative and has proved to be creative in value so far as the constitutional interpretation is concerned. It has been used wisely and sparingly so far only in such case where factual situations are ripe, or where legal issues are capable of being formatted precisely.

Over a period of 58 years only 14 references have been made to the Supreme Court on which the court refused to entertain only two references. Case after case various dimensions of Law and fact came in front of the court. It had lead down some new dimensions in the field of Law. Some gray areas are still awaited where an authoritative answer from the Supreme Court have not come. Therefore, a close study of new dimensions is the need of hour.

1. SCOPE AND COMPETENCE OF THE PRESIDENT TO CONSULT THE SUPREME COURT

The marginal note of Article 143 is worded as "Power of President to consult Supreme Court". Both clauses (1) & (2) empowers the President to refer to the opinion of the Supreme Court relating to the aspects contained therein. Article 74(1) mandates the President to act in accordance with the aid and advise of his council of ministers. Therefore, though the reference may go in the name of the President, in reality, the reference is by the council of ministers. But for that purpose, the Supreme Court cannot verify or examine as to whether the reference is by the President himself or on the advise of the council of ministers in view of the constitutional bar contained in clause (2) of Article 74 which mandates that the question whether any and if so what advise was tendered by the ministers to the President shall not be enquired into in any court.

But if the President consults the Supreme Court under Article 143 in the absence of an advise to that effect from the council of ministers, he will be committing a violation of the Constitution [that is, violation of Article 74(1)] for which he may be impeached. The competence of the President to consult the Supreme Court is not confined to matter in lists 1 and 3 of the seventh schedule on the ground that the executive power is co-extensive with that of the legislative power. The language of Article 143 is wide enough to empower the President to refer to the apex court for its advisory opinion on any question of law or fact which has arisen or is likely to arise, provided it appears to the President that the question referred is of such a nature and of such public importance that it is expedient to obtain the opinion of the Supreme Court upon it.

It is not necessary that the questions on which the opinion of the Supreme Court is sought must have actually arisen. It is competent for the President to make a reference under Article 143(1) at an anterior stage, namely, at the stage when the President is satisfied that the question is likely to arise. The satisfaction as to whether the question has arisen or is likely to arise and whether it is of such a nature and of such public importance that it is expedient to obtain the opinion of the Supreme Court upon it, is a matter entirely and essentially for the President to decide. It is for the President to determine what question or questions should be referred and if he does not have any serious doubt on any incidental question or questions, it is not for anybody else to contend that they have doubts. The parties appearing in a reference cannot go behind the order of reference and present new questions by raising doubts.

This issue was raised in *the Gujarat assembly election matter,*[1] it was opined that the truth or otherwise of the facts cannot be enquired or gone into nor can the court go into the question of bonafides or otherwise of the authority making the reference. The court cannot go behind the recital. It also cannot go into disputed questions of fact in its advisory jurisdiction under Article 143(1).

(A) Reference on a Question of Fact:

> Article 143(1) permits the President to refer for the opinion of the Supreme Court, even a question of fact. Among the ten references, excepting *Special Reference No. 1 of 1993,* all the references related to questions of law. The question of fact that was referred in this reference was that whether a Hindu temple or any Hindu religious structure existed prior to the construction of the *Ram Janmabhumi-Babri Masjid*? Therefore, this is the only reference wherein the President referred a question of fact to the Supreme Court under Article 143(1).

2. IS THE SUPREME COURT BOUND TO ANSWER THE REFERENCE

This issue was raised on the floor of the Constituent Assembly by *Shri H.V. Kamath* when Article 119 of the draft

1. In re Gujarat assembly election matter, (2002) 8 SCC 237.

constitution which corresponds to article 143 of the present Constitution came up for consideration. Shri Kamath while moving Amendment No. 1952 to the draft constitution, wanted a clarification from the assembly in the following words:[2]

> *"Sir, the point which I wish to raise in my Amendment No. 1952 is a simple one. The Article contemplates that the Supreme Court should report to the President its opinion or in its discretion it may withhold its opinion. I believe what is meant is that when once the President refers the matters to the Supreme Court. If that is not meant than the language is right. But if it is meant that once the President refers a matter to the Supreme Court, it must report its opinion thereon to the President, then the word "shall" must come in. I wanted a clarification on that point."*

Shri H.V Kamath did not move his amendment when *Dr. B.R. Ambedkar* pointed out that the Supreme Court is not bound. Therefore, the Supreme Court is not bound to answer the presidential reference made under Article 143(1). With regard to refusal to answer under Article 143(1), all opinions are unanimous in that the Supreme Court can refuse to answer a presidential reference under Article 143(1). Das, C.J. in *re Kerala Education Bill, 1957* opined that it is obligatory on the Supreme Court to entertain a reference and to report to the President it's opinion if the reference is under Article 143(2),but the court had under clause (1), a discretion in the matter and may in a proper case and for good reasons decline to express any opinion on the questions submitted to it. But Chief Justice Chandrachud opined to the contrary *in re Special Courts Bill, 1978* and held as follows:[3]

> *"The right of this court to decline to answer a reference does not flow merely out of the different phraseology used in clauses (1) and (2) of Article 143, in the sense that clause (1) provides that the court "may" report to the President its opinion on the question referred to it, while clause (2) provides that the court*

2. Constituent Assembly Debats, Vol. VIII, book no. 3 at 387 (1999).
3. A.I.R. 1979 S.C. 478.

> *"shall" report to the President its opinion on the question. Even in maters arising under clause (2), though that question does not arise in this reference, the court may be justified in returning the reference unanswered if it finds for a valid reason that the question is incapable of being answered."*

Gajendragadkar, C.J. in *Special reference No. 1 of 1964* opined to the same effect as that of Das, C.J. *in re Kerala Educational Bill*. The opinion of Gajendragadkar, C.J. is as follows:

> *"When a reference is received by this court under Article 143(1) this court may, in a given case, for sufficient and satisfactory reasons, respectfully refuse to make a report containing its answers on the questions framed by the President. Such a situation may perhaps arise if the questions formulated for the advisory opinion of this court are purely socio-economic or political questions which have no relation whatever with any of the provisions of the Constitution, or have otherwise no Constitutional significance. It is with a view to confer jurisdiction on this court to declinc to answer questions for such strong and compelling reasons that the Constitution has used the word 'may' in Article 143 (1) as distinct from Article 143(2) where the word used is 'shall'."*

The Supreme Court has no power to decline to answer whenever there is a reference to it under Article 143(2). But the court, undoubtedly, has power to refuse to give opinion under Article 143(1). In *Special Reference No. 1 of 1993* a five-judge bench unanimously refused to entertain a reference which was with regard to a question of fact.

The significance of the *Special Reference No. 1 of 1993* is that this is the only reference with regard to a question of fact and the President had unanswered it. It was only Chandrachud, C.J. who took a different view with regard to the answerability of the reference under Article 143(2). The observation of Das, C.J. Gajendragadkar, C.J. and Chandrachud, C.J. may be juxtaposed as follows:

In re Kerala Education Bill, 1957 (per Das, CJ)	*In re the Special Courts Bill 1978* (per Chandrachud, CJ)	*Special Reference No. 1 of 1964* (per Gajendragadkar, CJ)
"....It is worthy of note that, while under Clause (2) it is obligatory on this court to entertain a reference and to a report to the President its opinion thereon, this court has, under Clause (1), a discretion in the matter and may in a proper case and for good reasons decline to express any opinion on the question submitted to it....."	"....Even in matters arising under clause (2) though that question does not arise in this reference, the court may be justified in returning the reference unanswered if it finds for a valid reason that the question is incapable of being answered."	"...Whereas in the case of reference made under Article 143(2) it is the constitutional obligation of this court to make a report on that reference embodying its advisory opinion, in a reference made under Article 143(1) there is no such obligation."

3. IS THE OPINION "LAW DECLARED" WITHIN THE MEANING OF ARTICLE 141

There are conflicting authorities on this question. An authoritative answer from the Supreme Court is still awaited. *In re allocation of Lands and Building,*[4] and *in re Levy of Estate Duty*[5] the Federal Court held that advisory opinion do not have binding force of law. In *Attorney General for Ontario* v. *Attorney General for Canada*[6] the Judicial Committee of the Privy Council went to the extent of saying that opinions expressed in advisory jurisdiction will have no more effect than the opinion of the law officers. Same observations in the Supreme Court's judgment in *U.P. Legislature Case*[7] and *St. Xavier's College* v. *State of Gujarat*[8] are also relied upon for

4. A.I.R. 1943, F.C. 13.
5. A.I.R. 1943, F.C. 73.
6. (1912) A.C. 571, 589.
7. A.I.R. 1965 S.C. 745.
8. A.I.R. 1974 S.C. 1381.

the view that advisory opinion is not binding as law declared under Article 141.

But in the *Province of Madras* v. *M/s Boddu Paidanna and Sons*[9] Federal Court held that advisory opinion given by it in the Central Provinces Case[10] was binding. In *Ram Kishore Sen* v. *Union of India*[11] the High Court of Calcutta held that opinion given by Supreme Court under Article 143 is binding as law declared by it under Article 141.

In *Chhabidas Mehta* v. *Legislative Assembly of Gujarat State,*[12] Chief Justice Bhagwati speaking for the bench observed.

> *"It is no doubt true that the majority opinion was expressed by the Supreme Court Court in its advisory jurisdiction under Article 143 but we do not see why on that account it ceases to be law declared by the Supreme Court within the meaning of Article 141. The Constitution has conferred diverse jurisdictions on the Supreme Court. There is the original jurisdiction under Article 131; then there is the appellate jurisdiction under Article 132, 133, 134 and 136, there is also writ jurisdiction under Article 32; and lastly, there is advisory jurisdiction under Article 143. A point of law may arise for consideration in any of these jurisdictions and where such point of law is considered and the Supreme Court expresses what in its considered view is the correct position in regard to such point of law, it is clearly and indubitably a declaration of law by the Supreme Court. It is not material which jurisdiction provides the occasion for declaration of the law."*

His lordship said that the word "declared" in Article 141 should be given its plain natural meaning and so construed it has a wide connotation.

In *Hardwari Lal* v. *Election Commission of India*[13] the Punjab High Court following *Chhabidas Mehta's* case held that advisory

9. A.I.R. 1942. F.C. 33
10. A.I.R. 1939 F.C.I.
11. A.I.R. 1965 Cal. 282.
12. (1970) 2 Guj. L.R. 729.
13. (1977) 2 I.L.R. Punj. and Har. 269.

opinions under Article 143 are law declared under Article 141 and, therefore binding.

The question came to be considered by the Supreme Court in a reference case regarding Special Court Bill[14] and speaking for majority *Chandrachud, C.J.* observed:

> *"We are inclined to the view that though it is always open to this Court to re-examine the question already decided by it and to overrule, if necessary, the view earlier taken by it. In so far as all other Courts in the territory of India are concerned they ought to be bound by the view expressed by this Court even in the exercise of its advisory jurisdiction under Article 143 (1) of the Constitution."*[15]

This opinion of the Supreme Court cannot be treated as authoritative on this point for the following reasons:

1. The opinion is not categorical. The Chief Justice himself said that the question may be more fully considered on a future occasion.
2. The above opinion is itself expressed in exercise of advisory jurisdiction.

This question was again left open by the Supreme Court *in the Matter of Cauvery Water Disputes Tribunal*[16] on two grounds:

(1) That the question was not in terms of reference.
(2) That opinion expressed by it in this case will again the advisory.

However, there are sufficient reasons in favour of the view that opinion rendered by the Supreme Court may be treated as law declared by it under Article 141.

14. *In re* Special Courts Bill, A.I.R. 1979 S.C. 478.
15. *Ibid.*, p. 519.
16. A.I.R. 1992 S.C. 522.

The following points may be particularly noted:

(1) The word "declared" in Article 141 is wide enough in its natural meaning to include advisory opinion by the Supreme Court.

(2) The cases under Canadian or American Constitution cannot be treated as authoritative because in the Constitutions of these countries there is no provision parallel to Article 141.

(3) The Supreme Court is not bound to give opinion under Article 143(1) but once it gives opinion its pronouncement on a point of law is nothing less than declaration of law under Article 141.

(4) Doubtful questions of law are referred to the Supreme Court under Article 143 to clarify the law and avoid unnecessary litigation. If the courts in the country are free not to follow the advisory opinion and make their own assessments the very purpose for which the opinion was taken will be defeated because different interpretations by various courts will perpetuate the confusion.

(5) When the Supreme Court has to render advisory opinion under Article 143 the matter is considered by the Bench of not less than five judges and the experience shows that the Court issues notice to all interested parties and hears every one who desires to be heard. It follows almost the same procedure as in exercise of original jurisdiction and gives its opinion after more deliberations than in most of the cases of actual controversies between the two parties. If such well considered opinion is to bind none it will amount to exercise in futility, wastage of not only money and labour on the part of the State and other interested persons but also precious time of the highest Court of the country which is already overburdened.

(6) It is also illogical to treat an *ex-parte* judgment in actual dispute as binding but such well considered opinion as not binding on any Court.[17]

17. Prabhudat *v.* Suryakant, A.I.R. 1979, Bom. 166.

4. DOES THE ADVISORY OPINION BIND THE PRESIDENT

The marginal note of Article 143 shows that the President is not bound by the opinion of the Supreme Court. The marginal note of Article 143 reads "Power of President to Consult Supreme Court". The word consult shows beyond doubt that the President is not bound to give effect to the opinion. The next reason as to why the president is not bound by the advice of the Supreme Court in that the opinion cannot be enforced or executed. Article 142 which deals with the enforcement of decrees and orders of Supreme Court, under clause (1) states that only decree and orders of the Supreme Court can be enforced. Since an opinion is neither to decree nor an order, it cannot be enforced. When this is the legal and the constitutional position, the Supreme Court in *Special Reference No. 1 of 1993* observed:

We record at the outset the statements of the Attorney General that :

(1) ***
(2) the Union of India shall accept and treat as binding the answers of this court to the questions set out in the reference.

With regard to statement (2) recorded by the nine-judge reference bench, it is submitted that, when the constitutional position is that the President is not bound by the opinion, no concession can be given to the contrary. Late Mr. Seervai who appeared for U.P. Vidhan Sabha in *Special Reference No. 1 of 1964* argued that no party is bound by the opinion of the Supreme Court in a presidential reference under Article 143(1) and his arguments were stated by Gajendragadkar, C.J. in following words:[18]

Mr. Seervai began his arguments by pointing out the fact that in dealing with a reference under Article 143(1), the court is

18. *In re* Special Courts Bill, A.I.R. 1979 S.C. 478.

> *not exercising what may be described as its judicial function. There are no parties before the court in such a reference is, therefore advisory, and so, he contends that though he appears before us in the present reference on behalf of the House, he wants to make it clear that the House does not submit to the jurisdiction of this court in any manner in respect of the area of controversy conversed by the questions. In other words, he stated that his appearance before us was without prejudice to his main contention that the question about the existence and extent of the powers, privileges and immunities of the House, as well as the question about the exercise of the powers and privileges were entirely and exclusively within the jurisdiction of the House, and whatever this court may say will not preclude the House from deciding for itself the points referred to us under this reference. This stand was based on the ground that the opinion expressed by us is advisory and not in the nature of judicial adjudication between the parties before the court as such.*

Gajendragadkar, C.J.[19] answered the above contention in the following words:

> *"It may be that technically, the advisory opinion rendered by this court on the reference made to it by the President may not amount to judicial adjudication properly so-called and since there are no parties as such before the court in the Reference nobody would be bound by our answers . . . the advisory opinion rendered by us in the present Reference Proceedings is not adjudication properly so-called and would bind no parties as such."*

Thus the above observations clearly shows that the President is not bound by whatever the Supreme Court says in its advisory jurisdiction. *Late Mr. Seervai* recorded in his classical work "Constitutional Law of India"[20] as to what transpired in *Keshav Singh:*

---

19. *In re* Special Courts Bill, A.I.R. 1979 S.C. 478.
20. H.M. Seervai, Constitutional Law of India, Vol. II, 2175 (4th Edn.).

"Reverting to Justice Subba Rao's question, I replied: "very well, let me tell you that we will not be bound by anything you say. I make it clear to you, as I made it clear to the Chief Justice in his Chamber, that the Assembly will not be bound by anything you say." Justice Subba Rao asked me "You mean that you will not obey our orders?" I replied, "yes the Assembly will not obey your orders."

The above extract form late Mr. Seervai's commentaries on the Constitutional Law of India shows that the President is not bound by the advisory opinion of the Supreme Court. But in *Special Reference No. 1 of 1998* the Attorney General submitted before the court that the Union of India will accept and treat as binding the answers of the Supreme Court to the questions set out in the reference. What is the effect of this concession when the constitutional position is that the Union of India is not bound by the reference? Khanna, J. in *Kesavananda Bharti vs. State of Kerala*[21] made some observations regarding this issue as under:[22]

"Matters relating to construction of an Article of the Constitution or the Constitutional validity of an impugned provision have to be decided in the light of the relevant provisions and a concession made by the State Counsel or the opposite counsel would not absolve the Court from determining the matter independently of the concession. A counsel may sometimes make a concession in order to secure favourable verdict on another important point, such a concession would, however, not be binding upon another counsel. It is well-settled that admission or concession, made on a point of law by the Counsel is not binding upon the parties represented by thc Counsel, far less would such admission or concession was erroneous and not justified in law. It may, therefore, be laid down as a broad proposition that Constitutional matters cannot be disposed of in terms of agreement or

21. (1973) 4 SCC 225.
22. *Id.* at 820.

compromise between the parties, nor can the decision in such disputes in order to be binding upon others be based upon a concession even though the concession emanates from the State Counsel. The concession has, to be made good and justified in the light of the relevant provisions."

Therefore, though the Attorney General submitted that the Union of India would be bound by the reference, the Union of India is not bound by the opinion since an opinion is not "law declared" within the meaning of Article 141 of the Constitution. There cannot be estoppel against the Constitution.

5. IS THE OPINION BINDING ON THE SUPREME COURT

In *Ahmedabad St. Xavier's College Society* v. *State of Gujarat*[23] (which was decided by a bench of nine judges), Reddy, J. (for himself and Alagiriswami, J.) categorically held that the report which the Supreme Court makes to the President is not binding on the Supreme Court in any subsequent matter where, in a concrete case an analogous provision may be called in question, though it is entitled to great weight. If a smaller bench of the Supreme Court disagrees with the opinion of a larger bench since the smaller bench is not bound by an opinion, it may be technically correct, but it will be an anomalous situation that a smaller bench can overrule a decision rendered by a larger bench merely on the ground that the larger bench only gave opinion to the President.

To avoid the above stated situation, a five-judge bench in an appeal, referred a matter to a bench of nine judges where it could have referred it to a bench of seven judges. The reason as to why the five-judge bench referred the case to a nine-judges bench is to give weight and respect to the opinion rendered.

23. AIR 1978 SC 441.

6. IS THE OPINION BINDING ON HIGH COURT AND OTHER COURTS IN THE COUNTRY

This question was answered in affirmative by *Chandrachud, C.J.* in *re Special Courts Bill, 1978.*[24] He said:

> *"It would be strange that a decision given by this Court on a question of law in a dispute between two private parties should be binding on all courts in this country but the advisory opinion should bind no one at all, even if, as in the instant case, it is given after issuing notice to all interested parties, after hearing everyone concerned who desired to be heard, and after a full consideration of the questions raised in the reference."*

Almost everything that could possibly be urged in favour of and against the Bill was urged before us and to think that our opinion is an exercise in futility in deeply frustrating. While saying this, we are not unmindful of the view expressed by an eminent writer that although the advisory opinion given by the Supreme Court has high persuasive authority, it is not law declared by it within the meaning of Article 141.[25]

A nine-judge bench of the Supreme Court in *Supreme Court Advocates-on-Record Association* v. *Union of India*[26] construed the constitutional provisions regarding the appointment of judges to the higher judiciary and the transfer of judges of high courts. Five years after this decision was rendered, the President of India referred nine questions for the consideration of the Supreme Court and the reference recited that doubts had arisen about the interpretation of the law laid down by the Supreme Court in *Judges Case II.* A nine-judge bench entertained the reference and answered the questions. It is respectfully submitted that the Supreme Court ought not to have entertained the reference as it will tantamount to sitting in appeal over its own judgment and this aspect was stated

24. (1979) 1 SCC 380.
25. Seervai, H.M. : *Constitutional Law of India.* (New Delhi, Tripathi Publication, 1992) Vol. II, Page 1415 Para 25, 68.
26. (1993) 4 SCC 441.

with great clarity by Sawant, J. *in re Couvery Water Disputes Tribunal*:[27]

> *"When this court in its adjudicatory jurisdiction pronounces its authoritative opinion on a question of law, it cannot be said that there is any doubt about the question of law or the same is res integra so as to require the President to know what the true position of law on the question is. The decision of this court on a question of law is binding on all courts and authorities. Hence under the said clause the President can refer a question of law only when this court has not decided it. Secondly, a decision given by this court can be reviewed only under Article 137 read with Rule 1 of Order 40 of the Supreme Court Rules, 1966 and on the conditions mentioned therein. When, further, this court overrules the view of law expressed by it in an earlier case, it does not do so sitting in appeal and exercising an appellate jurisdiction over the earlier decision."*

It does so in exercise of its inherent power and only in exceptional circumstances such as when the earlier decision is per incuriam or is delivered in the absence of relevant material facts or if it is manifestly wrong and productive of public mischief. Under the Constitution such appellate jurisdiction does not vest in this court, nor can it be vested in it by the President under Article 143. To accept Shri Nariman's contention would mean that the advisory jurisdiction under Article 143 is also an appellate jurisdiction of this court over its own decision between the same parties and the executive has a power to ask this court to revise its decision. If such power is read in Article 143 it would be a serious inroad into the independence of judiciary.

Therefore, it is submitted that though it was specifically observed that the Union of India is not asking for reconsideration of the judgment in *Judges Case II*, yet it had the effect of the opinion bench sitting as an appellate court over its own judgment pronounced in *Judges Case II*.

27. *Supra* n. 8 at 145.

7. DOES THE ADVISORY OPINION BIND THE CHIEF JUSTICE OF INDIA

In *Special Reference No. 1 of 1998* a nine-judge bench of this Supreme Court answered certain questions of law and opinion was given on the role of the Chief Justice of India in the matter of appointment of judges to the higher judiciary and transfer of high court judges. It is submitted that an advisory opinion binds no one, as there is no litigant involved in a Presidential reference under Article 143. Same was the view taken by Gajendragadkar, C.J. *in re Keshav Singh* wherein the learned Chief Justice opined that the opinion tendered by the Supreme Court under Article 143(1) binds no one. In *Special Ref. No. 1 of 1998*, the Chief Justice of India was not a party and thus he cannot be said to be bound by the opinion given therein.

8. CAN THE SUPREME COURT MODIFY ITS EARLIER JUDGMENT IN AN ADVISORY OPINION

In *Supreme Court Advocate-on-Record Association* v. *Union of India*[28] a nine-judge by a majority of 7 to 2 held that in matters of appointment of judges to the Supreme Court under Article 124(2), the views of the collegium consisting of the Chief Justice of India and two senior most judges of the Supreme Court will have primacy. This was modified in *Special Ref. No. 1 of 1998*. The collegium's membership was altered from Chief Justice of India plus two senior most judges to Chief Justice of India plus four senior most judges of the Supreme Court. Since the law declared by the Supreme Court is contained in *Judges Case II*, it cannot be altered in an advisory opinion, which does not have the effect of declaring the law. Therefore, it is respectfully submitted that the alteration of the judgment of the Supreme Court in an advisory opinion has no effect. When a judgment of the Supreme Court rendered inter parties and an opinion of the Supreme Court under Article 143(1) conflicts, the judgment will prevail and not the opinion.

28. (1993) 4 SCC 441.

9. POINTS OF CONCLUSION

1. This Article confers upon the President the power to consult the Supreme Court upon any question of public importance as the President may think fit, whether of law or of fact and whether or not such questions relate to the functions and duties of the President. The President's opinion as to the question being of public importance is not open to question.
2. It is not necessary that the question on which the opinion of the Court is sought must have arisen actually. It is competent for the President to make a reference at an anterior stage, namely, when he is satisfied that such question 'is likely to arise'.
3. Clause (1) of Act, 143 empowers the President to refer to the Supreme Court a question of law or fact which has arisen or is likely to arise. In case, the Court has already pronounced a judgment on a question of law then it can not be said that a doubt exists regarding that question. The President can refer a question of law only when the Supreme Court has not decided it. The advisory jurisdiction under Art. 143 is not an appellate jurisdiction of the Supreme court over its own decisions. The Executive has no power to ask the Supreme Court to revise its decision.
4. While under Cl. (2), it is obligatory on the Supreme Court to entertain a reference and to report to the President its opinion thereon, the Court has, under Cl. (1), a discretion in the matter and may, in a proper case, decline to express any opinion on the questions submitted to it, e.g.,

   (i) Where the question referred to is a political one, as distinguished from the constitutional validity of a Bill or Act.
   (ii) Where it is incapable of being answered.
   (iii) Where the question is hypothetical or speculative or superfluous. But the mere possibility that a pending Bill may undergo

changes in course of legislation, would not make the question of constitutionality of a pending Bill hypothetical.

(iv) Where it is vague, unless the vagueness is cleared by the written briefs and submissions of the parties before the Court.

(v) Where the Court considers that the question does not arise in the facts and circumstances of the case.

5. It is for the President to determine what question should be referred, including a pending Bill, on the other hand, the Supreme court cannot go beyond the questions referred and discuss other questions because any doubts may have arisen relating to them.
6. A reference on the question of constitutionality of a pending Bill neither encroaches upon the functions and privileges of the legislature, nor supplants Art. 32 of the Constitution.
7. If the reference raises a question of law or fact which is justiciable, the Court can not refuse to give its opinion on the mere ground of expedience or propriety.
8. It is neither obligatory for the Supreme Court to give its opinion under Cl. (1) whenever the President makes a reference, nor for the President to act upon the opinion pronounced by the Supreme Court.
9. In its advisory jurisdiction under Art. 143, the Supreme Court can not go into disputed questions of fact, or inquire into the truth or otherwise of the recitals in the Order of Reference or the bonafides of the order of reference.

6

Consultative Jurisdictions Impact on Indian Legal System

With the delivery and communication of an advisory opinion the task of the court is over. Thereafter it rests with the requesting organ to accept it and to implement it in action. The extent of this reception and the effect given to the opinions depends upon their nature, apart from political considerations. Thereupon depends also their effect on the court. The opinions are regarded by the requesting bodies by the court itself on being of equal authority with the judgments.

The Court has made significant contribution towards the development of law through its opinions. The Court plays an important part in the development of law through its advisory jurisdiction as it does through its judgments in cases. A prominent law expert[1] once suggested that the president might use the court in helping to develop law through advisory opinions. The primary and immediate effect of an advisory opinion in the resolution of the difficulty that leads to the request for it. But there are other long range effects that

1. Sloan: *Advisory jurisdiction*, 1962 ed. at p. 840.

necessarily flow from its authoritative character. The opinions produce effects upon the court and, like judgments, are a means of developing law. The great majority of the opinions given by the Supreme court were effective several of them facilitated the work of the legal system in India and some led to the settlement of disputes which has given rise to requests:

1. IN THE DELHI LAWS ACT REFERENCE

The Delhi Laws Act case was the first one in which the question of delegation of legislative power was considered by the Supreme Court. It is worth nothing that each of the seven judges who participated in the decision gave separate opinion. All of them were agreed on a few basic propositions, viz., from a practical point of view, the Parliament should have power to delegate legislative power to the executive. The judges, however, differed on drawing the limits which the Parliament could delegate its legislative powers to the executive, and expressed mainly two views, (i) the Parliament is free to delegate its legislative power to any extent subject to the limitation that it must not efface itself or abdicate its powers.[2] (ii) the Parliament could not delegate to another agency its 'essential' legislative function, which meant the formulation of policy and enacting it into a binding rule of conduct.[3]

Under the first view the Parliament would enjoy much more freedom to delegate its legislative power than under the second one. Nevertheless, a reading of the Court's opinion on the Delhi Laws Act does establish definitely as to which of the views had the support of a majority of judges, for the various opinions delivered therein are too repetitive, discursive and vague. The Supreme Court, thus, failed to evolve a clear and articulate principle regarding the permissible limits within which the Parliament could delegate its legislative powers. It in course of time, however, has become settled through several later judicial pronouncements.[4]

2. Per Fazal Ali, Shastri and Das, JJ.
3. Per Kania, Mahajan and Mukherjee, JJ.
4. Bagla *v*. State of M.P., A.I.R. 1954 SC 465. Raj Narain *v*. Chairman, Patna Administration Committee, A.I.R. 1954 S.C 569.

The prevailing principle is that essential powers of legislation can not be delegated. The legislature can not delegate its function of laying down legislative-policy in respect of a bill and its formulation as rule of conduct. The Legislature must declare the policy of the law and the legal principles which are to control any given cases and must provide a standard to guide the officials to execute the law.

The Delhi Laws Act Reference case, however, proved to be very useful in the sense that it gave timely guidance to the Central Executive regarding the scope and extent of its legislative powers under the Act, and other related legislation, thus avoiding embarrassment to the Government and hardship to the people which might have been occasioned if subsequently any Act extended to Delhi or any other Part C State were to be declared *ultra vires* of the Constitution, thus, disturbing the manifold rights and titles, which would have come into existence before such a judicial declaration.

2. IN THE KERALA EDUCATION BILL REFERENCE

The Kerala Educational Bill Reference[5] was made in a politically heated situation. The Central Government made a skillful use of the provision of seeking advisory opinion of Supreme Court. The Reference saved the Central Government from political embarrassment as well as mollified public opinion and helped in the removal of the lacunae in the Bill as discovered by the Supreme Court.

On the issue of the Kerala Education Bill, the Central Government had not much of the choice. Had it sought amendments in the Bill by the Kerala Assembly on its own accord, its political motives would have been questioned because the Government at the Centre and the State belonged to two different political parties. Therefore, an objective assessment of the Bill by the Supreme Court was the alternative available. The controversy was couched in legalistic and Constitutional terms and the reference did not raise any political issue, although the motivation behind the reference might have been political. On the whole, however, the matter

5. A.I.R. 1958 S.C. 956 at p. 992.

may be said to be the precursor of healthy conventions in the area if federalism, in so far as even when the Centre could have vetoed the Bill but it did not, without seeking an opinion of a forum whose objectivity and impartiality could not be challenged by any body.

The Court, in the course of the opinion, laid down certain important principles regarding the interpretation of the Constitution as follows:

1. In determining the scope and ambit of the fundamental rights relied on by or on behalf of any person or body, the Court may not entirely ignore the directive principles of a state policy, but should adopt the principle of harmonious construction, and should attempt to give effect to both as much as possible.
2. The protection of Article 30(1) extends to the educational institutions or minorities, religious or linguistic, whether established before or after the commencement of the Constitution. It also extends to aided schools, where there are scholars from outside the minority community. For, Article 29(2) precludes aided schools from denying admissions on the grounds only of religion, language, caste, race or any of them.
3. The ambit of the right conferred by Article 30(1) is to be determined from the point of view of the educational institutions itself. The Constitution does not lay down any restrictions as regards subjects to be taught therein.
4. The true intention of Article 30(1) is to equip minorities with a shield whereby they could defend themselves against attacks by the majorities, religious or linguistic and not to arm them with a sword whereby they could compel the majorities to grant concession.

This reference has been cited in many cases. In *St. Xavier's College* v. *State of Gujarat*[6] Supreme Court followed the view of

6. AIR 1974 SC at p. 1389.

Kerala educational bill reference that the regularity measure by the State should not restrict the right of administration but facilitate it through the instrumentality of the management of the minority institution. In case of *Uni Krishnan* v. *State of A.P.*[7] honourable court was agree with Kerala's reference that right to recognition or affiliation is not a fundamental right.

In a landmark decision in *T.M.A. Pai Foundation* v. *State of Karnataka*[8] an 11-judge Constitution Bench following the reference of Kerala held that State Government and universities cannot regulate the admission policy of unaided educational institutions run by linguistic and religious minorities but state governments and universities can specify academic qualifications for students and make rules and regulations for maintaining academic standards again, in a landmark judgment of *P.A. Inamdar* v. *State of Maharashtra*[9] Kerala reference has been cited. Supreme Court held that neither in the judgment of TMA Pai nor in Kerala Education Bill decision there is any thing which would allow the state to regulate or control admissions in the unaided educational institutions. Thus, the private unaided professional institutions (minority and non-minority) cannot be forced to accept reservation policy of the State.

The reference has been used for interpretation of Anglo-Indians under article 366(2). In case of *State of Bombay* v. *Bombay Education Society*[10] reference is followed. In this case an order of state government which prevented the Anglo Indian School to admit students of other communities was held unconstitutional on ground that it prevented the Anglo Indian School from performing this constitutional obligation of admitting at least 40% students of other communities. Under Article 337 the State cannot impose any other obligation on the Anglo Indian Schools on a condition to receive grants.

The reference of Kerala educational bill is used in explaining the relationship between directive principles of state policy and fundamental rights. The Supreme Court observed

7. (1993) ISCC at p. 645.
8. AIR 2003 SC at p. 355.
9. AIR 2005 SC at p. 3286.
10. AIR 1954 SC at p. 561.

that though the directive principles cannot override the fundamental rights, nevertheless in determining the scope and ambit of fundamental rights the court may not entirely ignore the directive principles but should adopt the principles of harmonious construction and should attempt to give effect to both as much as possible.

3. IN THE BERUBARI REFERENCE

By this reference, the highest Court of the land was called upon to advice the President as to how an agreement with a foreign country which involved cession of territory, could be implemented while dwelling over the matter, the Court considered the scope and extent of Article 3 of the Constitution. Clause (c) of the Article deals with the diminution of the area of any State and this was the only clause relevant for the purpose of the reference. The Court rejected the Attorney General's contention that clause (c) of Article 3 was wide enough to cover even cession of Indian territory to a foreign State.

It was held that when the Constitution did not expressly provide for acquisition of foreign territory, it must not have intended to provide for cession of Indian Territory to a foreign country by implication under Article 3(c). The Court concluded that a part of the Territory of India could not be ceded by an ordinary Act of the Parliament, but it could only be done by an amendment of the Constitution under Article 368.

As a result of this opinion, the Constitution (Ninth Amendment) Act was passed and the Agreement was implemented. Amendment was made in the First Schedule to cede some Indian territory to Pakistan as envisaged in the Agreement.

The opinion on the Reference came in for consideration in *Ram Kishore Sen's case*.[11] In this case, the demarcation of boundaries which miserably affected a number of people residing in the demarcated areas of Berubari was challenged. It was contended that there must be a law passed by Parliament

11. Ram Kishore Sen and Others *v.* Union of India, AIR 1985 Cal. 282.

under Entry 14, List-I, Schedule VII[12] of the Constitution or also Article 3 should be amended so as to exclude its operation in the case of cession of territory to a foreign power. The opinion of the Supreme Court in the *Berubari Union's case* was, it was argued, wrong and was not binding upon the Calcutta High Court, being an advisory opinion. But the Calcutta High Court did not agree with this contention and, upholding the opinion on the Reference, held that a Parliament's statute, in addition to amendment of the First Schedule of the Constitution was not necessary. The question of amending Article 3 did not arise.

The opinion was considered and followed in *Bhansali's case* as well.[13] However, according to one commentator[14] on Constitutional law this judgment was clearly wrong, and that an amendment of the Constitution was absolutely unnecessary, because a law under Article 3 would have been adequate to implement the Agreement.

Again the opinion of the court is cited for interpretation of preamble of the constitution. In this context court has opined that the preamble of the constitution in a key to open the mind of the makers and shows the general purpose for which they made the several provisions in the constitution.

4. IN THE SEA CUSTOMS ACT REFERENCE

The Reference, the fourth one under the present Constitution, dealt with a knotty problem of Centre-State relationship in financial matters. The opinion nicely explained the word 'property' in Articles 285 and 289 to mean property itself, not the various aspects of property, i.e., manufacture, gift and import or export. The majority of the Judges propounded the theory that the Central Government could levy customs duty on goods imported or exported or an excise duty on the

12. Seventh Schedule, List 1, Entry-14 Provides:
"Entering into treaties and agreement with foreign countries and implementing of treaties, agreements and conventions with foreign countries".
13. S.R. Bhansali *v.* Union of India, AIR 1973 Raj 48 at p. 50.
14. Navshirvan H. Jhabvala, "The Constitution of India", p. 226.

goods produced or manufactured by a State Government irrespective of whether it was used or not for purposes of trade or business.

To exempt the export or import made by a State from customs duty would seriously impair the power of Parliament to regulate foreign trade by using its taxing powers. Similarly, exempting manufacture of goods by a State from union taxation would adversely affect the Central power to regulate inter-State commerce. Article 289, the majority opinion of the Court held, bars imposition of Central taxes on property and not those taxes which may indirectly affect or are in respect of income or property. The customs duty is a tax on 'import or export' and excise on 'production or manufacture' and none of these taxes are on property as such. Fortunately, majority opinion is almost in line with the position in other sister federation.[15]

A principle that the Centre was under obligation to share its revenues with the States, was established by the Court in its opinion. All revenues occurring in the states from their taxes is exclusively used by them, but all taxes by the Centre are not meant for its exclusive use. The Centre is required to share some of its taxes with the States. Therefore, Union's revenue raising capacity should not be impaired by interpreting the exemption in favour of the States broadly.

The import and export duties were a well recognised mode of controlling trade with countries and the exclusive power to legislate in respect of foreign trade would be impaired if such duties could not be levied on goods imported or exported by States. In this opinion the majority evolved the norms that on a true interpretation of Article 289(1) the immunity granted to the States in respect of union taxation could not be extended to the customs and excise duties intended to be imposed on the State Governments.

The issue well deserved the Presidential Reference to the Supreme Court and the opinion given on it is a everlasting impact on the validity of the Indian federalism in Indian circumstances. In the older federation under the Government of India Act, 1935, the Federal Court tried to give more and

15. U.S.A., Canada and Australia.

more autonomy to the Provinces. Unlike the Federal Court, the Supreme Court has declined to accept the doctrine of autonomous State rights because it would amount to weakening the Centre and the Constitutional fabric as well. Keeping in view the situation, circumstances and the peculiar federal set-up in India the Supreme Court has contributed to establish certain norms to provide the federal structure with a strong 'bias towards the Centre.

5. IN THE KESHAV SINGH REFERENCE

While evaluating the opinion of the Supreme Court, a reference to the decision of the Allahabad High Court on the *habeas corpus* petition of Keshav Singh, will be fully relevant after its final hearing in 1965, dismissing the petition, the Allahabad High Court ruled that the U.P. Assembly had power to commit a person for its contempt like the House of Commons in England. It held that the detention of the petition did not violate the provisions of Articles 22(2) of the Constitution. Their Lordships remarked further, "Once we have come to the conclusion that the Legislative Assembly has power and jurisdiction to commit for its contempt and to impose the sentence, we can not go into the question of the correctness, propriety or legality of the Commitment.[16]

This Court can not in a petition under Article 226 of the Constitution sit in appeal over the power of the Legislative Assembly committing the petitioner for its contempt." But what is important is that the High Court went into the facts of the case which it found insufficient for arriving at the conclusion that the commitment of the petitioner for contempt was malafide. In fact, the High Court regarded the action of the Legislation Assembly as *justiciable* before a court of law.

This view of the High Court contradicts the view of the Supreme Court expressed in its advisory opinion delivered by it on September 30, 1964 and is in line with the *Searchlight case*[17] and the minority opinion of Justice A.K. Sarkar. It would, however, be pointed out that a common trend runs through all

16. AIR 1965 SC 745.
17. M.S.M. Sharma *v.* Sri Krishna Sinha, AIR 1959 SC 395.

these judgments and that is that the judiciary in India has not treated the question as beyond its pale and purview. It has reserved to itself the right to look into all cases of breach of privileges of the Legislature and decide them on merits while admitting the power of the legislature to commit for its contempt like the mother of Parliaments. It has also permitted the suppression of Article 19(1)(a) by the privileges of the Legislatures.

The difference of opinion among the judges has been that some of them have regarded the punitive action taken by the Legislatures as being in conformity with the Articles dealing with fundamental right while others have regarded it as violative of them.

A similar dispute arose in 1984 in Ecnada privilege issue case. It has once again made the question of codification of privileges matter of serious discussion. The chief editor of a Telegu Newspaper Ecnada was found guilty of contempt of the Andhra Pradesh legislative council for publishing an item—"Elders commotion"—in his newspaper and was ordered by the house to appear before it for admonition.

The Supreme Court had issued an order to the secretary of the house not to arrest him. He refused to appear in the house unless arrested and taken. Despite the courts stay order, the council proceeded with the discussion of the matter and during the discussion the members expressed the view that the house was Supreme and sovereign in the matter of privileges and the court had no place in the matter and it should not surrender to the Supreme Court and the Editor should be arrested and brought before the house for admonition.

At this stage seeing that the matter was taking an ugly conflict between the legislature and the court, the Chief minister intervened and requested the house of postpone the deliberations on the subject as he had requested the President to refer to the matter to the Supreme Court for its advisory opinion. Although the matter had been diffused for the time being what could have become the worst constitutional confrontation between the legislative council of a state and the Supreme Court.

Once again there was a direct confrontation between the legislature and the court when the Tamil Nadu Assembly

Speaker issued warrants of arrest against the editor of Tamil Nadu daily "Kovai Mala Murasu". The privilege committee had directed the editor to appear before the Bar of the house to receive a reprimand for allegedly publishing a false report the AIADMK MLA had attacked a DMK MLA in the assembly for he sought to raise the issue of his life being in danger.

The Supreme Court stayed the summons issued by the speaker. The Speaker had taken the stand that he was not bound by the order of the court. The Attorney conceded before the court that he was not bound by the order of the court.

The Attorney conceded before the court that the resolution of the assembly constituted contempt of Court. Such actions like that of the Tamil Nadu assembly are calculated to destroy the very fabric of the constitution.

To sum up, it must be stated that there is, no doubt, a conflict between the provisions of the Constitution dealing with fundamental rights and those dealing with parliamentary rights and those dealing with parliamentary privileges. *K.M. Munshi*[18] himself, an active participant in Constitution making, has admitted that the framers could not foresee the conflict. So far four solutions have been suggested to remove the impasse. Renounded law expert *Shri K. Santhanam*[19] suggested that the legislatures should voluntarily surrender the right of arrest and imprisonment, "then the Parliament may enact a law by which the government can prosecute at the request of the Speaker or chairman any person who is considered guilty of contempt of the House of Legislature by its committee of privileges. As an alternative it is necessary to amend the Constitution deleting the reference to the House of Commons and adding a schedule of privileges or empowering the Parliament to formulate them by law."

A third suggestion has been that legislatures should not try the case of its own contempt just as no court of law should

18. CAD, Vol. VIII, p. 273.
19. Delivering his second lecture under the series "Conventions and Properties of Parliamentary Democracy in India" at the Indian Institute of Public Administration, New Delhi on September 30, 1964.

be allowed to try its contempt.[20] But such a suggestion, apart from being novel is not likely to find acceptance. The solution of the problem lies in amending the Constitution in such a way as to remove the conflict between privileges of the Legislature and fundamental rights of the people. Actually such a concept of rights is untenable in society. The fathers of the Constitution were over enthusiastic in calling them "fundamental." Otherwise they would have simply called them rights.

6. IN PRESIDENTIAL POLL REFERENCE

The problem related with the election to the highest office of the land deserved a Reference to the highest Court of the land for opinion.[21] Articles 62, 56, 70 and 71 of the Constitution came in for interpretation by the Court. It was held that the fixed term of the office mentioned in Article 56(1) as well as the mandate in Article 62(1) require that the election to fill a vacancy caused by the expiry of the term of the office should be completed before the expiry of the term. A reliance was put on the *Khare's case*.[22]

Article 62 of the Constitution was held to be a mandatory one. The Court interpreted Article 71(4) broadly and hold that the language of this clause was of a very wide amplitude. It was observed by the Court that the constitutional declaration under Article 71(4) made it manifest that the existence of any vacancy for any reason whatever (including due to the dissolution of a State Assembly) among members of the Electoral College could not be ground for questioning the Presidential election.

The Court rightly declined to consider hypothetical questions posed before it during the arguments. What would be the position, it was asked, if there was malafide dissolution of a State Assembly or if there was malafide refusal to hold

20. Bhanwar Lal Garg, "Defence of Peopl'e Rights" in Political Scientist, Ranchi, Vol. I (1965), No. 2, pp. 27-28.
21. AIR 1974 SC 1682 at p. 1692.
22. Khare *v.* Election Commission of India, A.I.R. 1958 SC 139; Babu Rao Patel *v.* Zakir Hussain, A.I.R. 1968 SC 904; S.K. Singh *v.* V.V. Giri, A.I.R. (1971).

elections thereto within a reasonable time or what would be the effect of a substantial number of State Assemblies on the Presidential election? The Court declined to answer any of these questions at the stage. The Court also refused to consider the constitutionally of the Eleventh Amendment Act, 1961 because it was not a referred problem before the Court.

This opinion of the Supreme Court also got criticism from some sections of the society. The opposition parties and some jurists criticised the opinion. Though Mr. Palkiwala[23] considered the opinion sound in law, he felt that the main issue remained undecided. According to him the unreferred and undecided questions were far more important then the simple issue which the Court decided. He felt that the Court had left open the problem as to what would be the position when a substantial number of State Assemblies were dissolved or even the Lok Sabha was dissolved. Secondly, the Court also did not consider the effect on the Presidential election of a malafide refusal to hold elections to a State Assembly where there was sufficient time to hold it before a Presidential election.

When informed about the opinion, the Prime Minister, Mrs. Gandhi expressed her satisfaction that no constitutional deadlock would now be created, her prediction proved true and in the light of the Supreme Court's opinion the Presidential election took place peacefully without any further litigation or opposition.

7. IN THE SPECIAL COURTS BILL REFERENCE

By the Reference the Government sought the Court's advice on a very sensitive issue. It had, on the one hand, made creation promises to the people and it had to live up to them. On the other hand, it had the charge of being vindictive against itself. The Supreme Court by answering the Reference helped the Government in adopting a proper and constitutional course to deal with the high political offenders.

During the course of hearing, the Court examined the implications of Articles 14 and 21 in the context of special

23. Supra n. 22 at p. 144.

courts. The Chief Justice, who delivered the majority opinion of the Court observed that a State, in the exercise of its governmental power had, of necessity, to make laws operating differently on different groups or classes of persons to attain particular ends. The Court ruled that the classification must not be arbitrary but must be rational. In order to pass the test, two conditions must be fulfilled, namely – (a) classification must be founded on an intelligible differentia which distinguishes those that are grouped together from others, and (b) differentia must have a rational relation to the object sought to be achieved by the Act. By applying these tests, the Court concluded, that the classification provided for by the Special Court will was valid.

One point deserves notice here. It was for the first time that a whole Bill was referred to the Court for advice regarding its constitutional validity and no specific questions were formulated. The Chief Justice Y.V. Chandrachud[24] observed that at one stage the Court was 'seriously considering the proposal that it should return the reference unanswered'. The Court was, indeed, asked to first find the 'technical lacunae' and then to help remove them. In a sense, the Court was expected to perform the combined functions of the law officers of the Union as well as of a Joint Select Committee. The point at issue was whether or not there should be limits at all to the process of institutional collaboration and accommodation between the Court and the Parliament.

Upendra Baxi, a constitutional commentator analyses[25] the circumstances in which the Reference was made. Just a few weeks earlier, Charan Singh and Raj Narain were asked to resign from the Cabinet. Elections to Parliamentary Board were due to take place. There was a wide diversity of views on the best course of action in regard to the emergency trails. Some demanded immediate legal action. Others felt that the issue must be dealt within a manner that the Opposition would not find opportunity to misrepresent Janta Party's commitment to the cause of human rights and the rule of law. The Party felt

24. *Supra* n. 23.
25. Upendra Baxi, "The Indian Supreme Court and Politics," *JILI,* Vol. XIII at p. 98.

that was not the suitable time for proposing such legislation. But Ram Jethmalani had given the notice of the Bill. Some time had to be bought. Hence the omnibus reference with lightening speed was made to the Court. The issue was skillfully transferred from the Cabinet to the Court.

It was, observes Upendra Baxi,[26] expedient or prudent for politicians to refer the matter to the Court but it was inexpedient and imprudent for the Court, to entertain the Reference. In matters affecting the rights of people in criminal proceedings, advisory jurisdiction should not be invoked or granted, because the liberty and life of affected people is at stake.

The Court should have declined the Reference. In a society which so recently had claimed to having seen the restoration of rule of law, the Union Government should not simply be allowed the plea that it could not determine one its own what was fair and just procedure for expeditious trials of those ousted for power. Politicians of all shades insist that Parliament is supreme, that it represents the general will of the people and that it should have the final authority of changing the Constitution. If the claim is genuine, elected politicians can never publicly maintain in a democracy that they are unable to decide even the basic elements of a process of fair trial without prior advice from the Supreme Court. On principle, this reference was wrong. The Government should not have made it in the first place. For the Supreme Court to entertain it was equally wrong.

In spite of all this, it would be fair to think that the Reference was made in all honesty. The Bill was based on a broader policy of social justice. Such a law was long over due. Beyond the constitutional aspect of ensuring speedy justice in a special category of offences, the Court rightly addressed itself to the larger question of ensuring the integrity of public office in all circumstances. The Chief Justice, Mr. Chandrachud,[27] expressed this concern in words which touched the heart of the matter. "Parliamentary democracy", he observed,

26. *Supra* n. 25.
27. AIR 1979 SC 478.

> "will see its halcyon days when the law will provide for a speedy trial of all offenders who misuse the public offices held by them. Purity of public life is a desired goal at all times and in all situations, emergency or no emergency."

But this wider principle, pointed out Justice Krishna Iyer, would not be adequately served by the 'truncated provision' of special courts to try emergency offences and it was to be hoped that the Government would turn its attention to placing on the statute book permanent legislation so that the "common man may know that when public power is abused for private profit or personal revenge, the rule of law shall rapidly run them down."

8. IN THE JAMMU AND KASHMIR RESETTLEMENT ACT REFERENCE

The Jammu and Kashmir Resettlement Act was introduced during the regime of former Chief Minister Sheikh Mohammad Abdullah and came into effect on October 6, 1982. It was termed by then opposition parties as "notorious bill number nine". The bill was presented to the then Jammu and Kashmir Governor B.K. Nehru. He consulted *Nani Palkhivala* who look the view that the bill would not stand scrutiny in any court. However, the Jammu and Kashmir Assembly passed the act, and it was referred to the Supreme Court as Presidential reference No. 1 of 1982.[28]

In October 2001 the Supreme Court returned without comment a 1982 reference by the President seeking its opinion on the validity of the Jammu and Kashmir Resettlement Act. The President had asked the court to decide whether the Jammu and Kashmir Assembly was competent to pass the Act, which grants the right of return to State subjects who fled to Pakistan after the Partition riots of 1947. Almost all of the people were from the Jammu region, which unlike Kashmir, saw bitter violence during the days of partition. Ever since the

28. Sp. re. no. (1) of 1982.

Supreme Court chose to reopen the two-decade-old issue, both the BJP and the N.C. have been busy cashing in on it by fuelling communal anxieties.

Sheikh Mohammad Abdullah[29] brought forward the Jammu and Kashmir Resettlement Act towards the end of his life, when he was seeking to reinvent the N.C. as a party of the Islamic Right. The Act allowed the refugees created by Partition to return to Jammu and Kashmir and reclaim their properties. While the idea of the Act is to offer an opportunity for communal reconciliation, its realisation could bring about exactly the opposite result. The reasons are not hard to see.

Jammu and Kashmir continues to refuse to grant full State subject rights to the many Hindu and Sikh refugees who came from what is now Pakistan Occupied Kashmir (POK). Legally, their children cannot seek admission in government-run institutions or employment. Although almost all such refugees have found ways to bypass the law, the obvious discrimination still rankles.

Hindu chauvinist groups in Jammu have been quick to make use of this volatile situation. For example, the BJP Member of the Legislative Assembly for the Hiranagar constituency, *Prem Lal*,[30] has claimed that the State government is "hell bent on changing the demography of the Jammu region". In a petition filed before the Supreme Court on November 29, 2002 the Panthers Party has argued that the Act will allow in even the "Taliban, with fraudulent certificates as descendents of anyone". This kind of rhetoric is falling on receptive ears. "Will the Pakistan government give us back the land and the homes we left in 1947?" asks *Mohinder Bakshi*,[31] whose family arrived in Kathua shortly after Partition.

Predictably, Hindu reaction has fuelled Muslim chauvinism. An N.C. politician from Rajouri, Tazeem Dar, made the typical, but bizarre claim that the Act will unite Muslims on both sides of the Line of Control (LoC) and thus

29. *Supra* n. 28
30. Ganjoo, R.C., "J&K newsletter unsettling Resettlement Act." available at www.organiser.org accessed on 7.18.2007.
31. Datar, P. Arvind, "J&K: legalised discrimination" available www.the hindu.com. accessed on 07.18.2007.

end the conflict in Jammu and Kashmir. Chief Minister Farooq Abdullah, for his part, has flatly refused to listen to criticism of his decision to make the Act applicable to Muslims in the State. "Leaving aside the Act itself," says CPI(M) State Secretary *Mohammad Yusuf Tarigami,*[32] "its implementation has nothing to do with communal reconciliation and everything to do with the worst kind of communal opportunism. The BJP and the N.C. are showing themselves to be two sides of the same coin."

No one is quite certain just how many refugees left the Jammu province in the wake of the riots of 1947. Along with their legal heirs, the figure could be as high as 200,000. Nor is it clear just how the Resettlement Act would actually work. Ironically, the refugees' property has all been leased out by the State government for periods of up to 99 years. More important, the Act itself will not automatically allow refugees from India to return, since the visa restrictions of the Union government will still apply. People's Democratic Party leader Mehbooba Mufti said: "No one in their right minds will want to come to the State, when everyone who can afford to get out is doing so."

Under other circumstances, the Resettlement Act would have enabled many people to return to the homes and lands they left under the most painful circumstances. Many families in Jammu have relatives across the border who may wish to return to spend their last years in the country where they grew up, surrounded by the kin from whom they were sundered. But the Act, sadly, is not about healing the wounds of 1947; it is about exploiting that tragedy.[33] The anger caused by the Act will allow the N.C. and the BJP to carve up neatly the votes of their respective communal constituencies. For the real victims of 1947, it will most likely do nothing at all.

32. Legal correspondent, "J&K Resettlement Act stayed". available at www.hindu.on.net.com. accessed on 07.17.2007.
33. Legal Correspondent, "J&K government to implement Resettlement Act," available www.times of india.india times.com accessed on 07.18.2007.

9. IN CAUVERY WATER DISPUTE REFERENCE

The Cauvery water dispute is one of the oldest dispute over water. The first dispute was in 1892 between the princely state of Mysore and Madras Presidency which imposed restrictions on Mysore to build storage reservoirs on the Cauvery. An agreement of 1924 was signed between two government formed the basis of all future negotiations since independence between the two states. Madras was definitely on a position of advantage in relation to Mysore since all major development projects in Mysore had to have the final approval of the Madras government.

Dispute comes into a new phase when on June 2, 1990 a tribunal known as "Cauvery Water Disputes Tribunal" was constituted by the central government. The tribunal gave an interim order in June 1991 directing the State of Karnataka to release a particular quantity of water for the State of Tamil Nadu. The Karnataka government resented the decision of the tribunal and promulgated an ordinance empowering. The government not to honour the interim order of the Tribunal.[34]

The Tamil Nadu government protested against the action of the Karnataka, hence the President made a reference to the Supreme Court under article 143 of the constitution. The court held that the Karnataka ordinance was unconstitutional as it nullifies the decision of the Tribunal appointed under the Central Act (The Inter-state Water Dispute Act, 1956) which has been enacted under Article 262 of the constitution. The ordinance is also against the principles of the rule of law as it has assumed the role of a judge in its own cause.

The Cauvery water disputes Tribunal was the country's first water tribunal to give an interim order. No other water tribunal, be it Narmada or Krishna had passed interim orders. The 205 TMC ft. water that it awarded to Tamil Nadu was arrived at after taking into account the 10 year availability of water from 1981 to 1990. It ignored two good years and two bad years. The remaining six years were considered the base for arriving at the figure after the opinion delivered in 1992, on

34. Subramanian, T.S., "An Award in sight" available at www.hindu.net.com accessed on 26.07.2007.

August 11, 1998 "The Cauvery River Authority (CRA)" was formed. It comprises the Prime Minister, and the Chief Minister of Tamil Nadu, Karnataka, Kerala and Pondicherry. It was to decide how to share the water in a distress year, aided by a monitoring committee consisting of officials and the Chief Secretaries and irrigation officials of four states.

After the opinion by the Supreme Court, the Cauvery Water disputes tribunal begins its working in 1992. The Tribunal chaired by N.P. Singh, with S.D. Agarwala and W.S. Roy as members. The cross-examination of witness cited by the four parties to the dispute concluded in December 2001, after eight years when the opinion was delivered. During the cross examination, nine witnesses cited by Tamil Nadu tendered evidence on the sharp fall in the inflow of Cauvery water into Tamil Nadu from the early 1980s. Karnataka cited eight witnesses. They contended that Tamil Nadu's water reading were wrong. The witnesses cited by Kerala wanted diversion of water from Cauvery basin for the generation of electricity.[35]

The Cauvery Water Disputes Tribunal announced its verdict on February 5, 2007. According to its verdict, Tamil Nadu gets 419 billion ft^3 (12 km^3) of Cauvery water while Karnataka gets 270 billion ft^3 (7.6 km^3). The actual release of water by Karnataka to Tamil Nadu is to be 192 billion ft^3 (5.4 km^3) annually. Further, Kerala will get 30 billion ft^3 and Puducherry 20 billion ft^3. The government of Karnataka, unhappy with the decision, filed a revision petition before the tribunal seeking a review. Following the final award of the tribunal, violence against Tamil population was anticipated in parts of Karnataka and consequently the city of Bangalore was put on high alert.

The Satluj-Yamuna canal reference is pending before the Supreme Court. Cauvery reference will work as a guiding lamp post for it.

10. IN RAM JANMABHOOMI REFERENCE

This was the first reference in which the President of

35. Document from International Water History Association, "Water and Civilization" available at www.iwha.polaire.net.

India had referred a question of fact. Before this, all the ten references was related to questions of law. There was a long-standing dispute relating to the disputed structure in Ayodhya which led to the communal tension and violence resulting in loss of many lives and destruction of property throughout the country. With a view to maintain communal harmony and fraternity amongst the people of India the Union Government issued an ordinance acquiring certain areas at Ayodhya which subsequently became an act. The question of fact referred to the Supreme Court for its advisory opinion.[36]

In Special Reference No. of 1993, the question referred to the Supreme Court for its advisory opinion was whether a Hindu temple or religious structure existed at a particular place in Ayodhya.

The Supreme Court refused to give its opinion on this reference for several reasons. According to the majority opinion, the matter under reference was already the subject-matter of litigation in the lower courts, wherein the dispute between the parties would be adjudicated, and, therefore, the reference made under Art. 143(1) became superfluous and unnecessary.

Two of the Judges (Ahmadi & Bharucha, J.J.) in a separate concurring opinion maintained that the Supreme Court could decline to answer a question referred to it under Art. 143 if it considers it to be not proper or possible to do so, but the Court must indicate its reasons. These learned Judges gave the following reasons for refusing to answer the reference in the instant case:

(1) The reference favoured one religious community and disfavoured another. The purpose of the reference was, therefore, opposed to secularism and was unconstitutional; the reference served no constitutional purpose.
(2) The Government proposed to use the Court's opinion as a springboard for negotiations. It did not propose to settle the dispute in terms of the Court's opinion.

---

36. Lal, Dr. B., Ayodhya and after, (Madhav Pub., 1992) at 179-80.

(3) To answer the reference it would be necessary to take evidence of experts, such as, historians, archaeologists and have them cross-examined.

(4) The principal protagonists of the two stands would not appear in the reference. Any opinion expressed by the Supreme Court would be criticised by one or both sides. This would impair the Court's credibility and compromise the dignity and honour of the Court.

The Court upheld the validity of the acquisition of 67 acres of land in Ayodhya. But it allowed revival of the title suit pertaining to the disputed site. There title cases are pending before the Allahabad High Court. Till the disposal of the dispute regarding the ownership of the land on which the Babri Masjid stood the government would act as a receiver of this portion of the land it cannot transfer this part of the acquired land to any third party and would return it to whoever was found to be the original owner by the Allahabad High Court.

Meanwhile, there are doubts about how independently the judiciary apparatus can still function in the present circumstances. When justice K.M. Pandey ordered the locks removed from the Mandir gate, on February 1, 1986, many secularists said that this was a Congress-sponsored *quid pro quo* with the Hindus in return for the infamous Muslim Women's Bill. That is of course a very serious allegation against the judge. What did happen, is that the Congress government first asked the VHP to file a petition to get the locks removed. When the VHP refused, the Congress moved one of its own people to file the petition, which was granted by the judge. This did not require any bribing or otherwise influencing of the judge; the argumentation of the petition was such that a positive Court ruling was virtually assured.[37]

Shortly before the Kar Seva, the same judge was refused a promotion by the Union Law Minister at the insistence of U.P. Chief Minister Mulayam Singh Yadav, against the advice

37. Document "Ram Janmabhoomi and the Courts", available at www.bharatvani.orgaccessed on 26.07.2007.

of the senior judges, which is normally followed by Mulayam, in the middle of his propaganda and military build-up to prevent the Kar Seva programme, justified his veto on the ground that justice Pandey is *a communalist.*

Lawyers and judges have protested against this interference. If a judge can be punished by the executive power for the contents of his Court rulings, then that is an intolerable breach of the separation of the legislative, executive and judicial powers, one of the cornerstones of a modern democratic polity. The secularists, champions of modernity against obscurantism, have in this case condoned this Ancient Regime practice by their silence. They have not stood up to remind Mulayam that, according to their own earlier opinion, justice K.M. Pande had only acted on government orders.

In January 1991, when Mulayam and the central government had become critically dependent on Congress support, and Congress did its best to placate the Hindu electorate as much as possible, justice K.M. Pandey was given his promotion after all.

The more fundamental question in the debate on the juridical dimension of the Ayodhya, is whether the issue involved can at all be adjudicated by a law court charged with checking legality in terms of the laws of the Indian Republic founded in 1947 and endowed with a Constitution in 1950. The VHP has rejected the authority of the Courts in this matter. The Babri Masjid groups have opposed this stand and demanded that the VHP abide by the Court verdict. But in October 1990, Immam Bukhari of the BMAC has also declared that if the court ruling goes against the Muslim demands, then he will not accept it, and an agitation against the verdict will be launched.

History teaches us lessons and it gives suggestions, how to deal with new circumstances. *Mahatma Gandhi*[38] during his last days on November 21, 1947 at a prayer meeting said :

> "I cannot help mentioning that according to the information received by me 137 mosques have been

38. Ajai and Shukuntala Singh, "How Mahatma Gandhi's Plan can solve Temple Issue", available at www.ajaishakuntala.tripond.com accessed on 26.07.2007.

destroyed in Delhi during the riots. Some of them have been converted into temples. There is one such mosque near Cannaught Place which can never remain unnoticed by any one. Today there is a tricolour flying over it. It has been changed into a temple by installing an idol in it. Desecrating in the mosques in this manner is a blot on Hinduism and Sikhism. It is gross adharma in my view. The blot which I have mentioned cannot be wiped out by saying that even the Muslims in Pakistan have desecrated the Hindu temples or changed them into mosques. In my view, any such act can only destroy religion, whether it is Hinduism, Sikhism or Islam."

The magic words are still relevant. We can take inspiration to solve the issue.

11. IN THE APPOINTMENT AND TRANSFER OF JUDGES REFERENCE

The independence and impartiality of the judiciary is one of the hall marks of the democratic set-up of Government. To give to the executive an unfettered discretion to decide the philosophy of the judges is to make the judiciary subservient to the executive.[39]

The Judges of the Supreme Court are appointed by the President. The Chief Justice of the Supreme Court is appointed by the President with the *consultation* of such of Judges of the Supreme Court and the High Courts as he deems necessary for the purpose. But in appointing other Judges, the President shall always consult the Chief Justice of India. He may consult such other Judges of the Supreme Court and High Courts as he may deem necessary.[40]

It should, however, be noted that the power of the President to appoint Judges is purely formal because in this matter he acts on the advice of the Council of Ministers. There was an apprehension that Executive may bring politics in the

39. AIR 1999 SC 1.
40. Article 124 (2).

appointment of Judges. The Indian constitution therefore does not leave the appointment of judges on the discretion of the Executive. The Executive under this Article is required to consult persons who are *ex-hypothesis* well qualified to give proper advice in matters of appointment of Judges.

Under Article 124(2) the President, in appointing other Judges of the Supreme Court is bound to consult the Chief Justice of India. But in appointing the Chief Justice of India he is not bound to consult anyone. The word 'may' used in Article 124 makes it clear that it is not mandatory on him to consult anyone.

Till 1973, the practice was to appoint the senior most Judge of the Supreme Court as the Chief Justice of India. This practice had virtually been transformed into a convention and was followed by the Executive without any exception. In 1956, the Law Commission headed by the then Attorney-General *M.C. Setalvad*[41] had criticised this practice and recommended that in appointing the Chief Justice of India the experience of a person as a judge, his administrative competence and merit should be judged and seniority should not only be the main consideration. The reports of the Law Commission were published as far back as in 1956. Since then 17 years had passed but no attempt was made by the Government to implement it. Instead, the Government continued to follow the principle of seniority as a matter of rule in appointing the Chief Justice of India.

On April 26, 1973, however, this 22 years old practice was suddenly broken by the Government within few hours of the delivery of the Judgment in the *Fundamental Rights case.*[42] Mr. A.N. Ray was appointed as Chief Justice of India superseding three of the senior colleagues. Justice Shelat, Hegde and Grover and eight hours after the swearing in ceremony of Mr. A.N. Ray, as the Chief Justice of India, the three Judges resigned from the Supreme Court. The action of the Government raised a great controversy. The Supreme Court Bar Association condemned the action of the Government in superseding the three eminent Judges of the

41. Law Commission Report, 1956.
42. (1973) 4 SCC 225.

Supreme Court. According to the resolution, the Government's action was a blatant and outrageous attempt and undermining the independence and impartiality of the judiciary and lowering the prestige and dignity of the Supreme Court.

(A) Supremacy of Executive: Judges Transfer Case I

Though according to the language used in Art. 124 the President is required to "consult" legal experts but prior to the decision of the Supreme Court on *S.C. Advocate-on-Record Association,*[43] it has always been interpreted that the President was not bound to act in accordance with such consultation. The meaning of the word 'consultation' came for the consideration of the Supreme Court in the *Sankalchand Sheth's* case,[44] which was related to the scope of Article 222 of the Constitution. It was held that the word *'consultation'* meant full and effective consultation. For a full and effective consultation it is necessary that the three constitutional functionaries *"must have for its consideration full and identical facts"* on the basis of which they would be able to take a decision. The President, however, has a right to differ from them and take a contrary view. Consultation does not mean concurrence and the President is not bound by it.

In *S.P. Gupta v. Union of India,*[45] popularly known as the *Judges Transfer case,* the Supreme Court unanimously agreed with the meaning of the term 'consultation' as explained by the majority in *Sankalchand Sheth's* case. The meaning of the word 'consultation' in Article 124(2) is the same as the meaning of the word 'consultation' in Article 212 and Article 222 of the consultation. The only ground on which the decision of the Government can be challenged is that it is based on *mala fide* and irrelevant considerations, that is, when constitutional functionaries expressed an opinion against the appointment.

This means that the ultimate power to appoint judges is vested in the Executive from whose dominance and subordination it was sought to be protected. The Supreme Court had abdicated its power by ruling that constitution

43. AIR 1994 SC 268.
44. AIR 1977, SC 2328
45. AIR 1982 SC 149.

functionaries had merely a consultative role and that power of appointment of Judges is *"solely and exclusively"* vested in the Central Government.

(B) Judicial Supremacy: S.C. Advocate on Record Association *v.* Union of India : Judges Transfer Case-II

In a historic judgment in *S.C. Advocate-on-Record Association* v. *Union of India*[46] popularly known as *Judges Transfer* case, a nine judge Court of the Supreme Court by a 7-2 majority overruled its earlier judgment in the *Judges Transfer* case (*S.P. Gupta* v. *Union of India*) and held that in the matter of appointment of the Judges of the Supreme Court and the High Courts the Chief Justice of India should have primacy. The matter was brought before the Court through a PIL writ petition filed by an advocate of the Supreme Court seeking relief of filling up vacancies in the higher judiciary.

The appointment of Chief Justice of India shall be on the basis of seniority. The Court has laid down detailed guidelines governing appointment and transfer of Judges and held that the greatest significance should be attached to the view of the Chief Justice of India formed after taking into account the views of two senior most Judges of the Supreme Court. It thus has, reduced to the minimum individual discretion conferred upon the Prime Minister and the Chief Justice of India so as to ensure that neither political bias nor personal favoritism nor animosity should play any part in the appointment of Judges of the Supreme Court and High Courts.

The selection should be made as a result of a participatory consultative process in which the executive should have power to act as a mere check on exercise of power by the Chief Justice of India. Mr. Justice Verma who delivered the majority judgment along with Mr. Justice A.N. Ray, Mr. Justice A.S. Anand and Mr. Justice S.P. Bhurucha[47] observed:

> *"Thus, the executive element in the appointment process has been reduced to minimum and political influence is eliminated.*

46. (1993) 4 SCC 441.
47. *Supra* n. 46 at p. 448.

It is for this reason that the word 'consultation' instead of 'concurrence' was used in the Constitution but that was done merely to indicate that absolute discretion was not given to any one, not even to the Chief Justice of India as an individual, much less to the executive".

(C) Sole Opinion of CJI without following Consultation Process: Not binding on Government: Judges Transfer Case-III

In re Presidential Reference[48] a nine-judges bench of the Supreme Court has unanimously held that the recommendation made by the Chief Justice of India on the appointment of Judges of the Supreme Court and the High Courts without following the consultation process are not binding on the Government. The Court also widened the scope of the Chief Justice's consultation process upholding the government's stand on consultation process, the Court gave its opinion on the nine questions raised by the President in his reference to the Supreme Court, under Art. 143 of the Constitution. The President had sought the Supreme Court's clarification on the consultation process, as laid down in *S.C. Advocates* case for the appointment and transfer of Judges following a controversy over the recommendation by former Chief Justice of India M.M. Punchchi. The BJP Government did not agree with his recommendation and referred the matter for the Supreme Court's opinion.

The Court held that the consultation process to be adopted by the Chief Justice of India requires consultation of *plurality of Judges*. The expressions "consultation with the Chief Justice of India" in Articles 217(1) and 222(1) of the Constitution of India require consultation of with plurality of Judges in the formation of opinion of the Chief Justice of India. The sole individual opinion of the Chief Justice of India does not constitute "consultation" within the meaning of the said articles.

The majority held that in regard to the appointment of judges to the Supreme Court under Art. 124(2), the Chief Justice of India should consult *"a collegium of four senior most*

48. AIR 1999 SC 1.

Judges of the Supreme Court" and made it clear that if "two judges give adverse opinion the Chief Justice should not send the recommendation to the Government." The collegium must include the successor Chief Justice of India. The opinion of the collegium must be in writing and the Chief Justice of India should send the recommendation to the President along with his own recommendations.

The recommendations of the collegium should be based on a consensus and unless the opinion is in conformity with that of the Chief Justice of India, no recommendation is to be made. In regard to the appointment of Judges of the High Courts, the Court held that the collegium should consist of the Chief Justice of India and any two senior most Judges of the Supreme Court. In regard to transfer of High Court Judge the Court held that in addition to the collegium of four Judges, the Chief Justice of India is required to consult Chief Justices of the two High Courts (one from which the Judge is being transferred and the other receiving him).

The Court held that the appointment of the Judges of higher court can be challenged only on the ground that the consultation power has not been in conformity with the guidelines laid down in the 1993 judgment and as per opinion given in 1999 decision, i.e. without consulting four senior most Judges of the Apex Court. The decision of the Supreme Court has struck a golden rule. It has made the consultation process more democratic and transparent.

D. Need for a National Judicial Commission

In a seminar in Delhi on judicial reforms held on Dec. 21, 1998 brought out sharp differences between those within the judiciary and those outside it. On the issue of appointment of judges of the higher judiciary the discussion showed that the Presidential reference had not settled the matter. The participants were broadly of the view that for the appointment and transfers in the context of the grant of exclusively primacy to the executive as in the First Judges Transfer case (1980) or to the judiciary as in the Second Judges Transfer case (1993) and affirmed in the Presidential reference (1998), a National Judicial Commission is necessary. In the First Judges Transfer case, *Justice Bhagwati*[49] had, in fact, suggested for the appointment of a Judicial Commission on the line of Australian Judicial Commission.

In fact a Bill was introduced in Lok Sabha by the National Front Government for setting up a National Judicial Commission in 1990 by the then Law Minister, Dinesh Goswami empowering the President to constitute a high level Judicial Commission for making recommendation for the appointment of a Judge to the Supreme Court (other than the Chief Justice of India), Chief Justice of High Courts and to the transfer of Judges from one High Court to another. However, the Constitution Amendment Bill lapsed consequent upon the dissolution of the Lok Sabha.

In the Indian context the controversy has arisen because the two sides—the Executive and the Judiciary—both trying to assert themselves in a tug of war for supremacy in the matter. However, both the sides have shown their filings on the matter.

It is, therefore, essential to evolve and establish a healthy convention so as to exclude the arbitrary interference of Executive in the matter of appointment of the Chief Justice of the Supreme Court and High Court. It is, therefore, suggested that a Judicial Committee, consisting of the Attorney-General, Law Minister, the President of the Bar Council of India, the President of the Supreme Court Bar Association and the Retiring Chief Justice of India, may be constituted and authorised to suggest a penal of names for the appointment of Judges of the Supreme Court and the High Courts. *Justice Bhagwati*[50] feels that the existing constitutional provisions are not adequate. He said:

> "It is unwise to entrust power in any significant or sensitive area to a single individual, however, high or important may be the office, which he is occupying."

At present it is left to the Central Government to select any one or more of the judges of the Supreme Court and the

49. Observation of Justice Bhagwati in National Seminar held on December 21, 1998 at New Delhi.
50. *Supra* n. 49.

High Courts for the purpose of consultation. This safeguard is not adequate. This change is essential for maintaining the independence of Judiciary.

The solution perhaps lies in a practice where neither side enjoys supremacy. A constitutional body reflecting the aspersions of all sections should be entrusted with the task of bringing in harmony between the two conflicting wings of the government. As suggested by the Law Commission in 1987, a National Judicial Service Commission should have the final say in matters of selection, promotion and transfer relating to the judiciary.

12. IN GUJARAT GAS REFERENCE[51]

The Gujarat Government enacted a law entitled the Gujarat Gas (Regulation of Transmission, Supply and Distribution) Act, 2001 empowering the State to regulate transmission, supply and distribution of gas in the State and the laying of pipeline, etc. This was avowedly done in the interest of general public and to promote gas industry in the State. But it was a strange law, which, in effect said that the Union Government had legislative competence to make laws on oil, but not on gas.

The Centre was of the opinion that the State had usurped the powers of the Union and a reference was made for the opinion the apex court by the President. On president reference seeking the Supreme Court's opinion on who should have jurisdiction over the gas pipelines the centre or the states a five-judge constitution Bench issued notices to all states and union territories. The Court comprising chief justice-designate justice S.P. Bharucha, justice G.B. Patnaik, Justice S. Rajendra Babu, Justice S.S.M. Quadri and Justice N. Santosh Hegde passed the order after the reference was made to it by Attorney General Soli Sorabjee.

Sorabjee[52] also said that a writ petition was filed by Association of Natural Gas Consumer Associations on the

51. SCC (2004) 4 at p. 489.
52. Singhvi, Dr. L.M.: *Jagadish Swarup's Constitution of India*, Vol. II, p. 2119.

fixation of gas prices for consumers. It issued notice to the association and Oil and Natural Gas Corporation (ONGC) and Gas Authority of India Limited (GAIL). The reference has raised the core question "whether Natural Gas in whatever physical form, including liquefied Natural Gas (LNG), is a union subject and the union has exclusive legislative competence to enact law on Natural Gas." The controversy stemmed from the fact that though the centre had been exercising control over the pipelines issue, the BJP-ruled State of Gujarat in April 2001 enacted Gujarat Gas (Regulation of Transmission, Supply and Distribution) Act.

The reference said that act empowered the Gujarat government to "provide for regulation of transmission, supply and distribution of gas, to promote gas industry in the State and for establishment of the Gujarat Gas Regulatory Authority, which shall, *inter alia*, have powers to decide as to who would lay pipelines." It said thus Gujarat made it mandatory that the existing companies having pipelines would require permission of the regulatory authority for taking up expansion or utilisation of excess capacity. The reference also seeks an answer to the query: "whether states have legislative competence to make laws on the subject of Natural Gas and LNG under entry 25 of list II of the seventh schedule to the constitution." As a corollary to the second question, the reference seeks the apex court's opinion "whether the state of Gujarat had legislative competence to enact the Gujarat Gas (Regulation of Transmission, Supply and Distribution) Act, 2001."

As per entry 53 of the union list, the Central Government has already enacted the Petroleum act, the Oil Fields (Regulation and Development) Act, the Oil Industry (Development) Act, 1974, and the Petroleum and Minerals Pipelines (Acquisition of Right to Use Land) Act. The reference says section 2 of the industries (Development and Regulation) Act, 1951, declares that it is expedient in the public interest that the union should take under control the industries specified in the first schedule.

Striking down the Act insofar as the provisions relating to Natural Gas or Liquefied Natural Gas (LNG) are concerned, the apex court has prevented a major mischief from taking place. Had such a law come into effect, it would have opened a Pandora's box and different states would have passed different laws.

Both oil and gas are mineral oil resources and trying to treat them separately was wrong, to say the least. The country requires balanced growth in supply, transmission and distribution of Natural Gas and LNG. This can be ensured only if the Centre alone has the legislative competence to enact such a law, as the court has opined. States would be competent to pass legislation only in respect of Gas and Gas-works for Industrial, medical and other similar purposes.

Some States tendency to view national resources as their exclusive wealth has been the bane of Indian polity. The most glaring example of it is the brazen waste of river waters which flows to the sea and the neighbouring countries while various States quibble about their claim on it. The emotive issue has been politicized to such an extent that it is almost impossible to enforce a reasonable solution. Sooner or later, a way will have to be found to treat such resources as belonging to the country and not any particular State.

13. IN GUJARAT ASSEMBLY ELECTION REFERENCE[53]

In the rapidly unedifying scenario in Gujarat, we have a political contretemps where constitutional functionaries are in avoidable operational conflict. The Election Commission has the plenary jurisdiction to decide on free and fair elections. After making a careful study and acting within its powers, the Commission has come to the conclusion that the conditions in the State warrant a date for the polls beyond early October, 2002. This decision being within Article 324 is *prima facie* valid. But a jurally bizarre impossible situation has been created by the astute action of the Chief Minister, with a majority in the House, to advise a pliant Governor to accept his hasty resignation and dissolve the Assembly.

This having been accomplished, a conundrum confrontation has sprung up because of Article 174 which lays down that six months shall not intervene between its (House)

53. (2002) 8 SCC 237: (2002) 8 JT 389.

last sitting in one session and the date for its first sitting in the next session. This six months span a parliamentary parameter is the maximum gap between two sitting of the House and inevitably the House having been dissolved, the newly-elected House has to become functional by October an impossible feat since the Election Commission declines to hold Election within the period.

The only obvious constitutional solution would be to bridge the gap by the imposition of President's rule by proclamation under Article 356.[54] Such a proclamation must have constitutional foundation on the score "that a situation has arisen in which the Government of the State cannot be carried on in accordance with the provisions of the Constitution." The Central Cabinet, on whose advice alone the President can act, is politically hesitant to exercise the powers under Article 356. There was perhaps political, communal mileage and vantage in hasty hustings, the very motive for the dissolution of the House. But the Commission, after an on-the-spot study conscientiously, was not in a mood to agree.

The opinion tendered by the five-member Constitution Bench of the Supreme Court on October 28, 2002[55] begin with a lengthy reasoning on why the presidential reference under Article 143 on the scope of Article 174 *vis-a-vis* Article 324 should be answered and not returned unanswered, as was urged by several Senior Counsel in their arguments. The questions posed in the reference, the Court said, were likely to arise in future and were of public importance.

However, as the Court ended up not answering any of these questions in its opinion, it would seem as though the Court saw merit in the plea to return the reference unanswered, without actually admitting it. While Article 174 deals with the interregnum between two sessions of a State legislature, Article 324 empowers the Election Commission (E.C.) to superintend, direct and control elections.

In his reference sent to the Supreme Court on August 19, President as advised by the Union Cabinet, had posed three

54. Dhavan, Rajeev, "The six months norm is dangerous in Gujarat" *Frontline*, Vol. XX, No. 18 (Sept. 13, 2002) at p. 16
55. *Supra* n. 53.

questions to be resolved by the court. First, is Article 174 subject to the decision of the E.C. under Article 324? Secondly, can the E.C. frame a schedule for elections to an Assembly on the premise that any infraction of the mandate of Article 174 would be remedied by resort to Article 356 by the President? Thirdly, is the E.C. under duty to carry out the mandate of Article 174 of the Constitution, by drawing upon all the requisite resources of the Union and the State to ensure free and fair elections?

These questions were based on the premise that Article 174(1), which stipulates that six months shall not intervene between the Assembly's last sitting in one session and the date appointed for its first sitting in the next session, would determine the date of the first sitting of a yet-to-be-constituted Assembly, following the holding of elections after the dissolution of the previous Assembly.

The main opinion, written by *Justice V.N. Khare*[56] on behalf of the Chief Justice, B.N. Kripal and Justice Ashok Bhan, and the two concurring opinions by Justices Arijit Pasayat and K.G. Balakrishnan found this basic premise faulty but proceeded to answer the reference. The E.C. too had endorsed this premise in its order, albeit with a caveat that under the circumstances found in Gujarat, in the aftermath of the post-Godhra riots against a minority community, Article 174(1) should yield to Article 324.

The Court justified its response to the reference on the grounds that a doubt had arisen in the mind of the President in regard to the interpretation of Article 174(1) of the Constitution, and that there was no earlier judgment by the apex court on the issue. But, it would seem that the Union government, which advised the President, was indeed convinced that the Article applied to a live as well as a dissolved Assembly.

The Court gave cogent reasons as to why the basic premise of the reference was not valid, thus vindicating to some extent the plea of some senior counsel to return the reference unanswered to the President. However, instead of returning the reference, the Court sought to explain why it

---

56. *Supra* n. 53 at p. 396.

could not answer any of the three queries, as posed by the President, because his basic assumption was wrong. Article 174(1), the Court opined, relates to an existing live and functional legislative Assembly and not to a dissolved one. This Article and Article 85 (the corresponding provision for Parliament) were not intended to provide any period of limitation for holding elections in order to constitute a new House, the Court said.

The Court pointed out that Articles 85 (1) and 174(1) were borrowed from Sections 19 (1) and 62(1) of the Government of India Act, 1935, which dealt with the frequencies of sessions of existing Houses of Parliament and State legislatures, and did not relate to dissolved Houses.

The Court concluded that they were visualised in the context of a scenario applicable only to a living and functional House and that the stipulation of a six-months intervening period between the two sessions is inapplicable to a dissolved House.[57]

Again, when Articles 85 and 174 were sought to be amended by the Constitution First Amendment Bill in 1951, the entire debate in Parliament revolved around propagation and summoning of the current session and the working of the existing Lok Sabha and State Assemblies, the Court point out.

Textually, Article 174(1) shows that the expression 'date appointed for its first sitting in the next session' cannot possibly refer to either an event after the dissolution of the House or to a new Legislative Assembly meeting for the first time after getting elected; when there is a session of the new Assembly after elections, the new Assembly will sit in its "first session" and not in the "next session", the Court explained. The omission of the phrase "after each general election" in Article 174 is a clear indication that it does not apply to a dissolved Assembly or a freshly elected one, the Court suggested.

Posing a hypothetical question, the Court said that if Article 174(1) applied to a dissolved Assembly, and if the

57. Quoting from Constituent Assembly Debates, when the Draft Articles 69 and 153 (corresponding to the current Articles 85 and 174) were discussed.

House was dissolved in the fifth month after the last day of sitting of the last session, the election will have to be held within one month so as to comply with its requirement, which would not have been the intention of the farmers of the Constitution. As no part of the dissolved House is carried forward to a new legislative Assembly, Article 174(1) does not link the last session of the dissolved House with the newly formed one, the Court reasoned.

The Court did not go into the merits of the application of Article 356, as suggested by the E.C. in its August 16, 2002 order, because it found that there was no infraction of the mandate of Articles 174(1) and 324 operate on different fields and neither of them is subject to each other.

The Court acknowledged that the E.C., in its interpretation of Article 174(1), was influenced mainly by the past practice of holding elections within six months of the last sitting of the dissolved House. "The gratuitous advice of application of Article 356 by the E.C. in its order was in all its sincerity, although now on our interpretation of Article 174(1), we find that it was misplaced".

After explaining why it could not answer any of the President's three questions, the Court, however, sought to answer a hypothetical question, which was not posed in the reference but was articulated during the hearing of the case. The Court found that the Representation of the People Act, 1951, has not provided any period of limitation to hold elections to constitute a fresh Assembly in the event of a premature dissolution of an Assembly.

The Court appears to have been carried away by imaginary concerns expressed by counsel for one of the national political parties and one of the States that in the absence of any period provided either in the Constitution or in the RPA, the E.C. may not hold elections at all and that in the event it would be the end of democracy. Examining related provisions in the Constitution and the RPA, the Court concluded:[58]

58. *Supra* n. 53 at p. 402.

> *"upon the premature dissolution of an Assembly, the E.C. was required to initiate immediate steps to hold elections in order to constitute a Legislative Assembly within six months from the date of such dissolution. "Ordinarily, law and order or public disorder should not be occasion for postponing the elections and it would be the duty and responsibility of all concerned to render all assistance, cooperation and aid to the E.C. for holding free and fair elections."*

The fixing of the "outer limit" by the Court for holding of elections by the E.C. in the case of a premature dissolution of an Assembly, has dismayed observers. The Court did not hear such a plea being advanced by any counsel, although Kapil Sibbal, representing the Congress (I), had suggested that in response to a specific query from the Court.

Logically, one can imagine an incident such as Godhra and the riots that followed it or even a serious earthquake or flood happening in a State after the dissolution of the Assembly, thus making it difficult for the E.C. to hold free and fair elections within six months. Under such circumstances, is there no way in which the E.C. can ensure and fair elections? Although the opinion of the Court is not binding on the constitutional functionaries, it seems to have overlooked such possibilities, thus inviting the criticism of being unreasonable.

Within an hour of the opinion being tendered by the Court, the E.C. announced the schedule for the Assembly elections in Gujarat. The State had have a one-day poll on December 12 and the counting of votes had taken on December 15. However, grim the law and order situation in the State, with the Supreme Court fixing an outer limit for holding elections, the E.C.'s hands appear to be tied.[59]

The Bhartiya Janta Party is pleased that the court's opinion did not go into the merits of Narendra Modi continuing as Chief Minister beyond six months without facing the State Assembly. The party is relieved that the coalition government headed by it at the Centre does not have to impose President's Rule in the State, as demanded by the

59. Krishna Iyer, V.B., "Gujarat Imbroglio : Some Reflections", *The Hindu*, Vol. XXV, (Aug. 24, 2002) at p. 11.

Opposition, to meet the constitutional crisis following the earlier perceived infraction of Article 174. For those who expected the court to pronounce on the non-accountability of the Modi regime since April 3, 2002 the last sitting of the dissolved Assembly, the opinion is bound to be a huge disappointment.

The Gujarat imbroglio brings to mind of *Dr. Ambedkar's*[60] pensive caution about the Constitution:

> *"I feel that it is workable, it is flexible and it is strong enough to hold the country together both in peace time and in war time. Indeed, if I may say so, if things go wrong under the new Constitution, the reason will not be that we had a bad Constitution. What we will have to say is, that Man was vile."*

14. IN SATLUJ-YAMUNA LINK CANAL REFERENCE

On July 22, 2004 President referred Punjab's Controversial Terminators of Agreements Act to the Supreme Court, starting what could prove to be the last legal round in India's largest running and most complex water dispute. In the coming months the Supreme Court will consider whether the act is constitutional and whether Punjab must obey 2002 order mandating that the SYL Canal be completed in a year. The act is unprecedented. It is the first time a State Government has sought to overturn a Supreme Court order through legislative means. Even the Karnataka assembly, which passed legislation on how much water it would release to Tamil Nadu from its reservoirs on the Cauvery. Sought to overturn only an award of a water disputes tribunal not a Judicial fiat.

The saddest part of the Saga, however is that the SYL Canal issue is in essence a straw man. The real problems facing in both Punjab and Haryana have to do with their colossally inefficient irrigation policies and the indiscriminate proliferation of water hungry crops such as paddy and sugarcane. While both states spend lakhs slugging it out in court whether they might consider doing their farmers any real favour.

60. CAD, Vol. VIII, p. 257.

7

Epilogue

1. CONCLUSION

Viewing from the amount of attention given to Article 119 of the draft constitution in the constituent assembly, it may be inferred that the constitution-makers thought the institution of advisory jurisdiction to be a procedural provision which was taken as it was from the Government of India Act, 1935. They never thought that the advisory jurisdiction of the Supreme Court would come to play such a significant role in the process of constitutional development. Certainly it is a provision which has at times, drawn attention from jurists, political thinkers and the press. It has been criticized, appreciated and sought to be modified by the constitutional experts.

Since its inception, the Supreme Court has had to exercise its advisory jurisdiction fourteen times. All the references involved important issues of constitutional significance and the Supreme Court by answering all these have served a very useful purpose. If we try to find out any general trend in the opinions given, we come to the conclusion that no general principles can be inferred.[1]

1. Agarwal, B.R., *The Supreme Court Practice and Procedure*, Metropolitan Book Co. Pvt. Ltd., 1975, p. 441.

Although in almost all reference cases, preliminary objections were raised, the court never yielded to them. The references were opposed on the grounds of being hypothetical, speculative and of doubtful maturity. Political or that the real questions were not included in the reference. *In the Special Court Bill reference,*[2] the court went too far in answering the reference. In this case the whole Bill was referred to the Court for advice regarding its constitutional validity and no specific questions were formulated. The Chief Justice Y.B. Chandrachud observed that at one stage the court was 'seriously' considering the proposal that it should return the reference 'unanswered'.

The Court was indeed asked to first find out the 'technical lacunae' and then to help remove them. Yet the Court accepted and answered the reference. In the *'Presidential Poll reference',*[3] the court was told that the reference did not include all and real questions on the issue. But the Court refused to go beyond the recitals of the reference and decided to entertain it. This ready willingness of the court to answer a Presidential reference has been viewed with caution.

The institution of a advisory jurisdiction established a channel between the Executive and the judiciary. This naturally raises doubts about the Executive-judiciary collaboration.[4] The question is whether the judiciary, armed with advisory jurisdiction, in India has been above politics. Charges of judicial intrusion in political affairs on account of this function of the Court have often been labeled.

The phrase 'likely to arise' has been interpreted to allow pending legislation to come before the court in reference proceedings. When a pending legislation is examined, we loose the benefit of a political judgment on the social needs which prompted the legislation.[5] Such political judgment should not be ignored, in its larger sense of an expression of the basic desires of the people, without running the risk of unnaturally

2. A.I.R. 1979 SC 478.
3. A.I.R. 1974 SC 1682.
4. Dharma Pratap, *The Advisory Jurisdiction of International Court,* The Clarandon Press, London, 1972, p. 252.
5. Frankfuter, *Anote on Advisory Opinion,* pp. 1004-05.

violating legal decisions from the deeper social and political trends of the Society. When a political judgment is by passed, we run the risk of embracing difficult and controversial questions. Whenever the action of a Government is examined before it takes place, the ebb and law of political controversy is likely to disturb the judicial claim.[6]

The requirement in Article 143, that the question referred be one of 'public importance', implies that the controversy prompting the reference will be contemporary and is likely to generate much political heat. The peculiar position of the instigating party as the Head of the State, taking instructions from the political head of the Government, makes the practice of referring hot political Issues to the Court an easy exercise.[7]

'Political issues' does not necessarily meant that the questions referred are political or are policy questions. It only means that the atmosphere in which the litigation arises is one of heated political controversy. Although the political heat may be in the background of a normal litigation, this fact does not dismiss the danger of such a practice in advisory opinions. The Courts reserve of prestige is not exhaustible. They must settle genuine private disputes, however, charged is the atmosphere. This is their job. But this does not mean that this is a good idea to encourage dipping into political controversy.

This danger of involvement in political controversy even when a legal and not a political question is involved, is clearly reflected in the advisory opinion practice of the international court of justice.[8] In such events the court took recourse to abstract questions and only by abstraction could the court avoid the political controversy which prompted the reference. But it should not be taken as a suggestion that the Indian Supreme Court should deal in abstractness.

The Court cannot really hope to avoid the heat of the political arena by dealing in abstraction any more then the

6. Hudson, *Advisory opinions of National & International Courts*, pp. 970-75.
7. Chitley, D.V. and Rao, S. Appu, *AIR Commentaries : The Indian Constitution with the Extensive, Analytical and Critical Commentaries*, The All India Reports Ltd., 1971 p. 473.
8. Doabia, H.S.T.S, *The Supreme Court on Constitution of India*, Wadhwa and Co., 1967, p. 1052.

Ostrich can effectively avoid his enemies by placing his head in the sand. If the situation is too volatile, that should honestly be considered as a factor in deciding whether or not to entertain the reference.

The Berubari reference provides an example of judicial involvement in political controversy. The issue was purely a legal one, "how does the government constitutionally cede territory if the situation was, in fact, one of cession?" However, this issue was one which had exacerbated public opinion for a long time. The real danger in this reference arises only if we assume that the opinion had favoured the Central Government's position and allowed a mere executive order to cede territory, instead of constitutional majority in the legislature.[9] The emotions in West Bengal ran very high, and could only have been vented on the Court. The alternative to West Bengal's displeasure is the dissatisfaction of the Centre at an adverse decision. Thus, there is the likelihood of loss of prestige on account of involvement in a political controversy. It is also likely that the public will view the use of an advisory opinion to be a political weapon rather than a source of removing doubts.

The Kerala Education Bill reference[10] also was made in a politically heated atmosphere. The purpose in raising the legal issue did not seem to be a genuine concern for the legality of the measure, as it had been in the Berubari reference. The legal doubts, however real, seemed, injected into the controversy as a means of carrying on the political struggle. The Government in Kerala, whose legislation was challenged, belonged to a different political party and it opposed the reference. They accused the Centre of discriminating in not referring other similar measures to the Court and of using the advisory jurisdiction for political ends. It appeared as though, having lost in the Assembly, the ruling party in the Centre attempted to win it in the Court.

In the Special Courts Bill reference[11] the atmosphere was charged with political feelings. There was a strong demand

9. Basu, D.D., *Commentary on the Constitution of India*, Wadha Publication, Nagpur, 1992, Vol. V, p. 1073.
10. A.I.R. 1958 SC 996.
11. A.I.R. 1979 SC 478.

from factions of the ruling party that the political offenders of the Emergency era should be tried expeditiously. On the other hand, the Indira Congress was labeling the charge of vindictiveness against the Government. The Government ventured to get its designs approved by the Court and the Court yielded to the executive designs. Constitutional experts aver that if it was prudent and expedient for the politicians to make the reference it was imprudent and inexpedient for the Court to entertain the same.

The Delhi Laws Act reference[12] was made in a context which could not cause too much excitement. The Customs Act reference, the *Keshav Singh case reference* and the Presidential Poll reference can be put in a category which did not cause much political heat. Of the four Federal Court opinions only the one of Central Provinces case generated much excitement. World War II and the struggle for independence made the other three cases, decided in 1941, 1943 and 1944, only of secondary importance.

In Ram Janmabhoomi reference,[13] again it is an example of judicial involvement in political controversy. There has been a long-standing dispute relating to the erstwhile Ram Janmabhoomi-Babri Masjid structure in Ayodhya which led to communal tension and violence from time to time and ultimately led to the destruction of the disputed structure on 6th December, 1992. The question raised before Court was whether a Hindu Temple or any Hindu religious structure existed prior to the construction of the Ram Janmabhoomi-Babri Masjid in the area on which the structure stood.

The Court held that Presidential reference seeking the Supreme Courts opinion on whether a temple originally existed at the site where the Babri Masjid subsequently stood was superfluous and unnecessary and opposed to secularism and favoured one religious community and, therefore, does not require to be answered.

In the Gujarat Assembly Election matter,[14] the atmosphere was charged with political feelings. The background was a

12. A.I.R. 1951 SC 332.
13. (1993) SCC 642.
14. (2002) 8 SCC 237.

spate of communal violence erupted in various parts of Gujarat in February, 2002. In these circumstances ruling party dissolved the Legislative Assembly and requested the election Commission to conduct fresh general election urgently so that the new legislative assembly would be able to have its first session on or before 3.10.2002. The Election Commission expressed its view that it was not in a position to conduct free and fair election until November/December, 2002. The main question raised before the Supreme Court was whether Article 174 is subject to the decision of the Election Commission of India under Article 324 as to the schedule of elections of the Assembly. The majority held that Article 174(1) of the Constitution relates to an existing live and functional Legislative Assembly and not to a dissolved Assembly.

An argument is advanced against the charge of the executive using the Court for political ends. It is that the Court's opinion is not known in advance. But it is no answer to the danger. If a battle is essentially political, however real the legal weapons in the battle may be, the party with one weapon in its arsenal which is denied to the other, will be suspected using it to its own advantage. The States of Kerala and West Bengal could not obtain the opinions of the Supreme Court.[15] They, therefore, suspected this move of the Centre. It is necessary to emphasis unwisdom of involving the Court in a constitutional question which arises because of political tactics not entirely free from suspicion.

The Court's willingness to hear a case despite the political background can not be treated simply as bowing in the face of an inevitable adjudication, but a deliberate policy decision that the dangers of a politically charged atmosphere are not worth worrying about. Although the responsibility for avoiding a reference involving heated political controversy must rest largely with the Government, it can safely be concluded that there is no danger yet. The Court's position is secure. But the prestige itself rests on a belief that the Court stands beyond party politics.[16]

15. Dawson, R. MacGreygor, *Democratic Government in Canada*, Univesity of Toronto Press, London, 1970, p. 492.
16. Dayal, S., *The Constitution of India*, Law Publishers, Allahabad, 1974, p. 341.

2. HOW FAR THE COURT HAS MAINTAINED ITS INDEPENDENCE

While dwelling over this point we find that the opinions of the Supreme Court so far have been both for and against the referring authority. The court does not appear to have been influenced by the wishes of the authority which referred the questions to it. If it accepted the stands taken by the Union Government in the *Presidential Poll reference,* the Special Courts Bill reference and partly in the references on the Kerala Education Bill and Sea Customs Act, it out rightly rejected the pleas of the Union Government in the Berubari case.

In the *Keshav Singh case,* the Court while accepting the right of the Legislature, which was not disputed, to commit persons for contempt committed within the House or by its members, emphatically refused to accede to the claim of the legislature that the Court had no jurisdiction to entertain any deal within a suitable manner a petition filed by a citizen claiming an infringement of his fundamental rights by the action of the legislature and asking for relief in respect of such infringement.[17]

This decision, establishing the independence of the higher judiciary in India and affirming the rights of the citizens to enforce his fundamental rights even against the action of the legislature has been welcomed by the public and the press generally. Its importance as a constitutional pronouncement has been appreciated throughout the Anglo-Saxon World. It can doubtlessly be said that the advisory opinions of the Supreme Court have never come in the way of the independence of the judiciary.[18]

By watching opinions of references we can infer that consultative jurisdiction should be used in four circumstances only.

(i) to enable the Government of India an authoritative

17. Rao, B. Shiva, *The Framing of India's Constitution: A Study,* IIPA, 1968, p. 453.
18. Hudson, M.O., "Advisory Opinions on National and International Courts", *Harvard Law Review,* 1924, p. 272.

opinion regarding the validity of a legislation before enactment or an executive action before its enforcement.

(ii) To deal with the problems of federalism.

(iii) Interpretation of the constitution.

(iv) The constitution creates some situations where legal rights exist but no legal remedies are available. There are matters which are excluded from the Supreme Court's jurisdiction i.e., Proviso to Article 131. The framers of the constitution though of providing an opportunity of judicial consideration by enacting Article 143.

3. SHOULD CONSULTATIVE JURISDICTION BE CONTINUED

A more careful examination of the specific arguments made in favour of advisory jurisdiction as they apply to the Indian context is necessary. Mainly two arguments are given in favour of the system : (1) the vital importance of avoiding the wastage of time and energy due to paralysis born of legal uncertainties, and (2) creation of judicial review. To the first argument it should be added that in order to save time, an advisory opinion must convincingly settle the dispute behind the reference. If it does not, more law suits will develop and the advisory opinion will have only added to the judicial work load. Indeed it may be seriously questioned whether the Delhi Laws Act lessened the litigation on the subject matter in dispute.

Besides the educational value of private litigation in different lower courts prior to the Supreme Court judgment should not be underestimated. The various legal positions may be elaborately explained and developed before the Supreme Court receives the question, thereby leading to a more considered judgment by the highest court in the country.[19]

The problem of saving non-judicial time has two facets. One is the expenditure of time and energy by the government

19. Popkin Willian, D., "Advisory Opinions in India", *Journal of the Indian Law Institute*, 1962, p. 252.

and the other involves the private sector. When the government passes a law, specially under modern economic conditions, a vast system of administration may come in its wake. If the law is unconstitutional this may all be a waste.

There may be cases where the *status quo* is so altered that the unscrambling is practically or totally impossible. *In the Berubari case* there was fear that the cession of land to Pakistan would create an unalterable situation once accomplished. *The Delhi Laws Act case* might have presented the same problem. Injury to the private sector may be caused by private parties, due to a reliance on some assumption concerning the law.

The Hindu women's rights case would have presented the same problem for the law as that case purported to change property rights. The title and interest in reality would depend on the validity of the statute involved. It is, however, true that each justification for advisory opinion carries its own danger. Anticipation of a dispute may result in vagueness and the creation of more doubts than are settled, thus causing a greater wastage of time and energy.

The second argument put forward in favour of the existence of advisory jurisdiction system in India is that it provides room for judicial review where none would otherwise be possible at any time. It is no longer a question of accelerating judicial scrutiny, but the existence of it at all. The Constitution[20] has created some situations where legal rights exist but no legal remedy is available.

Moreover, there are other situations under the Constitution where the Courts have been divested on the power to hear claims, but where the purpose appears to have been the denial of any substantive basis for a claim. The emphasis in all these latter cases on the creation of legislative competence to deal with certain areas, rather than on the ouster of the courts from examining a claim of legal right.[21] The Constitution makes a judgment in such cases that certain types of legislation are valid social objectives and are,

20. For instance, Articles 131 (Proviso) and 363, Art. 31(2), Art. 359(1), Art. 329, Art. 189(3) and Art. 199(3), Art. 361, etc.
21. Tromas, L.I., "Advisory Jurisdiction of the Supreme Court of India". *JIH*, 1963, at pp. 475-97.

therefore, not to be illegal. In these situations, the system of advisory jurisdiction may be helpful in obtaining a judicial decision.

But first it is to be ensured whether the Constitution allows such a practice. The language of the Constitution might be considered ambiguous. The procedural bars to judicial review in the articles noted earlier might exclude the Supreme Court even in its advisory capacity. Thus, 'no jurisdiction' might include a reference proceeding and an advisory opinion might be considered to 'call into question' that which was forbidden to be judicially heard. However, the Constitution nowhere speaks of the advisory 'jurisdiction' of the Supreme Court, it is more properly referred to as the consultative function to which a term like 'jurisdiction' does not apply.[22]

Indeed in the very case where jurisdiction is denied by Article 131, the Constitution requires an advisory opinion from the Court [clause (2) of Article 143] if the President so requests. Nor can an advisory opinion be considered to 'call anything into question' in any Court, for only the advice of the Court is sought. Whatever ambiguity may remain in this matter should be resolved in favour of allowing advisory opinions where there is a procedural bar to normal litigation.[23]

This is more consistent with the flexible and discretionary approach of the Indian courts in all matters of declaratory relief for infringed legal rights. Each case has then to be individually scrutinized to see if an advisory opinion should be given. If soundly used, however, an advisory opinion may dispel charges of unfairness in those situations where the government is most vulnerable, i.e., where the alleged unfairness is in an area where judicial review is also precluded.[24]

---

22. It is so described in Basu's Shorter Constitution of India (3rd ed. 1960) p. 300; and in the title of an article in *Trivandrum Law College Journal*, Madras 1955, Vol. I, p. 17 (Constitution of the Juridiciary with special reference in India).
23. Philips, P.D., "Advisory Opinions in India", *Australian Law Journal*, 1928-29, p. 73.
24. Aumann, F.R., "The Supreme Court and Advisory Opinion", *Ohio State University Law Journal*, (1937) pp. 94-98.

There is, to conclude, strong evidence in Article 143 itself that these justifications were part of the rationale for the creation and existence of the advisory opinion system in India. The provision of Article 143 that questions which are 'likely to arise' may be referred does indicate some willingness to depart from the stricter norms of maturity applicable in a regular case in the interests of preventing wastage of human energy and the requirement that a question be of public importance suggests that some political heat is tolerable in the interests of judicial settlement of an otherwise unmanageable dispute.

Both these provisions certainly demonstrate that advisory opinions are not meant to be as circumscribed in scope as the normal declaratory judgment.

One factor, in the Indian context makes the danger less serious and the utility of an advisory opinion greater, it is the immense prestige which the opinions of the higher Courts carry.[25] The predominating willingness to obey the Courts, 'judgment' means that greater risks may be taken with the goodwill which the judiciary possesses. More specially, the Court's role as advisor fits in readily with a traditionally non-litigous society accustomed to resort to the opinion of elders rather than to allow controversy to grow completely out of hand.

A constitutional commentator[26] is of the opinion that the basic nature of the Court as an authority to dispense with justice impartially according to law through properly instituted actions would not be frustrated by vesting it with consolatory function as long as the independence of the Court is the crido of our state polity. The singular eminence of the Judicial Committee of the Privy Council which is an advisory body to the Crown acting on judicial lines and principles may at once be called to mind. On the other hand, it may assist in the constitutional governance of the country by giving guidance to the executive and legislature to act in accordance with the constitution.

25. Allen, C.K., "Adminstrative Consultation of Judicary", *Law Quarterly Review*, 1951, p. 273.
26. Lily Isabel Thomas, "The advisory jurisdiction of the Supreme Court of India, JILI (1963), p. 475.

4. SUGGESTIONS

The institution of Consultative Jurisdiction established a channel between the executive and the Judiciary. Its importance as a constitutional pronouncement has been appreciated throughout the Anglo-Saxon world. For better working of the system, certain modifications in the provision may be suggested to make it more useful and less harmful.

1. Article 143 authorizes only the President, practically the Union Government to refer any question whether or not a Union subject to the Supreme Court. This power injudiciously, may result to grave injustice to the rights of the states and individual citizens. The President has sometimes made a reference not only regarding questions affecting the Union but also on questions affecting the states without their consent and even contrary to their wishes. President should be empowered to refer only issues which come within the Union Governments domain, or in regard to any issue involving state subjects or state rights, the President should make a reference only on the initiative of the State Government.

2. Article 143(1) empowers the President in his discretion to refer questions of both Law and Fact. It should be kept in mind that the similar provision,[27] in the old statute allowed only questions of law to be referred to the Court. The ad hoc committee on Supreme Court (1947) also recommended only questions of law for reference to the Court. It is understandable that what prompted the constituent Assembly to broaden the jurisdiction to include questions of fact also. The inspiration seems to come from the Canadian system,[28] where Governor-General can refer to the Supreme Court "Important questions of law or fact . . . touching any matter." It does not suit the Indian system.

The word fact may be meant to include anything and everything. Armed with such wide powers, the President may be tempted to make too frequent use of the advisory jurisdiction which may result in serious consequences. For instance, in *Ram Janmabhoomi reference* a question on fact was

27. Section 213 of the Govt. of India Act, 1935.
28. Section 55 of the Canadian Supreme Court Act, 1952.

asked before the court, whether a Hindu temple existed in the area on which the structure stood.

Court held that this question on fact was superfluous and unnecessary and opposed to secularism and favoured one religious community and, therefore, does not require to be answered. Again, in Jammu & Kashmir resettlement Act in 2001 the Supreme Court declined to give any comments on it. Infact, it was a mistake on the part of Constitution framers to have a broadened the scope of advisory jurisdiction of the Court. So, only question of law, therefore, should be allowed for reference to the Court and the word fact should be deleted.

3. In clause (2) of Article 143 the word 'shall' should be deleted, as it makes it obligatory upon the Supreme Court to answer a reference. The judiciary should not be bound to deliver an opinion if it wishes not to do so but should be free to judge whether or not to entertain a reference. The practice upto now shows that no reference has been made under clause (2) and even then the Supreme Court has not declined even a single reference. Compelling the Court to pronounce an opinion would be gross interference with the judicial independence of the Supreme Court.

4. Court should not go too far in giving opinion. In the Special Courts Bill,[29] the court went too far in answering the reference. In this case the whole Bill was referred to the Court for advice regarding its constitutional validity and no specific questions were formulated. The Chief Justice Y.B. Chandrachud observed that at one stage the court was seriously considering the proposal that it should return the reference 'unanswered'. The court was indeed asked to first find the 'technical lacunae' and then to help remove them. Yet the court accepted and answered the reference.

In the Presidential Poll reference,[30] the court was told that the reference did not include all and real questions on the issue. But the court refused to go beyond the recitals of the reference and decided to entertain it. This ready willingness of the court to answer a Presidential reference has been viewed with a caution.

29. A.I.R. 1979 SC 478.
30. A.I.R. 1974 SC 1682 (1974) 2 SCC 33.

5. Consultative jurisdiction should be invoked only sparingly and not frequently and only in such cases where factual situations are ripe, or where legal issues are capable of being formulated precisely and can be considered by the Court without much of a factual data and political questions should not be referred to the court for advice.

6. Opinions of Court on references must be delivered within stipulated time limit, otherwise they will be ineffective. *In Gujarat Assembly election matter*,[31] the President referred questions on 19.8.2002 and the opinion was delivered on October 28, 2002. In between this, Narendra Modi continued as a Chief Minister of Gujarat after October 3, he became the first head of the Government in the country since independence to remain in power without facing the legislature for six consecutive months. His continuance in power may not be violative of any constitutional provision, but involves serious questions such as lack of propriety and non-accountability.

7. Advisory jurisdiction by the Supreme Court can be beneficial to the country only if the court continues to be free from any executive pressure. Issues in which the central government is keenly interested are likely to be referred to the Supreme Court for its advice. Opinion expressed by the court in such cases will receive public credibility if its judicial independence is beyond question.

To conclude the institution is useful and should be continued. But the justification for its use must be carefully examined and weighed in the context of each case. The responsibility is of both the government as the questioner and the court in its capacity as guardian of the efficient working of the judicial system to see that its use does not become more of a danger to the long-term interests of justice than a benefit. The institution of consultative or advisory jurisdiction is good if used judiciously and infrequently.

> *"The institution is not faulty, the need is that the persons who run the institution behave properly."*
>
> —Dr. K.R. Narayanan
> Former President of India

31. (2002) 8 SCC 237, (2002) 8 LT 389.

APPENDIX A

THE REPORT OF AD HOC COMMITTEE ON SUPREME COURT, MAY 27, 1947

II. Advisory Jurisdiction of the Court

"11. There has been considerable difference of opinion amongst jurists and political thinkers as to the expediency of placing on the Supreme Court an obligation to advise the Head of the State on difficult questions of law. Inspite of arguments to the contrary, it was considered expedient to confer advisory jurisdiction upon the Federal Court under the existing Constitution by Section 213 of the Act. Having given our best consideration to the arguments pros and cons, we feel that it will be on the whole better to continue this jurisdiction even under the new Constitution. It may be assumed that such jurisdiction is scarcely likely to be unnecessarily evoked, and if , as we propose, the Court is to have a strength of ten or eleven judges, a pronouncement by a full Court may well be regarded as authoritative advice. This can be ensured by requiring that references to the Supreme Court for advice shall be dealt with by a full Court."

1. S. Vardhacharyar.
2. A. Krishnaswami Ayyar
3. B.L. Mittar.
4. K.M. Munshi
5. B.N. Rao

APPENDIX B

THE REPORT OF THE JOINT COMMITTEE ON INDIAN CONSTITUTIONAL REFORMS (SESSION 1933-34)

Volume I (Part I) page 195, para 327.

" 327. It is proposed that the Federal Court shall have a jurisdiction similar to that possessed by the Privy Council under Section 4 of the Judicial Committee Act, 1833 which provides that his Majesty may refer to the Committee for hearing or consideration any matters whatsoever as His Majesty may think fit, and that the Committee shall thereupon hear and consider the same, and shall advise His Majesty thereon. The expression used in the White Paper is "any judicial matter which the Governor General considers of such a nature and such public importance that it is expedient to obtain the opinion of the Court upon it", Exception was taken to the word 'justiciable' and we think perhaps that "any matter of law" would be preferable. We concur generally in the proposal and we are of the opinion that this advisory jurisdiction may often prove of great utility. We agree that it need not be limited to the federal sphere and that the right of referring any matter to the Court for an advisory opinion should be in the Governor-General's discretion."

APPENDIX C

RELATED ARTICLES OF CONSTITUTION OF INDIA, 1950

1. 143 Power of President to Consult Supreme Court

(1) If at any time it appears to the President that a question of law or fact has arisen, or is likely to arise, which is of such a nature and of such public importance that it is expedient to obtain the opinion of the Supreme Court upon it, he may refer the question to that Court for consideration and the Court may, after such hearing as it thinks fit, report to the President its opinion thereon.

(2) The President may, notwithstanding anything in [1][***] the proviso to Article 131, refer a dispute of the kind mentioned in the [2][said proviso] to the Supreme Court for opinion and the Supreme Court shall, after such hearing as it thinks fit, report to the President its opinion thereon.

2. 145. Rules of Court, Etc.

(1) Subject to the provisions of any law made by Parliament, the Supreme Court may from time to time, with the approval of the President, make rules for regulating generally the practice and procedure of the Court including:

(a) Rules as to the persons practising before the Court;
(b) Rules as to the procedure for hearing appeals and other mattters pertaining to appeals including the

1. The words, brackets and figure "clause (i) of" omitted by the Constitution (Seventh Amendment) Act, 1956, s. 29 and Sch.
2. Subs. by s. 29 and Sch., the Constitution (Seventh Amendment) Act, 1956, for "said clause".

time within which appeals to the Court are to be entered;

(c) Rules as to the proceedings in the Court for the enforcement of any of the rights conferred by Part III;

[3][(cc) Rules as to the proceedings in the Court under [4][Article 139A];]

(d) Rules as to the entertainment of appeals under sub-clause (c) of clause (1) of Article 134;

(e) Rules as to the conditions subject to which any judgment pronounced or order made by the Court may be reviewed and the procedure for such review including the time within which applications to the Court for such review are to be entered;

(f) Rules as to the costs of and incidental to any proceedings in the Court and as to the fees to be charged in respect of proceedings therein;

(g) Rules as to the granting of bail;

(h) Rules as to stay of proceedings;

(i) Rules providing for the summary determination of any appeal which appears to the Court to be frivolous or vexatious or brought for the purpose of delay; and

(j) Rules as to the procedure for inquiries referred to in clause (1) of article 317.

(2) Subject to the [5][provisions of [6][***] clause (3)], rules made under this article may fix the minimum number of Judges who are to sit for any purpose, and may provide for the powers of single Judges and Division Courts.

---

3. Ins. by s. 26, the Constitution (Forty-second Amendment) Act, 1976 (w.e.f. 1-2-1977).
4. Subs. by the Constitution (Forty-third Amendment) Act, 1977, s. 6, for "Articles 131A and 139A" (w.e.f. 13-4-1978).
5. Subs. by the Constitution (Forty-second Amendment) Act, 1976, s. 26, for "provisions of clause (3)" (w.e.f. 1-2-1977).
6. Certain words omitted by the Constitution (Forty-third Amendment) Act, 1977, s. 6 (w.e.f. 13-4-1978).

(3) [7][[***] The minimum number of Judges who are to sit for the purpose of deciding any case involving a substantial question of law as to the interpretation of this Constitution or for the purpose of hearing any reference under Article 143 shall be five:

Provided that, where the Court hearing an appeal under any of the provisions of this Chapter other than Article 132 consists of less than five Judges and in the course of the hearing of the appeal the Court is satisfied that the appeal involves a substantial question of law as to the interpretation of this Constitution the determination of which is necessary for the disposal of the appeal, such Court shall refer the question for opinion to a Court constituted as required by this clause for the purpose of deciding any case involving such a question and shall on receipt of the opinion dispose of the appeal in conformity with such opinion.

(4) No judgment shall be delivered by the Supreme Court save in open Court, and no report shall be made under Article 143 save in accordance with an opinion also delivered in open Court.

(5) No judgment and no such opinion shall be delivered by the Supreme Court save with the concurrence of a majority of the Judges present at the hearing of the case, but nothing in this clause shall be deemed to prevent a Judge who does not concur from delivering a dissenting judgment or opinion.

---

7. Subs. by the Constitution (Forty-second Amendment) Act, 1976, s. 26, for "The minimum number" (w.e.f. 131A. Exclusive jurisdiction of the Supreme Court in regard to questions as to constitutional validity of Central laws).

APPENDIX D

RELATED ARTICLES OF U.N.O.

CHAPTER XIV
THE INTERNATIONAL COURT OF JUSTICE

Article 92

The International Court of Justice shall be the principal judicial organ of the United Nations. It shall function in accordance with the annexed Statute, which is based upon the Statute of the Permanent Court of International Justice and forms an integral part of the present Charter.

Article 93

All Members of the United Nations are *ipso facto* parties to the Statute of the International Court of Justice.

A state which is not a Member of the United Nations may become a party to the Statute of the International Court of Justice on conditions to be determined in each case by the General Assembly upon the recommendation of the Security Council.

Article 94

Each Member of the United Nations undertakes to comply with the decision of the International Court of Justice in any case to which it is a party.

If any party to a case fails to perform the obligations incumbent upon it under a judgment rendered by the Court, the other party may have recourse to the Security Council, which may, if it deems necessary, make recommendations or decide upon measures to be taken to give effect to the judgment.

Article 95

Nothing in the present Charter shall prevent Members of the United Nations from entrusting the solution of their differences to other tribunals by virtue of agreements already in existence or which may be concluded in the future.

Article 96

The General Assembly or the Security Council may request the International Court of Justice to give an advisory opinion on any legal question.

Other organs of the United Nations and specialized agencies, which may at any time be so authorized by the General Assembly, may also request advisory opinions of the Court on legal questions arising within the scope of their activities.

APPENDIX E

STATUTE OF THE INTERNATIONAL COURT OF JUSTICE

Article 1

The International Court of Justice established by the Charter of the United Nations as the principal judicial organ of the United Nations shall be constituted and shall function in accordance with the provisions of the present Statute.

CHAPTER I

ORGANIZATION OF THE COURT

Article 2

The Court shall be composed of a body of independent judges, elected regardless of their nationality from among persons of high moral character, who possess the qualifications required in their respective countries for appointment to the highest judicial offices, or are jurisconsults of recognized competence in international law.

Article 3

1. The Court shall consist of fifteen members, no two of whom may be nationals of the same state.
2. A person who for the purposes of membership in the Court could be regarded as a national of more than one state shall be deemed to be a national of the one in which he ordinarily exercises civil and political rights.

Article 4

1. The members of the Court shall be elected by the General Assembly and by the Security Council from a list of persons nominated by the national groups in the Permanent Court of Arbitration, in accordance with the following provisions.
2. In the case of Members of the United Nations not represented in the Permanent Court of Arbitration, candidates shall be nominated by national groups appointed for this purpose by their governments under the same conditions as those prescribed for members of the Permanent Court of Arbitration by Article 44 of the Convention of The Hague of 1907 for the pacific settlement of international disputes.
3. The conditions under which a state which is a party to the present Statute but is not a Member of the United Nations may participate in electing the members of the Court shall, in the absence of a special agreement, be laid down by the General Assembly upon recommendation of the Security Council.

Article 5

1. At least three months before the date of the election, the Secretary-General of the United Nations shall address a written request to the members of the Permanent Court of Arbitration belonging to the states which are parties to the present Statute, and to the members of the national groups appointed under Article 4, paragraph 2, inviting them to undertake, within a given time, by national groups, the nomination of persons in a position to accept the duties of a member of the Court.
2. No group may nominate more than four persons, not more than two of whom shall be of their own nationality. In no case may the number of candidates nominated by a group be more than double the number of seats to be filled.

Article 6

Before making these nominations, each national group is recommended to consult its highest court of justice, its legal faculties and schools of law, and its national academies and national sections of international academies devoted to the study of law.

Article 7

1. The Secretary-General shall prepare a list in alphabetical order of all the persons thus nominated. Save as provided in Article 12, paragraph 2, these shall be the only persons eligible.
2. The Secretary-General shall submit this list to the General Assembly and to the Security Council.

Article 8

The General Assembly and the Security Council shall proceed independently of one another to elect the members of the Court.

Article 9

At every election, the electors shall bear in mind not only that the persons to be elected should individually possess the qualifications required, but also that in the body as a whole the representation of the main forms of civilization and of the principal legal systems of the world should be assured.

Article 10

1. Those candidates who obtain an absolute majority of votes in the General Assembly and in the Security Council shall be considered as elected.
2. Any vote of the Security Council, whether for the election of judges or for the appointment of members of the conference envisaged in Article 12, shall be taken without any distinction between permanent and non-permanent members of the Security Council.

3. In the event of more than one national of the same state obtaining an absolute majority of the votes both of the General Assembly and of the Security Council, the eldest of these only shall be considered as elected.

Article 11

If, after the first meeting held for the purpose of the election, one or more seats remain to be filled, a second and, if necessary, a third meeting shall take place.

Article 12

1. If, after the third meeting, one or more seats still remain unfilled, a joint conference consisting of six members, three appointed by the General Assembly and three by the Security Council, may be formed at any time at the request of either the General Assembly or the Security Council, for the purpose of choosing by the vote of an absolute majority one name for each seat still vacant, to submit to the General Assembly and the Security Council for their respective acceptance.
2. If the joint conference is unanimously agreed upon any person who fulfils the required conditions, he may be included in its list, even though he was not included in the list of nominations referred to in Article 7.
3. If the joint conference is satisfied that it will not be successful in procuring an election, those members of the Court who have already been elected shall, within a period to be fixed by the Security Council, proceed to fill the vacant seats by selection from among those candidates who have obtained votes either in the General Assembly or in the Security Council.
4. In the event of an equality of votes among the judges, the eldest judge shall have a casting vote.

Article 13

1. The members of the Court shall be elected for nine years and may be re-elected; provided, however, that of the judges elected at the first election, the terms of five judges shall expire at the end of three years and the terms of five more judges shall expire at the end of six years.
2. The judges whose terms are to expire at the end of the above-mentioned initial periods of three and six years shall be chosen by lot to be drawn by the Secretary-General immediately after the first election has been completed.
3. The members of the Court shall continue to discharge their duties until their places have been filled. Though replaced, they shall finish any cases which they may have begun.
4. In the case of the resignation of a member of the Court, the resignation shall be addressed to the President of the Court for transmission to the Secretary-General. This last notification makes the place vacant.

Article 14

Vacancies shall be filled by the same method as that laid down for the first election subject to the following provision: the Secretary-General shall, within one month of the occurrence of the vacancy, proceed to issue the invitations provided for in Article 5, and the date of the election shall be fixed by the Security Council.

Article 15

A member of the Court elected to replace a member whose term of office has not expired shall hold office for the remainder of his predecessor's term.

Article 16

1. No member of the Court may exercise any political

or administrative function, or engage in any other occupation of a professional nature.

2. Any doubt on this point shall be settled by the decision of the Court.

Article 17

1. No member of the Court may act as agent, counsel, or advocate in any case.
2. No member may participate in the decision of any case in which he has previously taken part as agent, counsel, or advocate for one of the parties, or as a member of a national or international court, or of a commission of enquiry, or in any other capacity.
3. Any doubt on this point shall be settled by the decision of the Court.

Article 18

1. No member of the Court can be dismissed unless, in the unanimous opinion of the other members, he has ceased to fulfil the required conditions.
2. Formal notification thereof shall be made to the Secretary-General by the Registrar.
3. This notification makes the place vacant.

Article 19

The members of the Court, when engaged on the business of the Court, shall enjoy diplomatic privileges and immunities.

Article 20

Every member of the Court shall, before taking up his duties, make a solemn declaration in open court that he will exercise his powers impartially and conscientiously.

Article 21

1. The Court shall elect its President and Vice-President for three years; they may be re-elected.
2. The Court shall appoint its Registrar and may

provide for the appointment of such other officers as may be necessary.

Article 22

1. The seat of the Court shall be established at The Hague. This, however, shall not prevent the Court from sitting and exercising its functions elsewhere whenever the Court considers it desirable.
2. The President and the Registrar shall reside at the seat of the Court.

Article 23

1. The Court shall remain permanently in session, except during the judicial vacations, the dates and duration of which shall be fixed by the Court.
2. Members of the Court are entitled to periodic leave, the dates and duration of which shall be fixed by the Court, having in mind the distance between The Hague and the home of each judge.
3. Members of the Court shall be bound, unless they are on leave or prevented from attending by illness or other serious reasons duly explained to the President, to hold themselves permanently at the disposal of the Court.

Article 24

1. If, for some special reason, a member of the Court considers that he should not take part in the decision of a particular case, he shall so inform the President.
2. If the President considers that for some special reason one of the members of the Court should not sit in a particular case, he shall give him notice accordingly.
3. If in any such case the member Court and the President disagree, the matter shall be settled by the decision of the Court.

Article 25

1. The full Court shall sit except when it is expressly provided otherwise in the present Statute.
2. Subject to the condition that the number of judges available to constitute the Court is not thereby reduced below eleven, the Rules of the Court may provide for allowing one or more judges, according to circumstances and in rotation, to be dispensed from sitting.
3. A quorum of nine judges shall suffice to constitute the Court.

Article 26

1. The Court may from time to time form one or more chambers, composed of three or more judges as the Court may determine, for dealing with particular categories of cases; for example, labour cases and cases relating to transit and communications.
2. The Court may at any time form a chamber for dealing with a particular case. The number of judges to constitute such a chamber shall be determined by the Court with the approval of the parties.
3. Cases shall be heard and determined by the chambers provided for in this Article if the parties so request.

Article 27

A judgment given by any of the chambers provided for in Articles 26 and 29 shall be considered as rendered by the Court.

Article 28

The chambers provided for in Articles 26 and 29 may, with the consent of the parties, sit and exercise their functions elsewhere than at The Hague.

Article 29

With a view to the speedy dispatch of business, the Court

shall form annually a chamber composed of five judges which, at the request of the parties, may hear and determine cases by summary procedure. In addition, two judges shall be selected for the purpose of replacing judges who find it impossible to sit.

Article 30

1. The Court shall frame rules for carrying out its functions. In particular, it shall lay down rules of procedure.
2. The Rules of the Court may provide for assessors to sit with the Court or with any of its chambers, without the right to vote.

Article 31

1. Judges of the nationality of each of the parties shall retain their right to sit in the case before the Court.
2. If the Court includes upon the Bench a judge of the nationality of one of the parties, any other party may choose a person to sit as judge. Such person shall be chosen preferably from among those persons who have been nominated as candidates as provided in Articles 4 and 5.
3. If the Court includes upon the Bench no judge of the nationality of the parties, each of these parties may proceed to choose a judge as provided in paragraph 2 of this Article.
4. The provisions of this Article shall apply to the case of Articles 26 and 29. In such cases, the President shall request one or, if necessary, two of the members of the Court forming the chamber to give place to the members of the Court of the nationality of the parties concerned, and, failing such, or if they are unable to be present, to the judges specially chosen by the parties.
5. Should there be several parties in the same interest, they shall, for the purpose of the preceding

provisions, be reckoned as one party only. Any doubt upon this point shall be settled by the decision of the Court.

6. Judges chosen as laid down in paragraphs 2, 3, and 4 of this Article shall fulfil the conditions required by Articles 2, 17 (paragraph 2), 20, and 24 of the present Statute. They shall take part in the decision on terms of complete equality with their colleagues.

Article 32

1. Each member of the Court shall receive an annual salary.
2. The President shall receive a special annual allowance.
3. The Vice-President shall receive a special allowance for every day on which he acts as President.
4. The judges chosen under Article 31, other than members of the Court, shall receive compensation for each day on which they exercise their functions.
5. These salaries, allowances, and compensation shall be fixed by the General Assembly. They may not be decreased during the term of office.
6. The salary of the Registrar shall be fixed by the General Assembly on the proposal of the Court.
7. Regulations made by the General Assembly shall fix the conditions under which retirement pensions may be given to members of the Court and to the Registrar, and the conditions under which members of the Court and the Registrar shall have their travelling expenses refunded.
8. The above salaries, allowances, and compensation shall be free of all taxation.

Article 33

The expenses of the Court shall be borne by the United Nations in such a manner as shall be decided by the General Assembly.

CHAPTER II

COMPETENCE OF THE COURT

Article 34

1. Only states may be parties in cases before the Court.
2. The Court, subject to and in conformity with its Rules, may request of public international organizations information relevant to cases before it, and shall receive such information presented by such organizations on their own initiative.
3. Whenever the construction of the constituent instrument of a public international organization or of an international convention adopted thereunder is in question in a case before the Court, the Registrar shall so notify the public international organization concerned and shall communicate to it copies of all the written proceedings.

Article 35

1. The Court shall be open to the states parties to the present Statute.
2. The conditions under which the Court shall be open to other states shall, subject to the special provisions contained in treaties in force, be laid down by the Security Council, but in no case shall such conditions place the parties in a position of inequality before the Court.
3. When a state which is not a Member of the United Nations is a party to a case, the Court shall fix the amount which that party is to contribute towards the expenses of the Court. This provision shall not apply if such state is bearing a share of the expenses of the Court

Article 36

1. The jurisdiction of the Court comprises all cases

which the parties refer to it and all matters specially provided for in the Charter of the United Nations or in treaties and conventions in force.

2. The states parties to the present Statute may at any time declare that they recognize as compulsory *ipso facto* and without special agreement, in relation to any other state accepting the same obligation, the jurisdiction of the Court in all legal disputes concerning:
   a. the interpretation of a treaty;
   b. any question of international law;
   c. the existence of any fact which, if established, would constitute a breach of an international obligation; and
   d. the nature or extent of the reparation to be made for the breach of an international obligation.
3. The declarations referred to above may be made unconditionally or on condition of reciprocity on the part of several or certain states, or for a certain time.
4. Such declarations shall be deposited with the Secretary-General of the United Nations, who shall transmit copies thereof to the parties to the Statute and to the Registrar of the Court.
5. Declarations made under Article 36 of the Statute of the Permanent Court of International Justice and which are still in force shall be deemed, as between the parties to the present Statute, to be acceptances of the compulsory jurisdiction of the International Court of Justice for the period which they still have to run and in accordance with their terms.
6. In the event of a dispute as to whether the Court has jurisdiction, the matter shall be settled by the decision of the Court.

Article 37

Whenever a treaty or convention in force provides for reference of a matter to a tribunal to have been instituted by the League of Nations, or to the Permanent Court of International Justice, the matter shall, as between the parties to the present Statute, be referred to the International Court of Justice.

Article 38

1. The Court, whose function is to decide in accordance with international law such disputes as are submitted to it, shall apply:
   a. international conventions, whether general or particular, establishing rules expressly recognized by the contesting states;
   b. international custom, as evidence of a general practice accepted as law;
   c. the general principles of law recognized by civilized nations; and
   d. subject to the provisions of Article 59, judicial decisions and the teachings of the most highly qualified publicists of the various nations, as subsidiary means for the determination of rules of law.
2. This provision shall not prejudice the power of the Court to decide a case *ex aequo et bono*, if the parties agree thereto.

CHAPTER III

PROCEDURE

Article 39

1. The official languages of the Court shall be French and English. If the parties agree that the case shall be conducted in French, the judgment shall be delivered in French. If the parties agree that the case shall be conducted in English, the judgment shall be delivered in English.
2. In the absence of an agreement as to which language shall be employed, each party may, in the pleadings, use the language which it prefers; the decision of the

Court shall be given in French and English. In this case the Court shall at the same time determine which of the two texts shall be considered as authoritative.

3. The Court shall, at the request of any party, authorize a language other than French or English to be used by that party.

Article 40

1. Cases are brought before the Court, as the case may be, either by the notification of the special agreement or by a written application addressed to the Registrar. In either case the subject of the dispute and the parties shall be indicated.
2. The Registrar shall forthwith communicate the application to all concerned.
3. He shall also notify the Members of the United Nations through the Secretary-General, and also any other states entitled to appear before the Court.

Article 41

1. The Court shall have the power to indicate, if it considers that circumstances so require, any provisional measures which ought to be taken to preserve the respective rights of either party.
2. Pending the final decision, notice of the measures suggested shall forthwith be given to the parties and to the Security Council

Article 42

1. The parties shall be represented by agents.
2. They may have the assistance of counsel or advocates before the Court.
3. The agents, counsel, and advocates of parties before the Court shall enjoy the privileges and immunities necessary to the independent exercise of their duties.

Article 43

1. The procedure shall consist of two parts: written and oral.
2. The written proceedings shall consist of the communication to the Court and to the parties of memorials, counter-memorials and, if necessary, replies; also all papers and documents in support.
3. These communications shall be made through the Registrar, in the order and within the time fixed by the Court.
4. A certified copy of every document produced by one party shall be communicated to the other party.
5. The oral proceedings shall consist of the hearing by the Court of witnesses, experts, agents, counsel, and advocates.

Article 44

1. For the service of all notices upon persons other than the agents, counsel, and advocates, the Court shall apply direct to the government of the state upon whose territory the notice has to be served.
2. The same provision shall apply whenever steps are to be taken to procure evidence on the spot.

Article 45

The hearing shall be under the control of the President or, if he is unable to preside, of the Vice-President; if neither is able to preside, the senior judge present shall preside.

Article 46

The hearing in Court shall be public, unless the Court shall decide otherwise, or unless the parties demand that the public be not admitted .

Article 47

1. Minutes shall be made at each hearing and signed by the Registrar and the President.

2. These minutes alone shall be authentic.

Article 48

The Court shall make orders for the conduct of the case, shall decide the form and time in which each party must conclude its arguments, and make all arrangements connected with the taking of evidence.

Article 49

The Court may, even before the hearing begins, call upon the agents to produce any document or to supply any explanations. Formal note shall be taken of any refusal.

Article 50

The Court may, at any time, entrust any individual, body, bureau, commission, or other organization that it may select, with the task of carrying out an enquiry or giving an expert opinion.

Article 51

During the hearing any relevant questions are to be put to the witnesses and experts under the conditions laid down by the Court in the rules of procedure referred to in Article 30.

Article 52

After the Court has received the proofs and evidence within the time specified for the purpose, it may refuse to accept any further oral or written evidence that one party may desire to present unless the other side consents.

Article 53

1. Whenever one of the parties does not appear before the Court, or fails to defend its case, the other party may call upon the Court to decide in favour of its claim.
2. The Court must, before doing so, satisfy itself, not only that it has jurisdiction in accordance with Articles 36 and 37, but also that the claim is well founded in fact and law.

Article 54

1. When, subject to the control of the Court, the agents, counsel, and advocates have completed their presentation of the case, the President shall declare the hearing closed.
2. The Court shall withdraw to consider the judgment.
3. The deliberations of the Court shall take place in private and remain secret.

Article 55

1. All questions shall be decided by a majority of the judges present.
2. In the event of an equality of votes, the President or the judge who acts in his place shall have a casting vote.

Article 56

1. The judgment shall state the reasons on which it is based.
2. It shall contain the names of the judges who have taken part in the decision.

Article 57

If the judgment does not represent in whole or in part the unanimous opinion of the judges, any judge shall be entitled to deliver a separate opinion.

Article 58

The judgment shall be signed by the President and by the Registrar. It shall be read in open court, due notice having been given to the agents.

Article 59

The decision of the Court has no binding force except between the parties and in respect of that particular case.

Article 60

The judgment is final and without appeal. In the event of dispute as to the meaning or scope of the judgment, the Court shall construe it upon the request of any party.

Article 61

1. An application for revision of a judgment may be made only when it is based upon the discovery of some fact of such a nature as to be a decisive factor, which fact was, when the judgment was given, unknown to the Court and also to the party claiming revision, always provided that such ignorance was not due to negligence.
2. The proceedings for revision shall be opened by a judgment of the Court expressly recording the existence of the new fact, recognizing that it has such a character as to lay the case open to revision, and declaring the application admissible on this ground.
3. The Court may require previous compliance with the terms of the judgment before it admits proceedings in revision.
4. The application for revision must be made at latest within six months of the discovery of the new fact.
5. No application for revision may be made after the lapse of ten years from the date of the judgment.

Article 62

1. Should a state consider that it has an interest of a legal nature which may be affected by the decision in the case, it may submit a request to the Court to be permitted to intervene.
2 It shall be for the Court to decide upon this request.

Article 63

1. Whenever the construction of a convention to which states other than those concerned in the case are

parties is in question, the Registrar shall notify all such states forthwith.

2. Every state so notified has the right to intervene in the proceedings; but if it uses this right, the construction given by the judgment will be equally binding upon it.

Article 64

Unless otherwise decided by the Court, each party shall bear its own costs.

CHAPTER IV

ADVISORY OPINIONS

Article 65

1. The Court may give an advisory opinion on any legal question at the request of whatever body may be authorized by or in accordance with the Charter of the United Nations to make such a request.
2. Questions upon which the advisory opinion of the Court is asked shall be laid before the Court by means of a written request containing an exact statement of the question upon which an opinion is required, and accompanied by all documents likely to throw light upon the question.

Article 66

1. The Registrar shall forthwith give notice of the request for an advisory opinion to all states entitled to appear before the Court.
2. The Registrar shall also, by means of a special and direct communication, notify any state entitled to appear before the Court or international organization considered by the Court, or, should it not be sitting, by the President, as likely to be able to furnish information on the question, that the Court will be prepared to receive, within a time limit to be fixed

by the President, written statements, or to hear, at a public sitting to be held for the purpose, oral statements relating to the question.

3. Should any such state entitled to appear before the Court have failed to receive the special communication referred to in paragraph 2 of this Article, such state may express a desire to submit a written statement or to be heard; and the Court will decide.
4. States and organizations having presented written or oral statements or both shall be permitted to comment on the statements made by other states or organizations in the form, to the extent, and within the time limits which the Court, or, should it not be sitting, the President, shall decide in each particular case. Accordingly, the Registrar shall in due time communicate any such written statements to states and organizations having submitted similar statements.

Article 67

The Court shall deliver its advisory opinions in open court, notice having been given to the Secretary-General and to the representatives of Members of the United Nations, of other states and of international organizations immediately concerned.

Article 68

In the exercise of its advisory functions the Court shall further be guided by the provisions of the present Statute which apply in contentious cases to the extent to which it recognizes them to be applicable.

Chapter V

AMENDMENT

Article 69

Amendments to the present Statute shall be effected by the same procedure as is provided by the Charter of the

United Nations for amendments to that Charter, subject however to any provisions which the General Assembly upon recommendation of the Security Council may adopt concerning the participation of states which are parties to the present Statute but are not Members of the United Nations.

Article 70

The Court shall have power to propose such amendments to the present Statute as it may deem necessary, through written communications to the Secretary-General, for consideration in conformity with the provisions of Article 69.

APPENDIX F

PROTOCOL NO. 2 TO THE CONVENTION FOR THE PROTECTION OF HUMAN RIGHTS AND FUNDAMENTAL FREEDOMS, CONFERRING UPON THE EUROPEAN COURT OF HUMAN RIGHTS COMPETENCE TO GIVE ADVISORY OPINIONS (European Treaty Series—No. 44)

Strasbourg, 6.5.1963

Protocol No. 2 (ETS No. 44) had been an integral part of the Convention since its entry into force on 21 September 1970. However, all provisions which had been amended or added by this Protocol are replaced by Protocol No. 11 (ETS No. 155), as from the date of its entry into force, on 1 November 1998.

Preamble

The member-States of the Council of Europe signatory hereto,

Having regard to the provisions of the Convention for the Protection of Human Rights and Fundamental Freedoms signed at Rome on 4th November 1950 (hereinafter referred to as "the Convention") and, in particular, Article 19 instituting, among other bodies, a European Court of Human Rights (hereinafter referred to as "the Court");

Considering that it is expedient to confer upon the Court competence to give advisory opinions subject to certain conditions, have agreed as follows:

Article 1

1. The Court may, at the request of the Committee of Ministers, give advisory opinions on legal questions concerning the interpretation of the Convention and the Protocols thereto.
2. Such opinions shall not deal with any question relating to the content or scope of the rights or freedoms defined in Section 1 of the Convention and in the Protocols thereto, or with any other question which the Commission, the Court or the Committee of Ministers might have to consider in consequence of any such proceedings as could be instituted in accordance with the Convention.
3. Decisions of the Committee of Ministers to request an advisory opinion of the Court shall require a two-thirds majority vote of the representatives entitled to sit on the Committee.

Article 2

The Court shall decide whether a request for an advisory opinion submitted by the Committee of Ministers is within its consultative competence as defined in Article 1 of this Protocol.

Article 3

1. For the consideration of requests for an advisory opinion, the Court shall sit in plenary session.
2. Reasons shall be given for advisory opinions of the Court.
3. If the advisory opinion does not represent in whole or in part the unanimous opinion of the judges, any judge shall be entitled to deliver a separate opinion.
4. Advisory opinions of the Court shall be communicated to the Committee of Ministers.

Article 4

The powers of the Court under Article 55 of the Convention shall extend to the drawing up of such rules and the determination of such procedure as the Court may think necessary for the purposes of this Protocol.

Article 5

1. This Protocol shall be open to signature by member-States of the Council of Europe, signatories to the Convention, who may become Parties to it by:
   a. signature without reservation in respect of ratification or acceptance; and
   b. signature with reservation in respect of ratification or acceptance, followed by ratification or acceptance.

   Instruments of ratification or acceptance shall be deposited with the Secretary General of the Council of Europe.
2. This Protocol shall enter into force as soon as all States Parties to the Convention shall have become Parties to the Protocol, in accordance with the provisions of paragraph 1 of this Article.
3. From the date of the entry into force of this Protocol, Articles 1 to 4 shall be considered an integral part of the Convention.
4. The Secretary General of the Council of Europe shall notify the member-States of the Council of:
   a. any signature without reservation in respect of ratification or acceptance;
   b. any signature with reservation in respect of ratification or acceptance;
   c. the deposit of any instrument of ratification or acceptance; and
   d. the date of entry into force of this Protocol in accordance with paragraph 2 of this Article.

In witness whereof, the undersigned, being duly authorised thereto, have signed this Protocol.

Done at Strasbourg, this 6th day of May 1963, in English and in French, both texts being equally authoritative, in a single copy which shall remain deposited in the archives of the Council of Europe. The Secretary General shall transmit certified copies to each of the signatory States.

APPENDIX G

PROTOCOL NO. 2 TO THE CONVENTION FOR THE PROTECTION OF HUMAN RIGHTS AND FUNDAMENTAL FREEDOMS, CONFERRING UPON THE EUROPEAN COURT OF HUMAN RIGHTS COMPETENCE TO GIVE ADVISORY OPINIONS (ETS NO. 44)

Explanatory Report

I. Protocol No. 2 to the European Convention for the Protection of Human Rights and Fundamental Freedoms was prepared within the framework of the Council of Europe by the Committee of Experts on Human Rights. It was opened for signature on 6 May 1963.

II. This document contains the text of the explanatory report and of the commentary of the Committee of Experts on Human Rights, which publication was authorised by the Committee of Ministers at the 139th Meeting of the Ministers' Deputies in March, 1965.

General Considerations

1. On 22nd January, 1960, the Consultative Assembly adopted Recommendation 232 on the "extention of the competence of the European Court of Human Rights as regards the interpretation of the Convention on Human Rights".
2. By Resolution (60) 20 of 15th September, 1960, the Committee of Ministers instructed the Committee of Experts to "determine whether it is desirable to

conclude an agreement on the basis of the proposals made in Recommendation 232 (1960) of the Consultative Assembly".

3. In the report which it prepared in April, 1961, the Committee of Experts expressed the view that it would be desirable to confer upon the European Court of Human Rights competence to give, subject to certain conditions, advisory opinions.
4. At its meeting in July, 1961, the Committee of Ministers in principle adopted the conclusions of the above-mentioned report and instructed the Committee of Experts to submit a draft Agreement based upon these conclusions.
5. The Committee of Expelts prepared the draft at its meetings held from 2nd to 11th October, 1961, from 2nd to 10th March, 1962 and from 1st to 7th June, 1962. On 5th March, 1962, a wide exchange of views was held on the matter at a joint meeting of members of the Committee of Experts and the Legal Committee of the Consultative Assembly.
6. The Committee of Experts in June, 1962 submitted a Report to the Committee of Ministers containing a draft Agreement confering on the Court of Human Rights competence to give advisory opinions.
7. Also in June, 1962, the European Commission of Human Rights sent to the Secretary General of the Council of Europe a letter proposing that the draft Agreement should confer on the Commission, as on the Committee of Ministers, the right to request advisory opinions from the Court.
8. The Minister's Deputies agreed at their 113th Meeting, held in September, 1962, to send the draft Agreement back to the Committee of Experts with new instructions to give an opinion on the proposals put forward by the Commission and also on the comments of certain delegations.
9. The Committee of Experts discussed these proposals and comments at the meeting held from 22nd to 27th October, 1962, under the Chairmanship of Mr. Ugo Caldarera, Italian Governmental Expert. In the

course of this meeting, Mr Petren, President of the Commission, explained the reasons which had led the Commission to submit proposals for amending the draft Agreement.

In addition, the Committee of Experts, after noting the model text for final clauses adopted in September, 1962, by the Ministers' Deputies, revised the wording of the final clauses of the draft in the light of that model text.

10. At the same meeting the Committee of Experts drew up a further Report which it submitted to the Committee of Ministers.

This included the final text of the Second Protocol and the comments of the Committee of Experts on:

- the proposals submitted by the Commission;
- the comments made by some of the Ministers' Deputies; and
- the changes made to the draft prepared in June, 1962.

COMMENTARY RELATING TO THE DRAFT PREPARED IN JUNE, 1962

Title

1. The following title has been given to the draft Agreement of which the Committee recommends the adoption: "(draft) Agreement conferring upon the European Court of Human Rights competence to give advisory opinions".

2. The draft includes a preamble and five Articles.

Preamble

3. The preamble calls for no comment.

Article 1

4. The purpose of this article is to define the consultative competence of the Court.

5. Paragraph 1 provides that the Court may, at the request of the Committee of Ministers, give advisory opinions on legal questions concerning the interpretation of the European Convention on Human Rights and the Protocols thereto.

6. The questions on which such opinions may be given must therefore have a legal character. The term legal questions" is to be understood as having the same meaning as is given to this term in similar international conventions.

As the Committee stated in its first report, this rules out, on the one hand, questions which would go beyond the mere interpretation of the text and tend by additions, improvements or corrections to modify its substance; and, on the other hand, questions whose solution would in any way involve matters of policy.

7. Only the Committee of Ministers shall have the right to request advisory opinions of the Court.

The Consultative Assembly, the European Commission of Human Rights and the Secretary General may submit proposals for requests for advisory opinions to the Committee of Ministers. In such cases it would be for the Committee of Ministers to decide whether the proposed request for an advisory opinion, by its purport, is capable of being submitted to the Court by application of paragraphs 1 and 2 of this article.

The Committee of Ministers would also be in a position to judge of the desirability of referring any such proposal to the Court.

8. The question was considered whether the text of the Agreement should not contain a provision determining what vote should be required for decisions of the Committee of Ministers on requests for advisory opinions from the Court.

The Legal Committee was of the opinion that such decisions should be taken by a majority of two-thirds of the members entitled to sit on the Committee (which is ihe majority provided for in Article 32 of the Convention) rather than by an unanimous vote.

Most of the Experts Shared this Opinion

Some experts considered that the question of voting in the

Committee of Ministers was part of the procedure for putting into operation the advisory competence conferred on the Court, and that the majority required for this vote should therefore be the subject of a statutory provision. They concluded that there was nothing to prevent the Committee inserting in the draft Agreement a provision on this point which might be worded as follows:

> "The decision of the Committee of Ministers to request the Court to give an advisory opinion shall be taken by a majority of two-thirds of the members entitled to sit on the Committee."

The majority of the experts thought it preferable not to include such a provision in the Agreement. They considered it was for the Committee of Ministers itself to determine what rules it would adopt in the matter (cf. Article 20 of the Statute of the Council of Europe).

9. The Court may exercise its consultative competence along within the limitations set out in paragraph 2 of Article 1. The object of those limitations is to prevent exercise of the consultative competence of the Court in questions which could come within the Court's primary function, namely, its judicial function. Under paragraph 2, the Court may not give an advisory opinion:

(a) on any question regarding the content or the scope of the rights and freedoms defined in Section 1 of the Convention and the Protocol thereto; or

(b) any other question which the Commission, Court or Committee of Ministers might have to consider in consequence of any such proceedings as could be instituted in accordance with the Convention.

10. As regards 9(a) above, the reasons for its inclusion are self-evident.

11. As regards 9(b) above, the Commission, the Court or the Committee of Ministers might, in consequence of the institution of proceedings, have to consider questions other

than those concerning the content or scope of rights and freedoms.

In the first place the Committee intended to exclude all questions of substance which, while they do not concern the content or scope of the rights and freedoms, involve obligations on the Contracting Parties.

Thus, Article 25, paragraph 1 of the Convention in fine provides that Contracting Parties which have recognised the right of individual application undertake not to hinder in any way the effective exercise of this right .

Article 57 stipulates that Contracting Parties must furnish, on request from the Secretary General, an explanation of the manner in which their internal law ensures the effective implementation of any of the provisions of the Convention.

According to Article 24 of the Convention any Contracting Party may refer to the Commission "any alleged breach" of the provisions of the Convention by another Contracting Party. Owing to the general terms in which this provision is cast, it would be possible for the bodies provided for by the Convention to have to consider breaches of the Convention which do not necessarily result from a violation of the rights and freedoms defined in Section 1 of the Convention and the Protocols, namely, violations of Articles 25, paragraph 1 and 57.

The Committee also intended to rule out questions of competence or of procedure which might come before one of the bodies provided for by the Convention in consequence of the institution of proceedings.

Thus, for example, the consultative competence of the Court does not extend to questions regarding the conditions of admissibility of applications before the Commission, which are defined in Articles 26 and 27 of the Convention.

The Committee has employed the phrase in French "par suite de introduction d'un recourse" ("in consequence of ..... proceedings") rather than the phrase "à l'occasion de 'introduction d'un recourse" ("in the course of proceedings") because it considered that the latter phrase was too wide.

The questions which are excluded are those which the Commission, the Court or the Committee of Ministers might have to consider in consequence of the institution of proceedings provided for in the Convention whether such proceedings are past, present, future or merely hypothetical.

The reference to the Commission in this text naturally includes a Sub-Commission (cf. Articles 29 and 30 of the convention).

Article 2

12. This article provides that the Court shall decide whether a request for an advisory opinion submitted by the Committee of Ministers is within its consultative competence as defined in the preceding article.

This provision is based upon Article 49 of the Convention which states that "in the event of disputes as to whether the Court has jurisdiction, the matter shall be settled by the decision of the court".

Thus, the Court has both the right and the obligation to refuse a request for an advisory opinion which the Committee of Ministers has asked to give if it comes to the conclusion that the request made is not within the scope of the Court's power as defined in this Agreement.

Article 3

13. Paragraph 1 of this article states that for the requests for an advisory opinion the Court shall sit in plenary session.

In its present form, Article 43 of the Convention provides that for consideration of cases brought before it, the Court shall consist of a Chamber composed of seven judges.

The Committee considered that the power conferred on the Court to give advisory opinions was such an important one that it ought to be exercised by the Court sitting in plenary session.

14. Paragraph 2 states that reasons shall be given for the advisory opinion of the Court.

This provision is based on Article 51, paragraph 1, of the Convention, which provides that reasons shall be given for the judgments of the Court.

15. Paragraph 3 provides that if the advisory opinion, in whole or in part, does not represent the unanimous opinion of the judges, any judge shall be entitled to deliver a separate opinion.

This paragraph is based upon Article 51, paragraph 2, of the Convention, Article 57 of the Statute of the International Court of Justice and also on Article 84, paragraph 2, of the Rules of Court of the International Court of Justice.

16. Paragraph 4 provides that an advisory opinion of the Court shall be communicated to the Committee of Ministers. This paragraph calls for no observations.

Article 4

17. The object of this article is to extend the powers of the Court laid down in Article 55 of the Convention to meet the purposes of the present Agreement.

Under Article 55, the Court has the power to draw up its own rules and determine its own procedure in respect of its jurisdiction in contentious matters.

The Court will also be able, by virtue of Article 4 of this Agreement, to exercise such power as regards its consultative competence if it thinks it necessary.

Article 5

18. This article contains the final clauses.

Paragraph 1 provides that the States signatories to the Convention may become Parties to the Agreement either by signature without reservation in respect of ratification , or by signature with reservation in respect of ratification followed by ratification.

This formula, which is intended to make it possible to speed up the entry into force of the Agreement, is based on similar clauses included in recent instruments concluded by the Council of Europe.[1]

1. See Article 7 of the Agreement on the exchange of war cripples, signed on 13th December, 1955; Article 5 of the Second Protocol to the General Agreement on Privileges and Immunities, signed on 15th December 1956; Article 8 of the European Agreement on Regulations governing the Movement of Persons, signed on 13th December, 1957; Article 6 of the European Arrangement on the exchange of television programmes, signed on 15th December, 1958; Article 7 of the European Agreement on the exchange of therapeutic substances, signed on 15th December, 1958; Article 8 of the European Agreement on the abolition of visas for refugees,

19. Paragraph 2 provides that this Agreement shall enter into force as soon as all States Parties to the Convention shall have signed it without reservation in respect of ratification or shall have ratified it.

Since the effect of this Agreement is to extend the competence of the Court as it is defined in the Convention, its entry into force will of necessity require the consent of all States which are Parties to the Convention.

20. Paragraph 3 concerns the notifications which must be made by the Secretary General and requires no comment.

FURTHER COMMENTARY RELATING TO THE DRAFT PREPARED IN OCTOBER, 1962

1. The Committee of Experts first considered whether the wording of the draft Protocol should not be reviewed in the light of the latest proposals presented by the European Court of Human Rights to the effect that two new articles, Articles 54 (bis) and 54 (ter), be incorporated in the Convention.

Article 54 (bis) would confer on the Court competence to give a prejudicial ruling, at the request of certain courts or tribunals, on any question of interpretation which might arise before these courts or tribunals.

Article 54 (ter) would confer on the Court competence to render an advisory opinion, at the request of a government, on any question of interpretation of the Convention which might arise in connection with a draft regulation or decree, a Bill or any projected legislation.

The Committee of Experts has not yet concluded its examination of these proposals.

While recognizing that there might be certain connections between the latter and the present draft, the majority of the Committee of Experts thought that there was no need to

---

signed on 20th April, 1959; Article 5 of the Agreement for the temporary importation of medical and surgical equipment, signed on 28th April, 1960; Article 7 of the European Arrangement for the protection of television broadcasts, signed on 22nd June, 1960; Article 9 of the Fourth Protocol to the General Agreement on Privileges and Immunities, signed on 16th December, 1961.

review the wording of the draft in the light of the Court's proposals.

2. The Committee of Experts also discussed whether the provisions of the Agreement should not be incorporated in the Convention in the form of additional Articles.

The Committee of Experts finally came to the conclusion that the Agreement should be presented to the States for signature in the form of a Protocol to the Convention.

It was agreed, however, that from the date of the entry into force of the Protocol, Articles 1 to 4 thereof should become an integral part of the Convention. This is specified in the new paragraph 3 of Article 5 of the draft.

The Committee of Experts was anxious to ensure that after the entry into force of the present Protocol, a State could not become a Party to the Convention without at the same time becoming a Party to the Protocol.

A number of experts thought that to this end it would be preferable to amend the text of the Convention.

Title

3. For the reasons explained in paragraph 2 of this commentary, the title of the Agreement has been changed to read as follows:

> "Protocol to the Convention for the Protection of Human Rights and Fundamental Freedoms, conferring upon the European Court of Human Rights competence to give advisory opinions"

Preamble

4. To conform with the model text of final clauses adopted by the Ministers' Deputies at their 113th Meeting, the experts made a purely drafting change to the first sentence of the Preamble.

Article 1, paragraph 1

5. For the reasons of principle set out in the report of June, 1962, the majority of the experts felt unable to adopt the Commission's proposal to the effect that the latter, like the

Committee of Ministers, should be able to apply directly to the Court for advisory opinions. They considered, in particular, that the Committee of Ministers, as a body representing the governments, was the one best qualified to appreciate the advisability of asking the Court for an advisory opinion.

6. Some experts expressed the view that the commission's proposals could be adopted. One of them made the following declaration on this point :[2]

> "There is no disadvantage in granting the Commission, concurrently with the Committee of Ministers, the power to request opinions of the Court. In fact, none of the principles laid down in the Human Rights Convention, or deriving from that instrument, imply that the right to request opinions on the interpretation of the Convention must be reserved to a single organ, in this case the Committee of Ministers. Moreover, since the Commission is an essential part of the machinery set-up by the Convention, it would be a logical extension of the idea which has inspired the granting of advisory competence to the Court that the right to invoke such competence should not be refused to the Commission or subjected to what appears to be the prior approval of the Committee of Ministers".

The material field of the Court's advisory powers has been so narrowly circumscribed in the draft of the Committee of Experts that the additional precaution, whereby any request for advisory opinion is channeled through the Committee of Ministers, appears excessive.

Article 1, paragraph 2

7. The majority of the experts took the view that the scope of the court's advisory powers could not be more precisely defined than in the present text.

8. The Committee considered that it would be useful to confer upon the Court competence to give advisory opinions within the limitations of the text adopted by the Commission.

2. This expert asked that his declaration should appear in extenso in this report.

Article 1, paragraph 3

9. After having again examined the matter, the Committee of Experts considered it preferable to insert a third paragraph in Article 1 of the Protocol, expressly stating that a decision of the Committee of Ministers to request an advisory opinion must be taken by a two-thirds majority vote of the representatives entitled to sit on the Committee.

Article 2

10. For the reasons set forth in paragraph 2 of this commentary, the word "Agreement" has been replaced by the word "Protocol".

Article 3

11. No comment.

Article 4

12. See comment in paragraph 10 of this commentary.

Article 5

13. General comment on Article 5. Referring to the model text of final clauses adopted by the Ministers' Deputies at their 113th Meeting, the Committee made a number of changes to the wording of this article. In paragraph 1, in particular, mention has been made of the procedure, not only of ratification, but also of acceptance.

Article 5, paragraph 2

14. One expert made some comments on paragraph 2 of Article 5.

The Committee of Experts considered that, for the reasons set forth at paragraph 19 in the Commentary to the draft Agreement, the present Protocol should not enter into force until all the States Parties to the Convention become Parties to this Protocol.

Article 5, paragraph 3

15. The reasons why the Committee decided to insert a third paragraph have already been set out in paragraph 2 of this commentary.

APPENDIX H

THE SUPREME COURT RULES, 1966

(Part V Order XXXVII)

Special Reference Under Article 143 of the Constitution

1. On the receipt by the Registrar of the Order of the President referring a question of law or fact to the Court under Article 143 of the Constitution the Registrar shall give notice to the Attorney-General for India to appear before the Court on a day specified in the notice to take the directions of the Court as to the parties who shall be served with notice of such reference, and the Court may, if it considers it desirable, order that notice of such reference, shall be served upon such parties as may be named in the order.
2. Subject to the directions of the Court the notice shall require all such parties served therewith as desired to be heard at the hearing of the reference to attendbefore the Court on the day fixed by the order to take the directions of the Court with respect to statements of facts and arguments and with respect, to the date of the hearing.
3. Subject to the provisions of this Order, on a reference under article 143 of the Constitution, the Court shall follow as nearly as may be the same procedure as is followed in proceedings before the Court in the exercise of its original jurisdiction, but with such

variations as may appear to the Court to be appropriate and as the Court may direct.

4. After the hearing of the reference under Article 143 of the Constitution the Registrar shall transmit to the President the report of the Court thereon.
5. The Court may make such order as it thinks fit as to the costs of all parties served with notice under these rules and appearing at the hearing of the reference under Article 143 of the Constitution.

Glossary

1. ACT

A set of rules and principles that determine a system of society's do's and don'ts; the institutions that legislate and enforce such rules. For example, when the party of the first part parties too hard, the party of the second part can sue.

2. AD-HOC

Ad-hoc is a Latin phrase which means "for this [purpose]". It generally signifies a solution designed for a specific problem or task, non-generalizable, and which cannot be adapted to other purposes.

Common examples are organizations, committees, and commissions created at the national or international level for a specific task. In other fields the term may refer, for example, to a tailor-made suit, a handcrafted network protocol or a purpose-specific equation. *ad-hoc* can also have connotations of a makeshift solution, inadequate planning, or improvised events. Other derivatives of the Latin include *ad-hoc, ad-hoc* and *ad-hoc.*

3. ADVISORY OPINION

An advisory opinion is an opinion issued by a court that does not have the effect of resolving a specific legal case, but merely advises on the constitutionality or interpretation of a law. Some countries have procedures by which the executive or legislative branches may certify important questions to the judiciary and obtain an advisory opinion. In other countries or specific jurisdictions, courts may be prohibited from issuing advisory opinions.

4. AMENDMENT

Amendment, in law, alteration of the provisions of a legal document. The term usually refers to the alteration of a statute or a constitution, but it is also applied in parliamentary law to proposed changes to a bill or motion under consideration, and in judicial procedure to the correction of errors. A statute may be amended by the passage of an act that is identified specifically as an amendment to it or by a new statute that renders some of its provisions nugatory. Written constitutions, however, for the most part must be amended by an exactly prescribed procedure. The Constitution of the United States, as provided in Article 5, may be amended when two-thirds of each house of Congress approves a proposed amendment (approval by the president is not required), and three-fourths of the states thereafter ratify it, sometimes within a set period. Congress decides whether state ratification shall be by vote of the legislatures or by popularly elected conventions. Only in the case of the Twenty-first Amendment (repealing prohibition) has the convention system been used. In many U.S. states, a proposed amendment to the state constitution must be submitted to the voters in a referendum.

5. ANGLO-SAXONS

Anglo-Saxons is the name collectively applied to the descendants of the Germanic people who settled in Britain between the late 4th and early 7th cents. Their backgrounds varied. Some came as mercenaries, others as invaders. They included, besides Angles and Saxons, Jutes and other groups. The eventual use of the name 'English' and 'England' for people and territory probably owes something to Bede, whose *History of the English People* dealt with the whole. He followed Pope Gregory I, who knew the people as Angles.

Much about the invasion and settlement is obscure, but for most of its history Anglo-Saxon England is one of the best-documented early medieval European societies. Besides Bede's *History*, historical sources include a number of saints' lives, and the *Anglo-Saxon Chronicle*. Many letters survive, those of the Anglo-Saxon missionary to the continent, Boniface, of particular importance. A great body of evidence relates to royal ideology, government, and administration: vernacular law codes (beginning with that of Æthelbert of Kent), charters, writs, and wills. Historians also benefit from the study of the language of vernacular texts, from that of place-names, of art (including sculpture), and of architecture. Archaeology, of burials, settlements, towns, kings' halls (Yeavering, Cheddar), monasteries, and churches, is critically important. Yet there are still uncertainties. Gaps in the evidence, problems of its interpretation and of reconciling different types, generate lively debate. Some may never be solved: it is salutary to realize how important subjects depend on chance survivals or discoveries—the ship-burial at Sutton Hoo.

6. APPELLATE JURISDICTION

Appellate jurisdiction is the power of a court to review decisions and change outcomes of decisions of lower courts. Most appellate jurisdiction is legislatively created, and may consist of appeals by leave of the appellate court or by right. Depending on the type of case and the decision below, appellate review primarily consists of: an entirely new hearing (a trial de novo); a hearing where the appellate court gives deference to factual findings of the lower court; or review of particular legal rulings made by the lower court (an appeal on the record).

7. ARTICLES

Series or sub-divisions of individual and distinct sections of a document, statute, or other writing, such as the Articles of Confederation. Codes or systems of rules created by written agreements of parties or by statute that establish standards of legally acceptable behaviour in a business relationship, such as articles of incorporation or articles of partnership. Writings that embody contractual terms of agreements between parties.

8. ATTORNEY GENERAL

Chief law-enforcement officer of a state and legal adviser to the chief executive. The office dates to the Middle Ages but did not assume its modern form until the 16th century. In the U.S., the position dates to the Judiciary Act of 1789. Head of the Department of Justice and a member of the cabinet, the attorney general oversees all the government's law business and acts as the president's legal adviser. Every U.S. state also has an attorney general.

9. AUTONOMY

Autonomy (Ancient Greek: áõôïíüìïò *autonomos*, Modern Greek: áõôïíïìßá *autonomia*, from *auto* "self" + *nomos*, "law": one who gives oneself his/her own law) is a concept found in moral, political, and bioethical philosophy. Within these contexts, it refers to the capacity of a rational individual to make an informed, un-coerced decision. In moral and political philosophy, autonomy is often used as the basis for determining moral responsibility for one's actions. One of the best known philosophical theories of autonomy was developed by Kant. In medicine, respect for the autonomy of patients is an important goal, though it can conflict with a competing ethical principle, namely beneficence. Politically, it is also used to refer to the self-governing of a people.

Autonomy [Gr.,=self-rule], in a political sense, limited self-government, short of independence, of a political state or, more frequently, of a sub-division. The term is also used for other self-governing units, such as a parish, a corporation, or a religious sect. A test of autonomy is the recognition that the group may make the rules governing its internal affairs. Political autonomy is frequently based on cultural and ethnic differences. Autonomy within empires has frequently been a prelude to independence, as in the case of the evolution of the British Empire into the Commonwealth of Nations, containing both autonomous and completely sovereign states. Autonomy as in the former Soviet "autonomous" republics and regions in Russia, providing local control over cultural and economic affairs, often is perceived as inadequate by nationalists, who sometimes have demanded independence, as in Chechnya. The same has proven true in Slovakia, and provides impetus for terrorism by Basque, Corsican, and Welsh extremists.

10. BENCH

A forum of justice comprised of the judge or judges of a court. The seat of the court occupied by the judges. The bench is used to refer to a group of judges as a collective whole. It is a tribunal or place where justice is administered. To appear before the full bench means to appear before the entire group of judges of the court.

11. BILL

Proposed legislation which has not yet been enacted. In the United Kingdom Parliament there are two types of bill: public and private. Public bills presented by ministers in the House of Commons, which take up the most parliamentary time, follow a set procedure, which is also followed for other public bills and private bills but with some variations. A bill initially is merely a short title, usually with an explanatory memorandum signed on the back by the minister in charge. It is read for the first time in the House of Commons. Upon passing, a complete draft of parts or chapters, classes, and schedules is drawn up and submitted for a second reading in the House. Here members debate the general principle and purposes of the bill. If the vote to confirm the second reading is won the bill is then committed to a standing committee to debate the detail. Complex bills may be referred to a select committee first, which then passes its recommendations to the standing committee. For some bills, notably finance bills, the detail is debated by a committee of the whole house and/or a standing committee. A bill is then reported to the House complete with suggested amendments from the committee stage. During the report stage these and any further amendments are debated in the House. Ultimately, the bill complete with agreed amendments is then given its third reading, and upon passing is submitted to the House of Lords. Generally, the Lords agree suggested amendments to the bill after which it is returned to the Commons. Members may then debate only the amendments suggested by the Lords and pass on their views. This continues until agreement is reached. The bill in its final form is then taken to the monarch by the clerks of the House of Lords for royal assent. When this is received the bill becomes an act and a date of commencement for the act coming into force may be set. A bill may be defeated on a vote at any of the three readings in the House of Commons and by the House of Lords. A bill may also be lost by being talked out in the Commons and in committee. Governments anxious to prevent this resort to the guillotine procedure, by which a time limit for each stage of a bill's passage is set. Ultimately, the Commons has supremacy under the 1911 and 1949 Parliament Acts and can override a Lords' veto by passing a bill twice in successive sessions.

12. CABINET

Body of senior ministers or, in the U.S., advisers to a chief executive, whose members also serve as the heads of government departments. The cabinet has become an integral part of parliamentary government in many countries, though its form varies. It developed from the British Privy Council, when King Charles II and Queen Anne regularly consulted the council's leading members to reach decisions before meeting with the unwieldy full council. The modern British cabinet consists of departmental ministers, drawn from the members of Parliament and appointed by the prime minister. In the U.S., the cabinet serves as an advisory group to the president without the sanction of law. Members' appointments are subject to Senate approval, and the U.S. Constitution sets cabinet members' order of succession to the presidency. The cabinet includes the secretaries of State, Treasury, Defense, Interior, Agriculture, Commerce, Labour, Health and Human Services, Housing and Urban Development, Transportation, Education, Energy, and Veterans Affairs and the Attorney General.

A cabinet is a body of high-ranking members of government, typically representing the executive branch. It can also sometimes be referred to as the council of ministers, an executive council, or an executive committee.

13. CHARTER

Document granting certain specified rights, powers, privileges, or functions from the sovereign power of a state to a person, corporation, city, or other unit of local organization. In Magna Carta (1215), King John granted certain liberties to the English people. Elsewhere in medieval Europe, monarchs issued charters to towns, guilds, universities, and other institutions, granting the institution certain privileges and sometimes specifying how they should conduct their internal affairs. Later, charters were granted to overseas trading companies (e.g., the British East India Co.), granting them monopolies in certain areas. Britain's colonies in North America were established by charter. Modern charters may be corporate or municipal. A corporate charter, issued by a governmental body, grants individuals the power to form a corporation, or limited-liability company. A municipal charter is a law that creates a new political sub-division and allows the people within it to organize themselves into a municipal corporation, in effect delegating to the people the powers of local self-government.

14. COMMONWEALTH

Free association of sovereign states consisting of Britain and many of its former dependencies who have chosen to maintain ties of friendship and cooperation. It was established in 1931 by the Statute of Westminster as the British Commonwealth of Nations. Later its name was changed and it was redefined to include independent nations. Most of the dependent states that gained independence after 1947 chose Commonwealth membership. The British monarch serves as its symbolic head, and meetings of the more than 50 Commonwealth heads of government take place every two years.

15. COMMONWEALTH OF NATIONS

The present Commonwealth comprises Britain and most of her old empire: 54 states, scattered over all the inhabited continents, with a population estimated (in 1994) at 1.4 billion. Mozambique, not a former British colony, was admitted as a special case in 1995.

The term 'commonwealth', in this context, dates from the early 20th century and grew out of the realization that several of Britain's older-established colonies were already self-governing in all essential respects. To call them 'colonies', or an 'empire', appeared to undervalue their real independence, and the new word was felt by some to express better the form the empire would take: a federation of equal nation states. This development was not to everyone's liking, however. Enthusiasts for the 'commonwealth ideal' had generally envisaged the dominions taking an equal share in the formulation of policies that would then be common to them all: instead it came to mean that they would have equal rights to separate policies of their own.

This privilege was established in the early 1920s, after disputes within the Commonwealth over the Washington naval conference of 1921-2 and the Chanak affair in 1922. In 1923 Canada became the first dominion to conclude a treaty with a foreign power (the Halibut Fish treaty) without reference to Britain; and the pattern for the future was set. It was formalized by an important pronouncement of the 1926 imperial conference, defining dominion status; and by the 1931 statute of Westminster, which confirmed the dominions' legislative autonomy. For the moment this only applied to colonies of European settlement, and not to the 'non-white' colonies. That changed in 1947, when the newly independent nation of India was admitted to the Commonwealth. That established the multiracial character of the Commonwealth as it exists today.

As decolonization progressed, other ex-colonies followed. Many old imperialists regarded this process with pride. Some of them saw the new Commonwealth as the culmination of the empire. In a way it was, for there had always been a strong tradition of what was called 'trusteeship' in British imperial thought. The idea that the Commonwealth could be a kind of empire-substitute, however, was soon shattered. The newest members regarded their hard-won national independence jealously, and there were sharp clashes between members, especially over the issue of apartheid, which forced South Africa to leave in 1961. So the Commonwealth became much less than the united 'third force' in the world that the imperial optimists had envisaged.

As it stands now, it is totally unlike any other international organization of states. It has a secretariat, and a secretary-general (set-up in 1965), but little else in common. It has no power, no united policy, no common principles, and no shared institutions. Most member states are parliamentary democracies, but not all. Most have retained English legal forms, but not all. Most play cricket, but not all. The single constitutional feature common to all member-states is that they acknowledge the British monarch as symbolic head of the Commonwealth, but fewer than half recognize her or him as the head of their own states. It was once thought of as an economic unit, a potential free (or preferential) trade area, but that was never convincing, and collapsed when Britain joined the European Economic Community in 1973.

Nevertheless the Commonwealth still serves a purpose, as a forum for informal discussion and co-operation between nations of widely disparate cultures. That function is served by a host of specialist Commonwealth institutions (the Commonwealth Institute in London, the Commonwealth Parliamentary Association, the Association of Commonwealth Universities, the Commonwealth of Learning); and by biennial conferences of Commonwealth heads of government. The ideal it represents still flickers, albeit fitfully.

16. CONSTITUTION OF INDIA

The *Constitution of India* is the supreme law of India. It lays down the framework defining fundamental political principles, establishing the structure, procedures, powers and duties, of the government and spells out the fundamental rights, directive principles and duties of citizens. Passed by the Constituent Assembly on November 26, 1949, it came into effect on January 26, 1950. The date 26 January was chosen to commemorate the declaration of independence of 1930. It declares the Union of India to be a sovereign, democratic republic, assuring its citizens of justice, equality, and liberty; the words *"socialist"*, *"secular"* and *"integrity"* were added to the definition in 1976 by constitutional amendment. India celebrates the adoption of the constitution on January 26 each year as Republic Day. It is the longest written constitution of any sovereign country in the world, containing 444 articles, 12 schedules and 94 amendments, for a total of 117,369 words in the English language version. Besides the English version, there is an official Hindi translation. After coming into effect, the Constitution replaced the Government of India Act, 1935 as the governing document of India. Being the supreme law of the country, every law enacted by the government must conform to the constitution.

17. CONTEMPT

In law, wilful disobedience to or open disrespect of a court, judge, or legislative body. An act of disobedience to a court order may be treated as either criminal or civil contempt; sanctions for the latter end upon compliance with the order. An act or language that consists solely of an affront to a court or interferes with the conduct of its business constitutes criminal contempt; such contempt carries sanctions designed to punish as well as to coerce compliance. In the U.S., a congressional committee can compel the attendance of witnesses. Any witness failing to appear or otherwise obstructing the committee in the course of exercising its powers may be in contempt. Witnesses are, however, protected by the 5th Amendment against forced self-incrimination..

18. CONTEMPT OF COURT

Contempt of court is a court order which, in the context of a court trial or hearing, deems an individual as having been disrespectful of the court, its process, and its invested powers. Often stated simply as "in contempt" or a person "held in contempt", it is the highest remedy of a judge to impose sanctions on an individual for acts which excessively or in a wanton manner disrupt the normal process of a court hearing.

A finding of contempt of court may result from a failure to obey a lawful order of a court, showing disrespect for the judge, disruption of the proceedings through poor behaviour, or publication of material deemed likely to jeopardize a fair trial. A judge may impose sanctions such as a fine or jail for someone found guilty of contempt of court. Typically judges in common law systems have more extensive power to declare someone in contempt than judges in civil law systems.

In civil cases involving relations between private citizens, the intended victim of the act of contempt is usually the party for whose benefit the ruling was implemented, rather than the court.

A person found in contempt of court is called a "contemnor". To prove contempt, the prosecutor or complainant must prove the four elements of contempt:

- existence of a lawful order
- the contemnor's knowledge of the order
- the contemnor's ability to comply
- the contemnor's failure to comply

19. COURT

A court is a body, often a governmental institution, with the authority to adjudicate legal disputes and dispense civil, criminal, or administrative justice in accordance with rules of law. In common law and civil law states, courts are the central means for dispute resolution, and it is generally understood that all persons have an ability to bring their claims before a court. Similarly, those accused of a crime have the right to present their defense before a court. Court facilities range from a simple farmhouse for a village court in a rural community to huge buildings housing dozens of courtrooms in large cities.

Court is an official assembly with judicial authority to hear and determine disputes in particular cases. In early judicial tribunals, judges sat in enclosures (courts in an architectural sense), and lawyers and the general public remained outside a bar (hence the term *bar* in legal contexts). Modern British courts are divided into those trying criminal cases and those trying civil cases; a second distinction is made between inferior courts, or courts of first instance, and superior courts, or courts of appeal. In the U.S. each state has its own system of courts, usually consisting of a superior (appellate) court, trial courts of general jurisdiction, and specialized courts (e.g., probate courts). The U.S. also has a system of federal courts, established to adjudicate distinctively national questions and cases not appropriately tried in state courts. At the apex of the national system is the Supreme Court of the United States. The secondary level consists of the United States Courts of Appeals. United States District Courts form the tertiary level. Crimes committed by military figures may be tried in a court-martial. In the past, ecclesiastical courts had broad jurisdiction.

20. COURTS IN ENGLAND

In England, after the Norman Conquest (1066), royal authority was gradually extended over the feudal lords, and by the early 13th century, although purely local courts had not been abolished, the supremacy of the central courts that had evolved from the Curia Regis [Lat.,=king's court], namely, the Court of Exchequer, the Court of Common Pleas, and King's Bench, was established. The Court of Common Pleas heard cases between ordinary subjects of the king, while King's Bench heard cases involving persons of high rank and acted as a court of appeals. Soon itinerant royal courts were established to spare civil litigants the labour and expense of going to the capital at Westminster and to afford hearings to persons held on criminal charges in county jails. By the 14th cent. the principal function of the central courts was to hear appeals from the circuit courts.

Unity was at least temporarily disrupted by the emergence (16th century) of equity as a distinct body of law administered by the chancery. The conflict of jurisdiction continued to some extent until 1875, when the Judicature Act of 1873 went into effect. As presently constituted as a result of subsequent reforms, the courts of England and Wales consist of the Court of Appeal, the High Court (with civil jurisdiction), the Crown Court (with criminal jurisdiction), the county courts, and the magistrates' courts. The High Court is divided, purely for administrative purposes, into three divisions: Chancery, Family, and King's (or Queen's) Bench. Appeals may in some instances be taken from the court of appeal to the House of Lords. The judicial committee of the privy council hears appeals from overseas territories still under British domain and from some Commonwealth countries. Under the Constitutional Reform Act, 2005 a new Supreme Court for Great Britain and Northern Ireland will be created in 2009, ending the role of the House of Lords as the highest court of appeal.

21. COURTS IN THE UNITED STATES

In the United States there are two distinct systems of courts, federal and state. Each is supreme in its own sphere, but if a matter simultaneously affects the states and the federal government, the federal courts have the decisive power. The district court is the lowest federal court. Each state has at least one federal district, and some of the more populous states contain as many as four districts. There are 11 circuit courts of appeals (each with jurisdiction over a defined territory) and a court of appeals for the District of Columbia; these hear appeals from the district courts. There are, in addition, various specialized federal courts, including the Tax Court and the federal Court of Claims. Heading the federal court system is the U.S. Supreme Court.

The court systems of the states vary to some degree. At the bottom of a typical structure are local courts that have authority only in specific matters and jurisdictions (e.g., court of the justice of the peace, police court, and court of probate). County courts, or the equivalent, exercising general criminal and civil jurisdiction, are on the next level. All states have a highest court of appeals, and some also have intermediate appellate courts. In a few states separate courts of equity persist.

22. DIRECTIVE PRINCIPLES OF STATE POLICY

The *Directive Principles of State Policy* are guidelines to the central and state governments of India, to be kept in mind while framing laws and policies. These provisions, contained in Part IV of the Constitution of India, are not enforceable by any court, but the principles laid down therein are considered fundamental in the governance of the country, making it the duty of the State to apply these principles in making laws to establish a just society in the country. The principles have been inspired by the Directive Principles given in the Constitution of Ireland and also by the principles of Gandhism; and relate to social justice, economic welfare, foreign policy, and legal and administrative matters. Directive Principles are classified under the following categories: Gandhian, economic and socialistic, political and administrative, justice and legal, environmental, protection of monuments and peace and security.

23. ELECTION

Formal process by which voters make their political choices on public issues or candidates for public office. The use of elections in the modern era dates to the emergence of representative government in Europe and North America since the 17th century. Regular elections serve to hold leaders accountable for their performance and permit an exchange of influence between the governors and the governed. The availability of alternatives is a necessary condition. Votes may be secret or public.

24. ELECTION COMMISSION

The *Election Commission* of India is an autonomous, quasi-judiciary constitutional body of India. Its mission is to conduct free and fair elections in India. It was established on January 25, 1950 under Article 324 of the Constitution of India. The Election Commission is one of the four pillars of the Indian Constitution, the other three being the Supreme Court of India, the Union Public Service Commission and the Comptroller and Auditor General of India. The commission presently consists of a Chief Election Commissioner and two Election Commissioners, appointed by the president. Until October 1989, there was just one Chief Election Commissioner. In 1989, two Election Commissioners were appointed, but were removed again in January 1990. In 1991, however, the Parliament of India passed a law providing for the appointment of two Election Commissioners. This law was amended and renamed in 1993 as the Chief Election Commissioner and other Election Commissioners (Conditions of Service) Amendment Act, 1993. As of Tuesday, April 21, 2009, the CEC is Navin Chawla. The two Election Commissioners are S.Y. Quraishi and former Power Secretary V.S. Sampath. The Chief Election Commissioner may be removed from his office in like manner and on the like grounds as a judge of the Supreme Court. It means the Chief Election Commissioner may be removed from office by Parliament by passing a resolution to that effect, passed by special majority on the ground of proved misbehaviour. Other Election Commissioner may be removed by the President on the recommendation of the Chief Election Commissioner.

25. ENTRY

The act of making or entering a record; a setting down in writing of particulars; or that which is entered; an item. Generally synonymous with *recording*. Passage leading into a house or other building or to a room; a vestibule. The act of a merchant, trader, or other business-person in recording in his or her account books the facts and circumstances of a sale, loan, or other transaction. The books in which such memoranda are first (or originally) inscribed are called *books of original entry,* and are *prima facie* evidence for certain purposes.

In copyright law, depositing with the register of copyrights the printed title of a book, pamphlet, and so on, for the purpose of securing copyright on the same. In immigration law, any coming of an alien into the United States, from a foreign part or place or from an outlying possession, whether voluntary or otherwise. In criminal law, entry is the unlawful making of one's way into a dwelling or other house for the purpose of committing a crime therein. In cases of burglary, the least entry with the whole or any part of the body, hand, or foot, or with any instrument or weapon, introduced for the purpose of committing a felony, is sufficient to complete the offense.

In customs law, the entry of imported goods at the custom house consists in submitting them to the inspection of the revenue officers, together with a statement or description of such goods, and the original invoices of the same, for the purpose of estimating the duties to be paid thereon. In real property law, the right or authority to assert one's possessory interest or ownership in a piece of land by going onto the land.

26. EUROPEAN COURT OF HUMAN RIGHTS

The *European Court of Human Rights* (*ECHR*) (French: *Cour européenne des droits de l'homme*) in Strasbourg is an international judicial body established under the European Convention on Human Rights (ECHR) of 1950 to monitor respect of human rights by states. The European Convention on Human Rights, or formally named Convention for the Protection of Human Rights and Fundamental Freedoms, is a convention adopted by the Council of Europe. All 47 member states of the Council of Europe are parties to the Convention. Applications against Contracting Parties for human rights violations can be brought before the Court either by other States Parties or by individuals.

The Court was instituted as a permanent court with full-time judges on 1 November 1998, replacing the then existing enforcement mechanisms, which included the European Commission of Human Rights (created in 1954) and the European Court of Human Rights, which had been created in 1959. The Court delivered its first judgment in 1960, *Lawless* v. *Ireland*.

27. EUROPEAN COURT OF JUSTICE

The European Court of Justice (ECJ), which is based in Luxembourg, is an institution of the European Union (EU) and should not be confused with the European Court of Human Rights. The ECJ played a crucial part in the process of integration in Europe, particularly by interpreting the treaty basis of the Community, formally a species of international law, as internal law common to the member-states. A series of judgments (starting with *Van Gend en Loos* 26/62 [1963] ECR 1 and *Costa* v. *ENEL* 6/64 [1964] ECR 585) interpreted the Treaty of Rome as a constitution for Europe, based on the doctrines of the 'direct effect' and 'supremacy' of Community law. Initially 'direct effect' meant that without further domestic legislation some articles of the Treaty of Rome became national law. It allowed individuals to rely on Community law as such before national courts.

The doctrine of 'direct effect' raised the possibility of a conflict between Community and national law. The ECJ resolved this problem by developing the principle of the 'supremacy' of Community law. Another feature of the Community which marks it out from other international organizations is its capacity to pass secondary legislation (that is, rules with the force of law which are not passed directly by one or more legislatures, but are authorized by them). The ECJ has strengthened this capacity by applying doctrine of direct effect to some secondary legislation (*Van Duyn* v. *Home Office* 41/74 [1974] ECR 1337). Although they took place over the same period of time as a political crisis that increased the control of the member states in the Community's legislative process, these legal developments provoked little or no political criticism. The criticism that did emerge was mainly legal. However, even the courts of the most recalcitrant member states (Germany, Italy, and France) had more or less acknowledged the constitutional role of the ECJ by the middle of the 1980s.

28. FEDERAL COURT

The term *"federal court"*, when used by itself, can refer to any court of the national government in a country that has a federal system such as that of the United States (United States federal courts) or Mexico or to a particular federal court, such as the United States district courts. In some countries, a particular court, for example, the Federal Court of Canada, the Federal Court of Australia or the Federal Court of Justice of Germany.

29. GOVERNOR-GENERAL

A *governor-general,* also known as *governor-general,* is a vice-regal representative of a monarch in an independent realm or a major colonial circonscription. Depending on the political arrangement of the territory, a governor-general can be a governor of high rank, or a principal governor ranking above "ordinary" governors. Today, the title governor-general is used in the independent Commonwealth realms (those Commonwealth countries which share Queen Elizabeth II, as Sovereign), with the exception of the United Kingdom, which does not have a Governor-General, being the Sovereign's home realm.

In modern usage, the term "governor-general" originated in those British colonies which became self-governing Dominions within the British Empire (examples are Australia, Canada and New Zealand). With the exception of New Zealand, each of the previously constituent colonies of these federated colonies already had a Governor, and the Crown's representative to the federated Dominion was therefore given the superior title of Governor-General. New Zealand was granted Dominion status in 1907, but as it had never been a federal state there was no pressing need to change the gubernatorial title. It was not until 28 June 1917 that Earl of Liverpool was appointed the first Governor-General of New Zealand. Another non-federal state, Newfoundland, was a Dominion for 16 years with the Kings's representative retaining the title of Governor throughout this time. Since the 1950s, the title governor general has been given to all representatives of the sovereign in independent Commonwealth realms. In these cases, the former office of colonial governor was altered (sometimes for the same incumbent) to become governor-general upon independence, as the nature of the office became an entirely independent constitutional representative of the monarch rather than a symbol of previous colonial rule. In these countries the governor general acts as the Monarch's representative, performing the ceremonial and constitutional functions of a Head of State.

30. GREAT BRITAIN

Great Britain, officially United Kingdom of Great Britain and Northern Ireland, constitutional monarchy (2005 est. pop. 60,441,000), 94,226 sq mi (244,044 sq km), on the British Isles, off W Europe. The country is often referred to simply as Britain. Technically, Great Britain comprises England (1991 pop. 46,382,050), 50,334 sq mi (130,365 sq km); Wales (1991 pop. 2,798,200), 8,016 sq mi (20,761 sq km); and Scotland (1991 pop. 4,957,000), 30,414 sq mi (78,772 sq km) on the island of Great Britain, while the United Kingdom includes Great Britain as well as Northern Ireland (1991 pop. 1,577,836), 5,462 sq mi (14,146 sq km) on the island of Ireland. The Isle of Man (1991 pop. 69,788), 227 sq mi (588 sq km), in the Irish Sea and the Channel Islands (1991 pop. 145,821), 75 sq mi (195 sq km), in the English Channel, are dependencies of the crown, with their own systems of government. For physical geography and local administrative divisions, see England, Wales, Scotland, and Ireland, Northern.

31. HOUSE OF COMMONS

The *House of Commons* is the name of the elected lower house of the bicameral parliaments of the United Kingdom and Canada. In the UK and Canada, the Commons holds much more legislative power than the upper house of parliament (the House of Lords and the Canadian Senate, respectively). The leader of the majority party in the House of Commons usually becomes the prime minister. Since 2005, the House of Commons of the United Kingdom has had 646 elected members; this will increase to 650 at the next General Election. The Canadian House of Commons has 308 members. The Commons' functions are to consider through debate new laws and changes to existing ones, authorise taxes, and provide scrutiny of the policy and expenditure of the Government. It has the power to give a Government a vote of no confidence. Historically, there have also been Houses of Commons in Ireland and North Carolina (United States).

The British House of Commons was created to serve as the political power base and voice for the free subjects of the realm, originally selected from the business and merchant classes of each local area to represent all the Sovereign's subjects who were not Lords Temporal or Spiritual. These estates are represented in the House of Lords. The name of the House does not originate from the fact that it represented the 'common' people, but rather from the fact that the constituencies represented were based on the commons (land areas) of England. The House of Commons was thus elected while members of the upper house were derived from hereditary title and descent, family lineage, or a service to the realm that warranted special recognition, such as the Law and Spiritual Lords. Throughout their histories, the British and Canadian Houses of Commons have become increasingly representative, as suffrage has been extended. Both bodies are now elected via universal adult suffrage. In both countries, the House of Commons may be prorogued for election only by the Crown, represented outside of the United Kingdom by the Governor General of each Commonwealth realm.

32. HOUSE OF LORDS

The Upper House of Britain's bicameral Parliament. From

the 13th and 14th centuries it was the house of the aristocracy. Until 1999 its membership included clergy, hereditary peers, life peers (peers appointed by the prime minister since 1958), and the judges of the Supreme Court of Judicature (Britain's final court of appeal). Though it predates the House of Commons and dominated it for centuries, its power has gradually diminished. Its power to affect revenue bills was constrained by the Parliament Act of 1911, and in 1949 its power to delay by more than a year the enactment of any bill passed by the Commons was revoked. In 1999 the hereditary peers lost their right to sit in the House of Lords, though an interim reform retains their voice in a more limited fashion. The body's chief value has been to provide additional consideration to bills that may be not be well formulated its largest city is London.

33. INTERIM ORDER

The term *interim order* refers to an order passed by a court during the pendency of the litigation. It is generally passed by the Court to ensure Status quo. The rationale for such orders to be passed by the Courts lie are best explained by Latin legal maxim "*Actus curiae neminem gravabit*" which translated to (English) stand for "*an act of the court shall prejudice no one*". Therefore to ensure that the interests of none of the party to the litigation are harmed, the court may pass an interim order. Interim orders passed by the court may be of various courts. The nature of the order essentially depends on the direction passed by the Court and on these basis they may be classified as under:

- Restraining order (also called *Injunction*), which are passed to stop either party from acting in a particular manner during the pendency of the civil action. These are essential passed by the court to prevent situations in which either party may suffer a harm because the other party did/continued an act which was the matter in issue and
- Directive order, which are passed to direct either part to continue to act in a particular manner till the conclusion of the trial or till further orders. These

may be passed if the non-continuation of the act would cause harm to the other party.

In public international law, the "rough equivalent" of an interim order is a provisional measure of protection, which can be "indicated" by the International Court of Justice. The manner and exercise of powers by the courts are prescribed under the laws of most nations. These may be either enacted by legislation in the form of procedural laws of the country (as done by, for example, the United Kingdom under the Civil Procedure Rules, 1998 or are left by the legislature for the courts to determine for themselves (for example, the Federal Rules of Civil Procedure). It is under these procedural laws that the power to issue interim orders may be conferred on the courts. In India, interim orders may be passed by civil courts in matters before them. Such orders can be passed either under the *Specific Relief Act* passed by the Parliament of India in 1963 or in terms of Section 151 of the *Civil Procedure Code* of 1908, which recognises and retains some *inherent powers* with the civil courts. However, the latter provision is usually seldom exercised. In terms of the 1963 Act, an interim order may be passed by the court only if the following conditions are satisfied;

1. Where there is a *prima facie* case in favour of the party seeking the order,
2. Irreparable damage may be caused to the party if the order is not passed and such damage may not be ascertained in terms of money and payable as damages, and
3. Where the balance of convenience lies with the party requesting for the order.

34. INTERNATIONAL COURT OF JUSTICE

Principal judicial body of the United Nations, located at The Hague. Its predecessor organization was the Permanent Court of International Justice, the judicial body of the League of Nations. Its first session was held in 1946. Its jurisdiction is limited to disputes between states willing to accept its authority on matters of international law. Its decisions are binding, but it has no enforcement power; appeals must be made to the UN Security Council. Its 15-member body of judges, each of whom serves a nine-year term, is elected by countries party to the court's founding statute. No two judges may come from the same country.

35. JUDICIAL COMMITTEE OF THE PRIVY COUNCIL

The *Judicial Committee of the Privy Council (JCPC)* is one of the highest courts in the United Kingdom, established by the Judicial Committee Act, 1833. It replaced the *Court of Delegates*. It is also the highest court of appeal (or court of last resort) for several independent Commonwealth countries, the UK overseas territories, and the British Crown dependencies. It is simply referred to as the *Privy Council,* as appeals are in fact made to the Queen as *Her Majesty in Council,* who then refers the case to the Judicial Committee for "advice". The panel of judges hearing a particular case (typically five members) is known as "the Board". It meets in the Privy Council Chamber in Downing Street.

In Commonwealth republics, appeals are made directly to the Judicial Committee instead. In the case of Brunei, the appeal is made to the local Sultan, who is advised by the Judicial Committee. Formerly the Judicial Committee gave a single piece of advice, but since the 1960s dissenting opinions have been allowed. In July 2007, the Judicial Committee held that it had power to depart from precedent if it concluded that one of its own previous decisions was incorrect.

The judicial system of the United Kingdom is unusual in having no single highest national court; the Judicial Committee is the highest court of appeal in some cases, while in most others the highest court of appeal is the House of Lords. In Scotland the highest court in criminal cases is the High Court of Justiciary, in civil cases the House of Lords, and the Judicial Committee of the Privy Council for matters arising from Scottish devolution.

36. JUDICIAL REVIEW

Examination by a country's courts of the actions of the legislative, executive, and administrative branches of government to ensure that those actions conform to the provisions of the constitution. Actions that do not conform are unconstitutional and therefore null and void. The practice is usually considered to have begun with the ruling by the Supreme Court of the United States in *Marbury* v. *Madison* (1803). Several constitutions drafted in Europe and Asia after World War II incorporated judicial review. Especially subject to scrutiny in the U.S. have been actions bearing on civil rights (or civil liberty), due process of law, equal protection under the law, freedom of religion, freedom of speech, and rights of privacy.

37. JURISDICTION

In law, *jurisdiction* (from the Latin *ius, iuris* meaning "law" and *dicere* meaning "to speak") is the practical authority granted to a formally constituted body or to a political leader to deal with and make pronouncements on legal matters and, by implication, to administer justice within a defined area of responsibility.

Alternatively, jurisdiction is the authority given to a legal body, or to a political leader to adjudicate and enforce legal matters.

Jurisdiction draws its substance from public international law, conflict of laws, constitutional law and the powers of the executive and legislative branches of government to allocate resources to best serve the needs of its native society.

There are three main types of judicial jurisdiction, personal (*personam*), territorial (*locum*), and subject matter (*subjectam*):

- *Personal* jurisdiction is an authority over a person, regardless of his location.
- *Territorial* jurisdiction is an authority confined to a bounded space, including all those present therein, and events which occur there.
- *Subject Matter* jurisdiction is an authority over the subject of the legal questions involved in the case.

Best examples of judicial jurisdiction are: appellate jurisdiction, in which a superior court has power to correct legal errors made in a lower court; concurrent jurisdiction, in which a suit might be brought to any of two or more courts; and federal jurisdiction. A court may also have authority to operate within a certain territory. Summary jurisdiction, in which a magistrate or judge has power to conduct proceedings resulting in a conviction without jury trial, is limited in the U.S. to petty offenses.

The geographic area over which authority extends; legal authority; the authority to hear and determine causes of action.

Jurisdiction generally describes any authority over a certain area or certain persons. In the law, jurisdiction sometimes refers to a particular geographic area containing a defined legal authority. For example, the federal government is a jurisdiction unto itself. Its power spans the entire United States. Each state is also a jurisdiction unto itself with power to pass its own laws. Smaller geographic areas, such as counties and cities, are separate jurisdictions to the extent that they have powers independent of the federal and state governments.

Jurisdiction also may refer to the origin of a court's authority. A court may be designated either as a court of general jurisdiction or as a court of special jurisdiction. A court of general jurisdiction is a trial court that is empowered to hear all cases that are not specifically reserved for courts of special jurisdiction. A court of special jurisdiction is empowered to hear only certain kinds of cases.

Courts of general jurisdiction are often called district courts or superior courts. In New York, however, the court of general jurisdiction is called the Supreme Court of New York. In most jurisdictions other trial courts of special jurisdiction exist apart from the courts of general jurisdiction; examples are probate, tax, traffic, juvenile, and, in some cities, drug courts. On the federal level, the district courts are courts of general jurisdiction. Federal courts of special jurisdiction include the Tax Court and the bankruptcy courts.

38. JUS

[*Latin, right; justice; law; the whole body of law; also a right.*] The term is used in two meanings:

Jus means *law,* considered in the abstract; that is, as

distinguished from any specific enactment, which we call, in a general sense, *the law.* Or it means the law taken as a system, an aggregate, a whole. Or it may designate some one particular system or body of particular laws; as in the phrases *jus civile, jus gentium, jus proetorium.*

In a second sense, *jus* signifies a*right;* that is, a power, privilege, faculty, or demand inherent in one person and incident upon another; or a capacity residing in one person of controlling, with the assent and assistance of the state, the actions of another. This is its meaning in the expressions *jus in rem, jus accrescendi, jus possessionis.*

39. LEGAL DOCTRINE

Legal doctrine is a framework, set of rules, procedural steps, or test, often established through precedent in the common law, through which judgments can be determined in a given legal case. A doctrine comes about when a judge makes a ruling where a process is outlined and applied, and allows for it to be equally applied to like cases. When enough judges make use of the process soon enough it becomes established as the *de facto* method of deciding like situations.

40. LEX

[*Latin, Law*] In medieval jurisprudence, a body or collection of various laws peculiar to a given nation or people; not a code in the modern sense, but an aggregation or collection of laws not codified or systematized. Also, a similar collection of laws relating to a general subject, and not peculiar to any one people.

In modern U.S. and English jurisprudence this term signifies a system or body of laws, written or unwritten, applicable to a particular case or question regarded as local or unique to a particular state, country, or jurisdiction.

41. MAJORITY

Full age; legal age; age at which a person is no longer a minor. The age at which, by law, a person is capable of being legally responsible for all of his or her acts (e.g. contractual obligations), and is entitled to the management of his or her own affairs and to the enjoyment of civic rights (e.g. right to vote). The opposite of minority. Also the *status* of a person who is a major in age. The greater number. The number greater than half of any total. The common-law age of majority is twenty-one although state legislatures may change this age by statute. Infants reach the age of majority on the first moment of the day preceding their twenty-first birthday. Minority is the period of time when a child.

42. MAXIM

A broad statement of principle, the truth and reasonableness of which are self-evident. A rule of equity, the system of justice that complements the common law. Maxims were originally quoted in Latin, and many of the Latin phrases are still familiar to lawyers today. The maxims were not written down in an organized code or enacted by legislatures, but they have been handed down through generations of judges. As a result, the wording of a maxim may vary from case to case. For example, it is a general rule that *equity does not aid a party at fault.*

43. OPINION

The reason given for a court's judgment, finding, or conclusion, as opposed to the decision, which is the judgment itself. See 107 P. 2d 1104, 1106, 1107. An opinion of a court implies its adoption by a majority of the judges. See 123 S.W. 2d 83, 85. Opinions are usually written by a single judge and if there were more than one judge deciding the matter, as in an appeal to a three-member appellate tribunal, other judges will join in the opinion. Concurring opinion one that is basically in accord with the majority opinion, but written to express a somewhat different view of the issues, to illuminate a particular judge's reasoning, to expound a principle which he holds in high esteem, etc. An opinion that concurs "in the result only" is one that entirely rejects the reasoning and conclusions concerning the law and/or the facts on the basis of which the majority reached its decision, and which expresses a different view, but has coincidentally led the judge or justice writing it to recommend the same disposition of the case (affirmance, dismissal, remand, etc.) as was agreed upon by the majority (or plurality).

Dissenting opinion one that disagrees with the disposition made of the case by the court, the facts or law on the basis of which the court arrived at its decision, and/or the principles of law announced by the court in deciding the case. Opinions may also be written which express a dissent "in part."

44. ORDER

Direction of a court or judge normally made or entered in writing, and not included in a judgment, which determines some point or directs some step in the proceedings. The decision of a court or judge is made in the form of an order. A court may issue an order after a motion of a party requesting the order, or the court itself may issue an order on its own discretion. For example, courts routinely issue scheduling orders, which set the timetable and procedure for managing a civil lawsuit. More substantive orders, however, typically are made following a motion by one of the parties.

45. PRESIDENT OF INDIA

The *President of India* or *Rashtrapati* (Sanskrit neologism, lit. "lord of the realm") is the head of state and first citizen of India, as well as the Supreme Commander of the Indian armed forces. In theory, the President possesses considerable power. With few exceptions, most of the authority vested in the President is in practice exercised by the Council of Ministers, headed by the Prime Minister.

The President is elected by the elected members of the Parliament of India (Lok Sabha and Rajya Sabha) as well as of the state legislatures (Vidhan Sabhas), and serves for a term of five years. Incumbents are permitted to stand for re-election. A formula. formula is used to allocate votes so there is a balance between the population of each state and the number of votes assembly members from a state can cast, and to give an equal balance between State Assembly members and National Parliament members. If no candidate receives a majority of votes there is a system by which losing candidates are eliminated from the contest and votes for them transferred to other candidates, until one gains a majority. The Vice-President is elected by a direct vote of all members (elected and nominated) of the Lok Sabha and Rajya Sabha.

46. PROCEDURE

The methods by which legal rights are enforced; the specific machinery for carrying on a lawsuit, including process, the pleadings, rules of evidence, and rules of civil procedure or criminal procedure. The form, manner, and order of steps taken in conducting a lawsuit are all regulated by procedural law, which regulates how the law will be administered.

47. SEPARATION OF POWERS

Division of the legislative, executive, and judicial functions of government among separate and independent bodies. Such a separation limits the possibility of arbitrary excesses by government, since the sanction of all three branches is required for the making, executing, and administering of laws. The concept received its first modern formulation in the work of Charles-Louis de Secondat, baron de La Brède et de Montesquieu, who declared it the best way to safeguard liberty; he influenced the framers of the Constitution of the United States, who in turn influenced the writers of 19th- and 20th-century constitutions.

48. SIR EDWARD COKE

Sir Edward Coke (born Feb. 1, 1552, Mileham, Norfolk, Eng.—died Sept. 3, 1634, Stoke Poges, Buckinghamshire) British jurist and politician. He became a lawyer in 1578 and was made solicitor general in 1592. His advance to the position of attorney general (1594) frustrated his great rival, Francis Bacon. As attorney general, he conducted several famous treason trials, prosecuting Robert Devereux, 2nd earl of Essex, and Henry Wriothesley, 3rd earl of Southampton (1600-01); Sir Walter Raleigh (1603); and the Gunpowder Plot conspirators (1605). Named chief justice of the Court of Common Pleas in 1606, Coke earned the ire of James I by declaring that the king's proclamation could not change the law (1610). He upset church leaders by limiting the jurisdiction of ecclesiastical courts. Appointed chief justice of the King's Bench by James I

(1613), he remained unswayed; he hinted at scandal in high places and defied a royal injunction in a case involving ecclesiastical privileges. He was dismissed in 1616, partly through Bacon's efforts. In 1620 he reentered Parliament (he had served in 1589), where he denounced interference with Parliament's liberties (1621) until he was imprisoned. In 1628 he helped frame the Petition of Right, a charter of liberties; this defense of the supremacy of the common law over royal prerogative had a profound influence on the English law and constitution. On his death his papers were seized by Charles I. His *Reports* (1600-15), taken together, are a monumental compendium of English common law, and his *Institutes of the Lawes of England* (4 Vols., 1628-44) is an important treatise.

49. STATUTE

Statute, in law, a formal, written enactment by the authorized powers of a state. The term is usually not applied to a written constitution but is restricted to the enactments of a legislature. Statute law is to be distinguished chiefly from common law, which may be defined as the body of legal rules derived from judicial decisions and custom. On most of the European continent all (or nearly all) the law is statutory and each field is subsumed by a code. In England and the United States, however, common law retains great importance, but with the expansion of government regulation there has been an immense growth in the statute law of those countries. In order to guide the courts many important statutes contain (usually in a preamble) a statement of the abuses that the legislation is intended to cure or of the general legislative intent. Statutes are classified in various ways. Public statutes (e.g., those establishing crimes) are universal in application, while private statutes (e.g., one compensating a named person for injury) are limited. Public statutes may be local, i.e., affecting only part of the area over which the legislature has authority, or general. Statutes that explain or clarify previous enactments or rules of common law are sometimes called declaratory statutes.

50. SUPREME COURT

A *Supreme Court* also called a *court of last resort* or *instance, court of final appeal* or *High Court,* is in some jurisdictions the highest judicial body within that jurisdiction's court system, whose rulings are not subject to further review by another court. The designations for such courts differ among jurisdictions. Courts of last resort typically function primarily as appellate courts, hearing appeals from the lower trial courts or intermediate-level appellate courts.

Many countries in fact have multiple "supreme courts," with each being the court of last resort for a particular geographical region or on a particular area of law. The United States, having a federal system of government, has a single Supreme Court of the United States, but each U.S. state furthermore has its own high court over which the U.S. Supreme Court only has jurisdiction on issues of federal law. Other jurisdictions follow the Austrian model of a separate constitutional court (first developed in the Czechoslovak constitution and Austrian Constitution of 1920). Furthermore, in e.g. Finland, Sweden, Czech Republic, Poland, and Taiwan, there is a separate Supreme Administrative Court whose decisions are final and whose jurisdiction does not overlap with the Supreme Court. The U.S. states of Texas and Oklahoma also divide subject matter jurisdiction among two separate courts of last resort, with one hearing criminal cases and the other civil cases.

In India, the Supreme Court of India was created on January 28, 1950 after the adoption of the Constitution. The Supreme Court is a constitutional authority independent from political interference. All judgments are binding across all states of India, the exception being the state of Jammu and Kashmir where the Indian Penal Code is not applicable. The court rulings take precedence over state High Courts. In extremely rare cases such as capital punishment, the decision may be passed on to the President of India for clemency petitions.

51. THE CONSTITUENT ASSEMBLY

The Constitution was drafted by the Constituent Assembly, which was elected by the elected members of the provincial assemblies. Jawaharlal Nehru, C. Rajagopalachari, Rajendra Prasad, Sardar Vallabhbhai Patel, Maulana Abul Kalam Azad, Shyama Prasad Mukherjee and N.R. Ghosh

[Nalini Ranjan Ghosh] were some important figures in the Assembly.

There were more than 30 members of the scheduled classes. Frank Anthony represented the Anglo-Indian community, and the Parsis were represented by H.P. Modi and R.K. Sidhwa. The Chairman of the Minorities Committee was Harendra Coomar Mookerjee, a distinguished Christian who represented all Christians other than Anglo-Indians. Ari Bahadur Gururng represented the Gorkha Community. Prominent jurists like Alladi Krishnaswamy Iyer, B.R. Ambedkar, Benegal Narsing Rau and K.M. Munshi Ganesh Mavlankar were also members of the Assembly. Sarojini Naidu, Hansa Mehta, Durgabai Deshmukh and Rajkumari Amrit Kaur were important women members. The first president of the Constituent Assembly was Sachidanand Sinha, later, Rajendra Prasad was elected president of the Constituent Assembly. The members of the Constituent Assembly met for the first time in the year 1946 on December 9.

52. UNION CABINET OF INDIA

The cabinet of ministers of the Government of India led by the Prime Minister of India is referred to as the Union Cabinet in India. The Prime Minister has the right to decide who he wants to include in his cabinet of ministers and what portfolio is assigned to them. The Union Cabinet is the most powerful executive body in India. The Union Cabinet has ministers of 3 types : (1) Cabinet Ministers, (2) State Ministers, (3) Deputy Ministers.

53. UNITED STATES PRESIDENTIAL CABINET

Under the doctrine of separation of powers, a cabinet under a presidential system of government is part of the executive branch. In theory, at least, they carry out policy rather than create it. In addition to administering his or her segment of the executive branch, a cabinet member is responsible for advising the head of government on areas within his or her purview. They are appointed by and serve at the pleasure of the head of government; they are strongly subordinate to the executive and can be replaced at any time. Normally, since they are appointed by the executive, they are members of the same political party, but the executive is free to select anyone, including opposition party members, subject to Congressional confirmation.

Normally, the legislature or a segment thereof must confirm the appointment of a cabinet member; this is but one of the many checks and balances built into a presidential system. The legislature may also remove a cabinet member through a usually difficult impeachment process.

54. WESTMINSTER CABINETS

Under the Westminster system, members of the cabinet are collectively responsible for all government policies. All ministers, whether senior and in the cabinet or junior ministers, must publicly support the policy of the government, regardless of any private reservations. Although, in theory, all cabinet decisions are taken collectively by the cabinet, in practice many decisions are delegated to the various sub-committees of the cabinet, which report to the full cabinet on their findings and recommendations. As these recommendations have already been agreed upon by those in the cabinet who hold affected ministerial portfolios, the recommendations are usually agreed to by the full cabinet with little further discussion.

55. WRIT

An order issued by a court requiring that something be done or giving authority to do a specified act. The development of English common law relied on the courts to issue writs that allowed persons to proceed with a legal action. Over time the courts also used writs to direct other courts, sheriffs, and attorneys to perform certain actions. In modern law, courts primarily use writs to grant extraordinary relief, to grant the right of appeal, or to grant the sheriff authority to seize property. Most other common-law writs were discarded in U.S. law, as the courts moved to simpler and more general methods of starting civil actions. U.S. courts commonly use several extraordinary writs, which are issued only when the courts believe that usual remedies have failed. The writ of *habeas corpus*, sometimes called the "great writ," is probably the best-known example of a writ.

Table of Cases

(A)

(B)

(C)

(D)

(E)

(G)

(H)

(I)

(N)

(P)

(R)

(S)

(T)

The Earl of Sheftbury's Case (1977) 86 ER 782

The Province of British Columbia *v.* The Attorney General of the Dominion of Canada 64 (Can) 377, 90

Tamil Nadu Cauvery Neerappasana Villai Porugal Vivasayigal Nala Urimal Padhugappa Sangam *v.* Union of India, (1990) 3 SCC 440, 137

T.M.A. Pai Foundation *v.* State of Karnataka AIR 2003 SC P. 335, 212

(U)

Uni Krishnan *v.* State of A.P. (1993) 1 SCC 645, 212

Union of India *v.* Paras Laminators (P) Ltd. (1990) 4 SCC 453: 1991 SCC (L&S) 208, 137, 145

(W)

Wellace Bross & Co. Ltd. *v.* CIT AIR 1948 PC 118: 75 1A 86.

Bibliography

1. Primary Sources

(a) Documents and Debate

The Constituent Assembly Debates, 1949.
The Parliamentary Debates, Indian Affairs, Lords (1934-45).
Parliamentary Debates, Indian Affairs Commons (1934-35).
Supreme Court of Canada Act 1906.
Commonwealth of Australia in Judiciary Act, 1903-19.
Finnish Constitution 1919.
Government of India Act 1935.
Constitution of Ireland 1927.
The Supreme Court Rules 1966.
Parliament Debates Lords (1934-35) Vol. 97C.
The Chairman's Draft Report (Lord Linlithgo) 1934.
All Pakistan Legal Decision 1955.
Gazette of Pakistan extraordinary Part III, Islamabad 2007.
The Charter of U.N.O.
Convention on the Privileges and Immunities of the United Nations of 1946.
Convention for the Protection of Human Rights and Fundamental Freedoms 1950.
Universal Declaration of Human Rights 1948.
The Kerala Education Bill 1957.
Delhi Laws Act 1912.
India-Pakistan Agreement of 1958.
Sea Customs Act 1878.

Central Exercise and Salt Act 1944.
The Delimitation Act 1972.
Presidential and Vice-Presidential Election Act 1962.
The Commission of Inquiry Act 1952.
Special Courts Bill 1978.
Jammu & Kashmir Resettlement Act 1982.
The River Board Act 1956.
Inter-State Water Dispute Act 1956.
Ayodhya Act 1993.
General Clause Act 1897.
Gujarat Gas (Regulation of Transmission, Supply and Distribution) Act 2001.
Representation of the People Act 1951.

(b) Books

Agarwal, B.R.: *The Supreme Court Practice and Procedure,* Metropolitan Book Co. Pvt. Ltd., Delhi, 1975.

Austin, G.: *The Indian Constitution: Cornerstone of a Nation,* Clarandon Press, Oxford, 1956.

Agarwal, Dr. H.O.: *International Law and Human Rights,* Central Law Publication, Allahabad, 2007.

Basu, D.D.: *Tagore Law Lectures on Limited Government and Judicial Review,* Sarkar and Sons Pvt. Ltd., Calcutta, 1972.

Basu, D.D.: *Introduction to the Constitution of India,* Wadhwa Publication, Nagpur, 2005.

Basu, D.D.: *Constitutional Law of India,* Practice Hall of India Pvt. Ltd., New Delhi, 1978.

Basu, D.D.: *Commentary on the Constitution of India,* Wadhwa Publication, Nagpur, 1992.

Basu, D.D.: *Annotated Constitution of India,* Practice Hall of India Pvt. Ltd., New Delhi, 1953.

Basu, D.D.: *Shorter Constitution of India,* Wadhwa Publication, Nagpur, 2001.

Chitley, D.V. and Rao, S. Appu : *A.I.R. Commentaries the Indian Constitution with the Extensive, Analytical and Critical Commentaries*. The All India Reports, Ltd., 1971.

Cowen, Z.: *Federal Jurisdiction in Australia,* Oxford University Press, London, 1959.

Dawson, R. Mac. Gregor : *The Government of Canada,* University of Toronto Press, London, 1970.

Dayal, S.: *The Constitution of India*, Law Publishers, Allahabad, 1975.

De. Smith S.A.: *Judicial Review of Legislation*, Eastern Book Co.; Lucknow 1975.

Dharma Pratap : *The Advisory Jurisdiction of International Court*, The Clarandon Press, London, 1972.

Dicey, A.V.: *Law of the Constitution*, MacMillan and Co. Ltd., London, 1959.

Dicey, A.V.: *An Introduction to the Study of the Law of Constitution*, MacMillan and Co. Ltd., London, 1961.

Dawson, R. MacGreygor : *Democratic Government in Canada*, University of Toronto Press, London, 1970.

Doabia, H.S.T.S.: *The Supreme Court on Constitution of India*, Wadhwa and Co., Nagpur, 1967.

Dauglas, W.O.: *Studies in the American and Indian Constitution Law (Marshall to Mukharjee)*, Eastern Law House, Calcutta, 1956.

Ghose, P.K.: *The Constitution of India, How it has been formed*, The World Press Pvt. Ltd., Calcutta, 1966.

Gladhill, A.: *The British Commonwealth, the Development of its Laws and Constitutions*, Stevens and Sons, London, 1967.

Gupta, S.P.: *Bhartiya Samvidhan* (in Hindi), 2002.

Halsbury, S.: *Laws of England*, Butterworth and Co., London, 1954.

Ilbert, C.: *Government of India*, Oxford University Press, London, 1915.

Jain, D.C.: *Parliamentary Privileges under the Indian Constitution*, Sterling Publishers Pvt. Ltd., New Delhi, 1975.

Jain, M.P. and S.N.: *Principles of Administrative Law*, Wadhwa Publication, Nagpur, 1997.

Jain, M.P.: *Indian Constitutional Law*, Wadhwa Publication, Nagpur, 2006.

Kennedy, W.P.M.: *The Constitution of Canada*, University of Toronto Press, London, 1970.

Kagzi, M.C.J.: *Constitution of India*, Metropolitan Book Co. Pvt. Ltd., New Delhi, 1984.

Keith, A.B.: *Constitutional Law*, Steven & Sons, London, 1959.

Kashyap, C. Subhash : *Our Constitution*, National Book Trust, New Delhi, 2002.

Kashyap, C. Subhash : *Our Parliament,* National Book Trust, New Delhi, 2002.

Liskin, Bora : *Canadian Constitutional Law,* The Carswell Co. Ltd., Toronto, 1975.

Maitland, F.W.: *Constitutional History of England,* Cambridge University Press, 1955.

Malika, S.: *Supreme Court on Constitutional Law,* Eastern Book Company, 1974.

Maxwell : *Interpretation of Statutes,* N.M. Tripathi Pvt. Ltd., Bombay, 1982.

Mukherji, Dr. P.B.: *The Indian Constitution; Change and Challenges,* Rupak Publisher, Calcutta, 1976.

May, Sir T.F.: *Parliamentary Practice,* Butterworths Co., London 1957.

Massey, I.P.: *Administrative Law,* 2001.

Paton, G.W.: *A text book of Jurisprudence,* Oxford University Press, London, 1972.

Prasad, A.: *Vidhi Shastra Ke Mulsiddhant,* Eastern Book Co., Lko. 2001.

Pandey, Dr. J.N.: *Constitutional Law of India,* Central Law Agency, Allahabad, 2007.

Pandey, G..S.: *Constitution of India,* University Book House Pvt. Ltd., Jaipur, 2007.

Seervai, H.M.: *Constitutional Law of India,* N.M. Tripathi Pvt. Ltd., Bombay, 1996.

Saharay, Dr. H.K.: *The Constitution of India; an analytical approach,* 1998.

Singh, J. Mahaveer: *Bharat Ka Samvidhan,* Eastern Book Co. Ltd., Lucknow, 1992.

Shukla, V.N.: *The Constitution of India,* Eastern Book Co. Ltd., Lko, 2001.

Singh, M.M.: *Constitution of India,* 1975.

Rao, B. Shiva: *The Framing of India's Constitution, A Study,* Indian Institute of Public Administration, Pub. 1968.

Raju, V.B.: *Constitution of India,* 1973.

Tripathi, Prof. P.K.: *Samvidhan Kay Tatva,* Govt. of India Publication, 1982.

Wheare, K.C.: *Federal Government,* Oxford University Press, 1953.

Wheare, K.C.: *Modern Constitutions*, Oxford University Press, 1969.

Hidayatullah, Justice M.: *Constitutional Law of India*, Govt. of India Pub., 1992

Mahajan, Vidyadhar: *Constitution of India*, Eastern Book Co. Lko, 1991.

Kapoor, S.K.: *International Law*, Central Law Agency, Allahabad, 2007.

Singhvi, Dr. L.M.: *Jagadish Swarup's—Constitution of India*, 2006.

(c) Journals/Periodicals

Aberhoworth : "Advisory function in the Federal Supreme Court", *George Town Law Journal*, Vol. 49, 1935, p. 101.

Allen, C.K.: "Administrative Consultation of Judiciary" *Law Quarterly Review*, Vol. 15, 1951, p. 97.

Aumann, F.R.: "The Supreme Court and Advisory Opinion", *Ohio State University Law Journal*, Vol. 37, 1937, p. 495.

Baxi, Upendra : "The Constitutional Quisksands of Keshavanand Bharti and the Twenty-fifth Amendment, *Supreme Court Case Journal*, Vol 259, 1974, p. 616..

Dubaue, H.A.: "The Duty of Judges as Constitutional Advisor." *American Law Review*, Vol. 52, 1980, p. 22.

Field, G.P.: "Advisory Opinions—Analysis", *Indian Law Journal*, Vol. 66, 1948-49, p. 205.

Foster, M.: "The Declaratory Judgment in Australia and the United States", *Melbourne University Law Review*, Vol. 40, 1957-58, p. 66.

Frank Foster F.: "A note on Advisory Opinion", *Harward Law Review*, Vol. 23, 1926, p. 12.

Frank Foster, F.: "Advisory Opinions", *Encyclopedia of Social Science*, Vol. 1, 1968, pp. 475-76.

Glovie, P.C. and Undergraff, C.M.: "Advisory Opinions", *Law Review*, Vol. 9, 1928, p. 98.

Gupta, S.C.: "Article 194 (3) and the triangle of Democracy", *Supreme Court Journal*, Vol. 115, 1965, p. 19.

Grinnel, F.W.: "Duty of the Court to give Advisory Opinions", *Massachusetts Law Quarterly Review*, Vol. 61, 1917, p. 73.

Hogemann, J.F.: "The Advisory Opinions in South Dakata", *South Dakota Law Review*, Vol. 9, 1971, p. 93.

Hudson, M.O.: "Advisory opinions on National and International Courts", *Harvard Law Review*, Vol. 41 1924, p. 83.

Note : "Advisory Opinions on the Constitutionality of Statute." *Harward Law Review*, Vol. 72, 1956, p. 93.

Note : "The Case of an Advisory Function in Federal Judiciary, *George Town Law*, Vol. 17, Journal, 1962, p. 201.

Note : "Extra Judicial Opinion", *Harvard Law Review*, Vol. 91, 1896, p. 272.

Phillips, P.D.: "Advisory Opinions in India", *Australian Law Journal*, Vol. 115, 1928-29, p. 19.

Popkin, William D.: "Advisory Opinions in India", *Journal of the Indian Law Institute*, Vol. 13, 1962, p. 194.

Smilarieh, T.A.: "Advisory opinions in Florida; An experiment in Inter-Governmental Cooperation", *University of Florida Law Review*,.Vol. 64, 1971-72, p. 119.

Stevens, G.N.: "Advisory Opinions: Present Status and Evaluation", *Washington Law Review*, Vol. 58, 1958, p. 206.

Tromas, L.I.: "Advisory Jurisdiction of the Supreme Court of India." *JIH*, Vol. 52, 1963, pp. 475-97.

Tripathi, P.K.: "Keshvananda Bharti vs. The State of Kerala, Who wins". *Supreme Court Cases Journal*, Vol. 1, 1974, p. 10.

Wager, W.J.: "Advisory Opinions in the Federal Judiciary: A Comparative Study," *Kannas City Law Review*, Vol. 42, 1952-53, p. 166.

Omar, Dr. Imtiaz.: "Reflections on the Advisory Jurisdiction of the PNG Supreme Court". available at: www.beta.austlii.edu.au, accessed on 25 Jan. 2006.

(d) Law Reports

All India Reporter (Relevant Volumes).

Supreme Court Cases (Relevant volumes).

Allahabad Law Journal. Federal Law Reports.

Report of the *ad hoc* committee on the Supreme Court, 1949.

Bharat's Law of India (1999).

Report of Joint Committee on the Indian Constitutional Reform (1934-35).

Supreme Court Journal.

2. Secondary Sources

Articles

Noorani, A.G.: "A historic document." *Frontline*, Vol. 20, No. 18 (Sept. 13, 2002) at p. (10-14).

Dhavan, Rajeev: "The six month norm is dangerous in Gujarat". *Frontline*, Vol. 20, No. 18 (Sept. 13, 2002) at p. 16.

Venkatesan, V.: "Care taker by default" *Frontline*, Vol. 20, No. 18 (Sept. 13, 2002) at pp. 17-18.

Venkatesan, V.: "In the Supreme Court" *Frontline* Vol. 12, No. 19 (Sept. 27, 2002) at p. 31.

Dhavan, Rajeev: "The Supreme Court reference". *The Hindu*, Vol. 25, (Aug. 23, 2002) at p. 12.

Singh, Prof. M.P.: "Conducting elections" *The Hindu*, Vol. 25 (Aug. 29, 2002) at p. 12.

Krishna Iyer, V.B.: "Gujarat Imbroglio Some Reflections", *The Hindu*, Vol. 25 (Aug. 24, 2002) at p. 11.

Tandon, Bishan: "*Laxman Rekha Khan Lang raha hai.*" Hidunstan, (Aug. 31, 2002).

Swami, Praveen: "A battle for water" *Frontline*, Vol. 20, Issue-03 available at www.Aonnet.com accessed on 19 July, 2007.

Swami, Praveen: "A Canal Crisis", *Frontline*, Vol. 12, issue 16, available at www.flonnet.com accessed on 19 July, 2007.

Document: "Protocol No. XI to the convention for the protection of Human Rights and fundamental freedoms, restructuring the control machinery established thereby." available at www.conventions.coe.inc/treaty/htm. accessed on 2 July, 2007.

Document: "Ramjanbhoomi and the Courts". available at www.bharatvani.org accessed on 26 July, 2007.

Ajai and Shukuntala, Singh : "How Mahatma Gandhi's Plan can solve Temple Issue". available at www.ajai-shakuntala.tripond.com accessed on 26 July, 2007.

Subramanian, T.S., "An award in Sight" available at *www.hinduonret.com* accessed on 26 July, 2007.

Legal Correspondent: "J&K Resettlement Act stayed." *The Hindu*, (New Delhi Ed.) Vol. 125, 02, Feb. 2002, p. 1, C-1.

Swami Praveen: "Communal Designs", *Frontline*, Vol. 18, Issue 25, 8 Dec. 2001.

Legal Correspondent, "Do states have right over natural gas: Centre to SC", *The Times of India* (New Delhi ed., 29 Oct. 2001), p. 1, C 1-3.

(b) News Dailies

The Hindu (2002-2009, Delhi Edn.)
The Times of India (Delhi Ed., 2002-09)
The Hindustan Times (Lko. Ed., 2000-09)
Hindustan (In Hindi, Lko. Ed., 2000-09)

(c) Magazines

Frontline (2002-09)
Outlook (2002-09)
India Today (2002-09)

(d) Dictionaries and Encyclopedias

Webster's new 20th Century Dictionary, 2003.
The Oxford Companion to Law by David M. Walker, Clarendon Press, Oxford, 1980.
The Chambers Dictionary (Deluxe, Ed. 1997) Allied Chambers (India) Ltd., New Delhi.
Bhargava's Concise Dictionary. Edited by Prof. R.C. Pathak (11th Edn. 1987).
Ballantine's Law Dictionary, 18th Ed. 2001.
Halsbury's Laws of England, Butterworth, London, 1974.
www.freedictionary.com (online)
www.answers.com (online)
www.wikipedia.com (online)
www.encyclopediabretanica.com (online)

(e) Libraries

R.M.L. National Law University, Lucknow.
Judicial Training and Research Institute (JTRI), Lucknow.
The Institute of Constitution and Parliamentary Studies, New Delhi.
Dr. R.U. Singh, Law Library, Lucknow University.
Tagore Central Library, Lucknow University.
Acharya Narendra Dev Library, Lucknow.
Government Advocates Library, High Court, Lucknow Bench, Lucknow.

State Law Officer's Library, Lucknow.
Rajya Suchana Kendra Library (Govt. of U.P.)
C.L.L. Library, Lucknow University.
B.H.U. Central Library, Banaras.
B.H.U. Law Library, Banaras.
Indian Law Institute Library, New Delhi.
Supreme Court Bar Association Library, New Delhi.
Supreme Court Judges Library, New Delhi.
India International Centre, New Delhi.

(f) Internet Websites Used

http//www.tribuneindia.com/2004/20040327/edit.htm.
time of India.indiatimes.com/articleshow/msid.cms.
hinduonnet.com/the hindu/the scrip/print.htm.
beta.austlii**:edu.au/au/special/alta 95/ozmar.html.
en.wikipedia.org/wiki/kaveri-River-Water-Dispute.
Pakistani.org/Pakistan/constitution/events/cjp-ref-2007.
123helpme.com/view.asp.
Scjudgments.com/guest/news/viewnewsdetail.asp.
deccanterald.com/archives/jan212004/n6.asp.
Indlaw.com/search/quick.aspx.
lawmin.nic.in/ncrwc/final report/v2b3-6.htm.
rediff.com/news/2007/feb/05cau.htm
innews.yahoo.com/070205/43.html.
iwha.polaire.net/cgi-bin.
dawn.com/2007/05/15/top2.htm.
parliament of india.nic.in
Indiacode.nic.in (Acts/Bare/Rules)
Legalserviceindia.com
Iawyearscollective.org.
commoncauseindia.org.
allahabadhighcourt.nic.in
bookfinder.com protection of Human rights and fundamental freedom.

Index